Life in Nelson's Navy

Poop lanthorne

Life in Nelson's Navy

by
DUDLEY POPE

Foreword by the Admiral of the Fleet
Sir John Fieldhouse

Flint lock for great guns

NAVAL INSTITUTE PRESS
Annapolis, Maryland

BLUEJACKET BOOKS

Originally published in Great Britain by Allen & Unwin Ltd.
First Bluejacket Books printing, 1996

ISBN 1-55750-516-0

Printed in the United States of America on acid-free paper ♾

03 02 01 00 99 98 97   8 7 6 5 4 3 2

Contents

List of Illustrations

Bar and chain shot

Foreword

by the Admiral of the Fleet Sir John Fieldhouse

I am delighted to have been asked to write the foreword for this edition of Dudley Pope's excellent book.

The magic of the 'Nelson touch' and the great battles fought and won by that remarkable man has captured the imagination and interest of generations of people throughout the world.

Away from the crash of cannon and the glory of victory, there is another story; that of the reality of life at sea in Nelson's navy, with its harsh discipline, corruption, poor victuals and the near constant battles with the elements that were the lot of the seamen of those times.

This other story is encapsulated in this book and Dudley Pope has painted a vivid picture of the life of the men who manned the wooden walls, which were in time of danger our sure shield.

I commend this story to all those who seek to learn more of the history of what the Royal Navy calls 'the greatest single factor' – the seaman.

Ministry of Defence,
Whitehall, London

Author's Foreword

Life at sea in Nelson's day is a subject which since Victorian times has been grossly distorted, particularly by romantic writers. For example, much is made of the fact that the press gang could seize a man from the bosom of his family and make him serve in the Royal Navy. He was of course paid the normal rate, and it is unlikely that any of his brothers would have been so unlucky as to be picked up at the same time. In the Second World War in Britain there was universal conscription.

It has been said that wounded seamen in the war against Napoleon were abandoned with their disabilities. Very soon after the end of the Second World War every man receiving a British pension for disabilities of 45 per cent or less, the author among them, had the pension stopped. This was done by a socialist government whose election pledge had been to give the ex-servicemen 'a square deal'. One and a half centuries had made little change.

Other subjects, such as flogging, discipline, leave and food, are dealt with later, but the important thing to bear in mind is that one must judge by the standards of the day.

The picture of a curly-haired midshipman not yet past his fifteenth birthday was often correct, but fifty per cent of a ship's midshipmen were likely to be in their thirties or forties – men who had failed their examination for lieutenant or, having passed, lacked the influence to get a job. There were, however, hundreds of young midshipmen who, before they were sixteen, had sailed in command of prizes with a crew of a dozen. Self-reliance appeared earlier in those days.

The life afloat, the routine on board the ships, and the administration of the Royal Navy of Nelson's day are an absorbing subject, but in modern times knowledge of it can be obtained only by exhaustive reading of original documents referring to all aspects of the period. These extend from the accounts of battles in ships' logs to the minutes of the courts martial of men ranging from admirals to ordinary seamen, from requests from surgeons for lime juice and pursers for beer to the claims of men declaring that they were American subjects and not liable to impressment, to pleas to admirals and ministers seeking patronage.

The autobiographies and biographies of those who served at the time give a good picture of the life, particularly because they range from seamen to admirals. It is fortunate that some retired seamen and petty officers wrote their memoirs (often with more skill and always with less inhibition than their seniors), so that we see the lower deck as well as the quarterdeck.

The manuals, almost all privately printed because there were no 'official' instruction books in those days, whether for sail handling, tactics, gunnery or the daily work afloat, tell us much about shipboard routine.

Fortunately, several families have kept much of the correspondence of their naval forebears, so that the historian can often glimpse not only a man's official life but his family life – the grumbles, hopes and fears, for example, that he might express to his wife.

No author who spends more than a quarter of a century studying the life at sea in the Nelson period, who does often exhaustive research in several countries for studies of particular great events (the Battles of Copenhagen and Trafalgar, for example), or a specific event concerning one ship (the *Hermione* mutiny) or one man (the trial and execution of Admiral the Hon. John Byng), can list all the documents and books he has consulted, but my bibliography gives a selection which may assist anyone doing further research.

I have also had the advantage of learning about handling a ship under sail because for the past twenty-five years I have been able to sail my own yacht (which is our home) into most of the ports of any consequence – British, Danish, Dutch, French, Spanish and Italian, from Copenhagen to the West Indies – which have had any importance in the Royal Navy's history.

For this reason the first person I must thank is my wife, who, literally, has been the 'mate' for more than twenty-five years. I have been very lucky because two men in particular tried to pass on to me their knowledge of the sailing navy before they too 'went over the standing part of the foresheet'. For many years Lieutenant-Colonel Harold Wyllie, the marine artist whose knowledge of the design, construction, rigging and handling of sailing ships of war was almost unrivalled, and who learned much from a father whose life his own almost duplicated, regularly passed on thousands of words of material from his files and his memory. He would recall a fact he thought I should know and, wherever in the world I happened to be, a letter would arrive, written in his tiny, neat handwriting. As often as not there would be sketches (some of which are used in this book) to elucidate a point. The reason for all this, apart from a close bond of affection which had grown up between us and our wives, was his wish that I should 'put it all down'. This book is in part what he wanted me to write and my only regret is that he did not live long enough to see it in print.

Commander W. B. Rowbotham, until his death, was just as kind. His knowledge of the administration of the Navy was unequalled. Until his death he read the manuscripts of all my books with care and interest and his typewriter, even more ancient than mine, would list any errors he noted or, more likely, would add more material.

These two men are simply those with whom I was most constantly in touch until their deaths, but I have been fortunate because many retired naval officers who served at sea in the last days of sail have passed on their reminiscences and papers.

Some of the material referred to above and which follows has provided the background for the series of novels I have been writing about Lieutenant, later Captain, Lord Ramage. It is perhaps unusual to devote the same standards of accuracy in technical detail to novels as to naval histories, but thanks to the material I have at my disposal it has been an easy task, and an enjoyable one.

The unique cutaway drawing of HMS *Victory* by Colin Mudie, and the line drawings by the late Harold Wyllie in the front matter and at the ends of chapters, were executed specially for the author.

DUDLEY POPE
Yacht *Ramage*
Leeward Islands

HMS *VICTORY*

Built to the design of Sir Thomas Slade, her keel was laid down at the Old Single Dock, Chatham, on July 23, 1759, and she was launched on May 7, 1765

PARTICULARS

Length on Gun Deck	186′ 0″
Length of Keel	151′ 1″
Moulded Breadth	50′ 6″
Extreme Breadth	51′ 10″
Depth in Hold	21′ 6″
Displacement (Approx.)	3,500 tons
Burthen	2,162 tons

ARMAMENT—1805

Lower Deck	30—32 pounders and 2—12 pounders
Middle Deck	28—24 pounders
Upper Deck	30—12 pounders
Quarter Deck	12—12 pounders
Forecastle	2—68 pounders (Carronades)

KEY TO DRAWING

1. Poop
2. Hammock Nettings
3. Mizenmast
4. Quarter Deck
5. Steering Wheels
6. Here Nelson Fell
7. Pikes
8. Mainmast
9. Gangway
10. Focsle
11. Carronades
12. Foremast
13. Captain Hardy's Cabin
14. Upper Deck
15. Nelson's Day Cabin
16. Nelson's Dining Cabin
17. Nelson's Sleeping Cabin with cot
18. Shot Garlands
19. Middle Deck
20. Wardroom
21. Tiller Head
22. Entry Port
23. Capstan Head
24. Galley and Stove
25. Lower Deck
26. Tiller
27. Chain and Elm Tree Pumps
28. Mooring Bitts
29. Manger
30. Orlop
31. Sick Bay
32. Aft Hanging Magazine
33. Lamp Room
34. Midshipman's Berth—here Nelson died
35. Forward Hanging Magazine
36. Powder Store
37. Powder Room
38. Aft Hold
39. Shot Locker
40. Well
41. Main Hold
42. Cable Store
43. Main Magazine
44. Filling Room

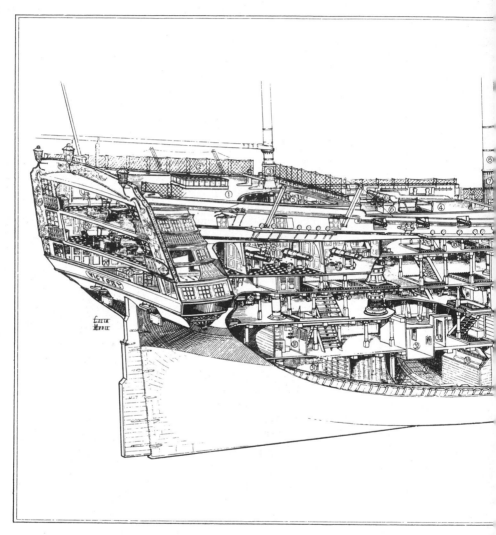

See key on previous page

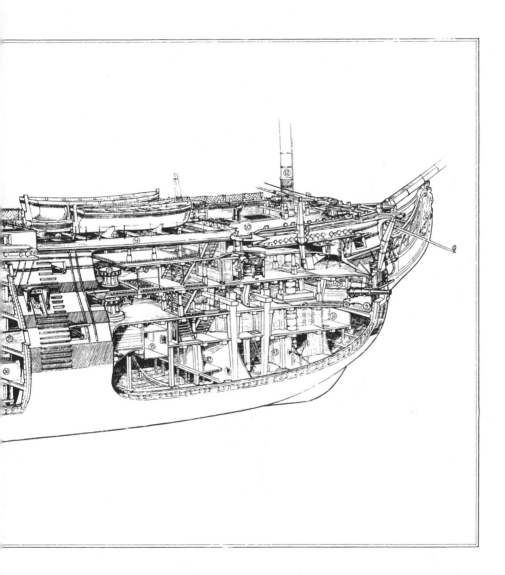

CHAPTER ONE

The Face of England

When news reached Britain on 24 June 1793 that the National Convention in Paris had executed Louis XVI, and the French Ambassador, M. Chauvelin, was ordered to leave the country, the Britain that found itself at war a few days later was a nation of only 8 million people, 750,000 of whom lived in London. With one brief interval the war was to last for the next twenty-two years, and, while almost every country in Europe was eventually involved, Britain would be the only country to fight the French from beginning to end.

For long periods there was nowhere she could fight the French on land, so the Royal Navy became the only weapon always in action: ships of war ranging from great three-deckers to tiny cutters cruised far and wide in the Channel and North Sea, the North and South Atlantic, Indian Ocean, East and West Indies, attacking or defending, patrolling or blockading, searching or protecting. Perhaps fittingly, a ship of the line carried a defeated Napoleon to his final exile.

The story of how these ships were built, manned, provisioned and kept at sea has usually been told as a bland mixture of Nelson's 'Band of Brothers' going into action to the tune of Heart of Oak with pink-cheeked young midshipmen waving their dirks in defiance of the Dons. In fact it is far more fascinating – a story of sea victories emerging from a mixture of courage, cowardice and corruption, nepotism, patronage and long-standing fraud by politicians and merchants, of revolting sicknesses which killed a hundred times more men than perished in battle.

Yet, without an understanding of the Britain that existed in the year the war began and of the standards, values and conditions of the people on land and at sea, how the Royal Navy functioned and finally left Britain the most powerful nation in the world will remain a mystery, considerably distorted by Victorian sentimentality and legend.

It has been fashionable to make much of the cruelty of flogging and the harshness of the press gangs which tore devoted husbands from their wives and sent them off to the war for years on end. Few people realise, however, that when the fleets mutinied at Spithead and the Nore four years after the war began neither flogging nor the press gangs were among the men's list of complaints. Even fewer stop to think that the press gangs took up very few men compared with, for example, the nation-wide conscription in Britain of the Second World War, which made every able-bodied man liable for service and was then extended to women as well. The soldier of 1940 captured at Dunkirk who spent the next five years in a German prison camp was in the same situation as the pressed sailor of 1797 who was taken prisoner and spent the next five years at some prison like Verdun. The press-ganged seaman who spent five years in a ship of the line in the East Indies would count himself luckier than a conscript of 1941 who was captured by the Japanese at Singapore and forced to build the Burma Road.

It is vital, in other words, to judge the Navy of Nelson's day by the standards of Nelson's day, and it would be wrong to think of those standards as always being lower than those of today. The men who tried to kill each other with sword, cutlass, musket or comparatively crude cannon and who fought by no convention other than honour would despise as unmanly the modern flame-thrower; the seamen who accepted false colours as a legitimate ruse of war but always hoisted their true colours before opening fire would scorn submarine warfare.

There is only one common denominator – the man himself. The soldier under Wellington waiting in the wet misery of a Spanish winter in 1810 to hold the heights of Torres Vedras was no colder, wetter or safer than the British, Polish, Indian, American, New Zealand and South African troops waiting in 1943 to storm the heights of Monte Cassino after a long wait in the cold and mud of an Italian winter. Whether serving under a Nelson or a Wellington, he grumbled, misbehaved, fought honourably or tried to run away, got drunk and chased women. There is no indication that his British descendants behaved much differently in the Crimea, the Boer War, or either of the two world wars. Some captains were sadists, whether commanding a wooden frigate or a steel destroyer, and some were almost worshipped by their men. Some admirals and generals sought glory rather than victory – they were not always the same thing – whatever the war.

In looking back at the Navy of Nelson's day we are looking back nearly two centuries, to a time when Britain fought for her life against an enemy who could see the cliffs of Dover on any clear day. We are in the same position as someone in 2125 who looks back at Britain as she faced Hitler across the Channel in 1940. The observer in 2125 will, among other things, learn that while German guns were firing shells across the twenty-one miles of the Channel the British were arming the young and the elderly civilians with pikes made of metal piping to which a bayonet was clipped; that schoolboys distinguished only by armbands guarded their villages against invasion, armed with 12-bore shotguns for which they had bought the cartridges out of their pocket money. Yet the country folk of Nelson's day had watched warily for Bonaparte's invasion in much the same way. The weapons were different but the people and the spirit were the same.

The seamen of Nelson's day naturally came, with a few exceptions, from the ordinary people of Britain, and in the 1790s these folk, according to a survey completed several years earlier, 'will endure long and hard labour, insomuch that after twelve hours' hard work, they will go in the evening to football, cricket, prison-base, wrestling, cudgel playing or some such-like vehement exercise for their recreation'.

Although claiming that they were 'as long-lived generally as the people of any nation in the world', the survey had to admit that 'on the other side, by reason of intemperance, and of an unhappy excess that has obtained in spiritous liquors, there is no part of the world wherein people are more subject to die suddenly'. The ordinary Englishman worked hard (he had little choice) and drank and played hard.

In a country where there was no national police system and in peacetime the standing army was kept small to avoid it becoming a force to overthrow the government, the mob held sway: an angry and ugly crowd yelling protests outside a politician's house and smashing his windows was an accepted sight, just as a degree of corruption was accepted in politics. (However, the First Lord of the

Admiralty, Lord Melville, was too blatant and was impeached for it just three months after Nelson was buried in St Paul's following his death at Trafalgar.)

If he was violent in his politics, the man of the mob was violent in his sports, most of which (judged by modern standards) were cruel; he lived in a cruel age. Cock-throwing caused no comment and a crowd usually gathered to watch a cockerel with one leg tied by a length of string attached to a peg in the ground. A man standing twenty-two yards away hurled a broomstick at it and often the cockerel was agile enough to dodge, but to win the bird the man had to knock it down and pick it up before it recovered.

Bull-baiting was popular; the bull was chained to a stake and anyone could – for a few pence – set his dog on it. Badger-baiting was usually part of the entertainment at an inn. The badger, an animal with very strong jaws, was usually secured to a stake by a chain through its tail and dogs were set on it while the crowd watched.

Cock-fighting was one of the most popular sports and a large variety of people, ranging from peers of the realm to labourers, bred their own fighting cocks. A labourer would walk into an inn with his favourite bird in a sack over his shoulder and challenge all comers for a barrel of ale. A town challenged another town, village challenged village, a sporting squire backed his fancy with a hundred guineas. Wearing spurs tipped with steel or silver, comb and wattles cut, wing feathers clipped, a prized Black Red, Birchin Yellow, Ginger Red or other favourite breed went into the pit and fought to the death for its owner's honour, guineas or ale. From these battles such phrases as 'main chance', 'battle royal' and 'pit against' became part of the language.

Yet animals were not the only ones involved in violent sports. Cudgel-playing was always good for a crowd and involved two men armed with long sticks fitted with basket handles. They swiped and parried until blood was drawn or one was a moment too slow and was sent sprawling unconscious. Boxing was fighting with bare fists (which were pickled in brine to harden them) with the barest minimum of rules, a fight usually ending only when one man collapsed or was knocked out – often after a couple of hours or more. The ring was formed by the onlookers, and men's knees were used as stools to rest the fighters. The man fighting the favourite usually faced a form of sabotage from the favourite's backers, who aimed surreptitious kicks at his shins.

These were the common sports, the frequent events happening of an evening in towns and villages. Horse racing was very popular whenever some horses could be collected at a reasonably flat field. It, too, was rough and tough: jockeys often concentrated as much on trying to tip rivals from their horses as on riding and the jockey on the favourite expected an irate crowd to set about him if he lost. It was a common complaint of a rider that a favourite running slow could cost him bruised shins and a couple of teeth knocked loose by livid punters. The actual races were usually a series of eliminating heats, ending in a final which was the real race of the day.

For those who had no money to spend or who preferred cheaper or quieter pursuits, there were, in addition to football and cricket, such games as skittles, quoits and bell-ringing, using small handbells. For the more athletic wealthy there was hunting the hare or the fox, the members of fashionable packs stoking themselves with stirrup cups and following a rigid tradition of never balking at a hedge.

Shooting was popular; partridge were preferred to pheasant for the unsporting but practical reason that a browning shot was the easiest and a covey of partridge thus made a better target than a rocketing pheasant. Spice was added by the chance of a sporting piece blowing up in its owner's face, while a bad flint, damp powder or sheer carelessness could produce a flash in the pan and immunity for the intended game. A fisherman's equipment for river or lake was much less complicated and hazardous: horse's hair, preferably from the tail of the beast, made excellent line.

The thirsty workman or seasoned toper had plenty of drink to choose from: in addition to wines and the age-old mead and metheglin, there were perry, cider, rum, ale (the varieties included Steponey, stick-back, scurvy-grass, sage and college ale), brandy made from malt or apples, and, of course, gin. For many of the working class, especially in London, gin was a temporary release from the misery of cold, hunger, squalor and poverty, for it was a very cheap drink. At first a national beverage, gin quickly became a national vice, an enlightened Bow Street magistrate half-way through the century reporting that it was 'the principal sustenance (if it may be so called) of more than 100,000 people in the Metropolis'. For those preferring less heady drinks there were tea, coffee, chocolate and sherbet.

The country was prosperous, obliged to import nothing for its day-to-day living except items like tea, sugar and rum. It had coal aplenty, brought in by colliers sailing it down the east coast to London. Its flocks of sheep provided wool and there was linen for making cloth and paper. Sturdy oaks grew near rivers so that the trunks when felled could be carried in barges down to shipyards. Sherwood Forest bestrode the River Trent, the Forest of Dean the Severn, Windsor Forest was beside the Thames, and the New Forest in Hampshire flanked the shipyards of the Solent and Spithead.

Britain was on the brink of further widespread scientific discoveries and industrial development: already chroniclers and advertisers were laying claim to 'the best clocks, watches, locks, barometers, thermometers, air pumps &c in the world' and boasting of 'curious telescopes, microscopes, perspectives, globes and sea compasses'. But the towns were far from being hemmed in by factories: much of the manufacturing was done in the home. Men, women and children often laboured long hours in their own houses, delivering whatever they manufactured to their employers' warehouses.

Individual industries were very localised, a particular district or county becoming famous for a specific product. Sussex, containing fewer than 30,000 houses, was famous for its fish while Bedfordshire with half that population produced quantities of wool, butter and cheese, the women weaving fine bone lace in their homes at Olney and Newport Pagnell, while those at Dunstable and Luton had a reputation for the quality of their straw hats. In Berkshire the town of Reading was famous for the canvas it produced for the sails of the ships of the Royal Navy. Oxfordshire had less than 25,000 houses and, while Woodstock was famous for its steel, Henley had a reputation for malt, Banbury for cheese, Whitney for blankets and Burford for saddles.

Kent was well populated and boasted excellent fruit. It produced woad and madder for the dyers, while gourmet and trencherman favoured succulent Fordwich trout from near Canterbury. The county town of Maidstone was noted for its thread and hops, while Faversham was busy trading with London, its sturdy little hoys and barges tacking and wearing up and down the rivers Swale and Thames whatever the weather.

Essex had more than 40,000 houses and produced saffron, especially from the fields round Walden, while Surrey, with the same number of houses, was well known for the Fuller's earth coming from near Reigate. In the Midlands the Five Towns of Staffordshire were producing rough, solid pottery, but Josiah Wedgwood's works at Burslem had revolutionised the industry, using scientific methods and fine clays (quantities of kaolin had been found in Cornwall). Until that time the rich had used glass, silver and pewter and the poor had wooden platters and mugs.

In the north of England, Yorkshire boasted fine herrings landed at Scarborough, knitted waistcoats, gloves and stockings made in Doncaster, and iron from Sheffield. The spur makers of Ripon had a ready market for their wares in the London shops, while liquorice from Pontefract was much prized. In Wales, Denbigh was famous for its tanners and glovers, while in Flintshire there was stone tough enough for cutting into millstones, and honey, used to make metheglin, was produced in its valleys.

Throughout the nation the influence of John Wesley was still spreading, particularly in Cornwall. The Church of England had been submerging itself in self-satisfaction, and the habit of many parsons of holding more than one living, leaving the work to under-paid curates, resulted in the Church losing touch with the needs of the people. Only a few decades earlier Archbishop Herring's visitation showed that of 711 clergymen in the diocese of York 335 had more than one parish – and that 393 of the 836 parishes did not have their rector living in the village. The twenty-six bishops represented votes in the House of Lords and they liked to be in London while Parliament was sitting. This, combined with bad travelling conditions and a disinclination to be far from well served dining tables, meant that all too frequently some of the bishops saw little of their diocese.

By modern standards, the country was governed with very few ministers, but the Government then as now had at its disposal hundreds of sinecures which brought their holders a regular income and were awarded like prizes or tips. The effect was to create a vast number of men and women who could be relied on to support the Government either by giving their votes at elections or, if they were MPs, in the House of Commons. And, of course, ministers often held several paid posts.

The Civil Service, though not then called that, was not large, despite the variety of taxes that were levied and their own bureaucratic skill in creating as many jobs as possible. The tax on chocolate, for instance, entailed an inspector-general at £500 a year, a Register (*sic*: registrar) of the Chocolate Seals at £80, a stamper of labels at £50, and 'three pasters for fixing on the said labels, each £50 per annum'. For the coffee duties, two surveyors were needed for the roasting-houses, with six clerks.

These government employees passed no examination to get their jobs and in many cases had little or nothing to do; most of them were receiving a type of pension, or remittance, earned through family relationship or influence, and where work was involved paid a deputy. In towns where there were a number of government employees – in a port, for instance, where in addition to Customs and Excise men there would be Navy yard employees as well as contractors and their dependants – the Government through its various departments could bring a great deal of influence to bear at election time. The ballot was not secret, and if a man voted against his employer's candidate he risked his job. In other constituencies the voters often gave their votes to the highest bidders. The number of voters in each of the constituencies sending members to the House of Commons varied from under half a dozen to more than a thousand and the fewer the voters the more effective and expensive the bribery or pressure.

The allocation of Parliamentary seats was absurd – a fifth of the Commons were elected by the four south-western counties, Cornwall, Somerset, Devon and Dorset. Cornwall, with under 30,000 houses, had forty-two members while Essex had only eight. Kent, with a larger population than Cornwall, had eighteen members. Devonshire returned thirty members – the same number as Yorkshire.

In a harsh age, the gallows was never far away, but, although human life had little value by modern standards, property was sacrosanct. Anyone caught laying his hands on someone else's property was punished severely, often by being sent to the gallows. A man could be hanged if he was found guilty (among more than 150 other charges) of 'stealing from the person' more than a shilling, horse stealing, housebreaking, rape, abducting with intent to marry, burglary, 'putting in fear', and highway robbery.

For coining money the guilty man could be drawn and quartered; for petit-treason – in cases, for instance, of a servant killing his master or a clergyman his prelate – the guilty person could be hanged and drawn. The penalty for felony was death; thus a man caught stealing half a crown could be hanged, and so could a man who stole a horse or a sheep. There were the usual anomalies in the law – a man who stole a basket of fruit could be hanged because the fruit had been harvested; another man stealing the same amount of fruit but picking it himself was guilty only of trespass.

Hangings were public and regarded as worthwhile entertainment, crowds assembling long before the time, waited on by piemen and fruit sellers. Dr Johnson, when hanging was transferred from the gibbet at Tyburn to outside the particular jail in which the condemned man was held, commented that 'The publick was gratified by a procession; the criminal supported by it. Why is all this to be swept away?' But not only the lawbreaker could find himself in jail: men were jailed by their creditors for debt, and of course they still owed the money when they were finally freed from the Marshalsea, the prison in which they usually found themselves.

In the field of science, man's curiosity about the world around him was beginning to yield tangible results. The existence of electricity had long been known but was still used mainly as a novelty. The Abbé Nollet, for instance, had used a Leyden jar to amuse the late French king, lining up 180 of the Royal Guards and giving them all a shock. He then lined up scores of Carthusian monks, each holding a wire connecting him to his neighbour, and at the appropriate moment the Abbé completed the circuit – it was a mile long – and the startled and electrified monks sprang into the air. Astronomy was by now firmly established and an accurate chronometer had been designed so that longitude could be calculated correctly. John Smeaton had built the third Eddystone lighthouse (completed in 1759, it would last until 1877).

Various hospitals had been founded – among them the Westminster (1720), Guy's (1724), St George's (1733), the London (1740) and the Middlesex (1745). St George's at Hyde Park Corner marked the western limit of London while the London Hospital, on the eastern border, was still within sight of green fields and farms. By modern standards it was easy to get into a hospital, although the cynic might add that once in it was difficult to get out again. A sick person wishing to become a patient had first to get a letter of recommendation from one of the governors. Failing that he had to put down a deposit of nineteen shillings and sixpence. This was not a charge for medical treatment – on the contrary, if he or she recovered it was returned to him. Should things not turn out so successfully, though, the beadle took a shilling for informing the next of kin, the porter a shilling for providing a burial certificate, the men who carried the body to the hospital gates needed two shillings, the matron a shilling for providing a black pall, and the steward a shilling for certifying the patient dead.

A live patient who had to go to the cutting ward (operating theatre) paid the sister half a crown, a shilling to her assistant, and a shilling to the sister of his own ward. The beadle and his assistant who carried the patient to the cutting ward and back each received sixpence. Yet the food eaten while a person was a patient was provided free.

The day-to-day social life of London revolved round the coffee houses, which were a happy combination of café and club (and occasionally brothel). For the price of a cup of coffee or chocolate a man could spend his whole day there, gossiping, debating, reading the newspapers, writing letters and – for most coffee houses acted as accommodation addresses – receiving them. Several coffee houses had a specialised clientele: city merchants tended to go to Garraways, Jonathan's or Lloyd's. In time of war a merchant sending goods by sea or a shipowner intending that one of his ships should join the next convoy to the West Indies could rely on the Admiralty sending word to Lloyd's. Booksellers patronised the Chapter coffee house, off Paternoster Row, while artists (and foreigners, who perhaps found artists more cosmopolitan than most other Britons) went to Old Slaughter's, in St Martin's Lane. Each coffee house usually had a sign outside illustrating its name, but one sign was universal, and that depicted a woman's hand holding a coffee pot. Coffee could be obtained on the premises – but its chief purpose was being a brothel.

Gambling was the national sport, whether a penny wagered on a dog baiting a bull or a fortune plunged at one of the fashionable clubs. The man of fashion usually chose White's in St James's Street or, if a Tory, the nearby Cocoa Tree. White's was the great place for gambling – Walpole wrote earlier that 'Lord Stavordale, not one and twenty, lost eleven thousand there last Tuesday, but recovered it by one great hand at hazard: he swore a great oath – Now, if I had been playing deep, I might have won millions.'

The Army was in a sorry pickle at the time the war began with M. Chauvelin going off down the Dover Road. Detested by the civilian population (the redcoats acted as the police in the case of riots), it was recruited from the scum of the country for the very good reason that no one else would join. Some of the officers were elegant fops attracted by the uniforms and bought their commissions without any military training, obtaining promotion by buying a higher rank from a willing seller. A wealthy man could buy a regiment and become its colonel, and it was fairly common for a family wanting a scallywag out of the country to buy a subaltern's commission in a regiment stationed abroad – advertisements for such commissions were frequently displayed in the newspapers, an escape for debtors and jilters. It was hardly surprising that the Army had the reputation of being the worse-officered in Europe. The officers were brave enough in time of war but usually ignorant of the most elementary tactics. In peacetime the science of soldiering did not have the cachet that it had in continental Europe; it was an occupation for gentlemen. In France, for instance, it was an occupation for professionals; the young Napoleon was studying as an artilleryman. Fortunately Britain had a proportion of dedicated officers who showed what could be done without patronage and who emerged later in the war.

The country's capital city was a confusion of noise, reeking squalor and poverty. A walk along many of London's streets meant a triple assault – on the nostrils from the stench of garbage lying in rotting heaps; on the ears from the clatter of horses' hooves and coachwheels on cobblestones, overlaid by pedlars and hucksters crying their wares, the shouts of the penny-post man, and scavengers clanging their bells; and on the conscience – more complacent than is usual today – from the persistent whine of beggars, ranging from consumptive children to their age-warped grandparents.

London was still a well defined city, although beginning to spread rapidly. Its western edge was Tyburn Lane (now Park Lane), running from Tyburn Turnpike (Marble Arch) to Hyde Park Corner. North of Tyburn Road (now the western end of Oxford Street), Marylebone was still little more than a hamlet. Portland Place had many vegetable gardens and Tottenham Court Road had houses for a few hundred yards and was then fields until the traveller arrived at Tottenham Court, a hamlet famous for its tea gardens.

On the east side of the metropolis Mile End Road ran through farms and fields; Mile End itself and Bethnal Green were slowly growing into large hamlets. The Ratcliff Highway and Upper Shadwell ran through fields and ropewalks and nearby was Execution Dock, where, until recent times, pirates had been hanged and their bodies left strung up in chains at the water's edge.

On the other side of the Thames, Jamaica Street (now Road) had shipyards on the Thames side and open fields to the south. Many of these fields were still tenter grounds, on which large wooden frames (tenters) used for making cloth were built, with the material stretched across them so that it dried evenly without shrinking (hence the phrase 'on tenterhooks').

The Old Kent Road ran up to London Bridge, mostly through fields and tenter grounds, but houses were being built. Beyond Borough to the westward were more fields, with timber-yards flanking the Thames. Back across the river again were Somerset House, Charing Cross and Whitehall. Millbank ended in the marshes of Pimlico, where men still occasionally shot snipe. And in Tothill Fields, among the cowsheds, there was a bear garden.

London, which had come to include Southwark and Westminster, sprawled east and west along the Thames for seven and a half miles, from Limehouse to Tothill Street, but there was a sharp division between the City proper and the most fashionable part of London in which the aristocracy lived. They had moved westward from the Covent Garden area to Hanover Square and then, under pressure from the City dwellers, to Grosvenor and Berkeley Squares. The City was self-contained administratively; its gates were shut promptly at ten o'clock at night, the watch patrolled the streets and suspected persons – particularly 'vagabonds, strumpets or nightwalkers' – were seized and taken off to a house of correction.

Yet although the streets of London might have been dirty they were noisy and cheerful: apart from passers-by and the usual crop of costermongers, pickpockets and beggars, there were wayside entertainers and hucksters of all ages and sexes. As soon as a lad was old enough to shout he was old enough to sell and the cries of street sellers were part of London life – 'Ye-o-o! Here's your fine Yarmouth bloaters!' – 'Penny a bunch, turnips!' – 'Wi-i-ild Hampshire rabbits!' – 'Long life candy – candy from herbs!'

Small boys would 'toss the pieman' – tossing a coin and leaving the pieman to call. If the pieman lost he handed over a pie without taking a penny; if he won he took the penny without handing over a pie. Apple women, straw pads on their crushed bonnets, would be carrying baskets on their heads. Other women, tawdry jewellery glittering on trays round their necks, would be crying the ritual

'Chewl-ree a penny, pick 'em and choose 'em!' Tea sellers cried the merits of their fresh green tea, but the odds were that it was old leaves, dried and then stained with a copper solution. There would probably be an old man in muddy boots selling cress lifted that morning from Pimlico Marshes; another man selling live linnets was up at daybreak checking his traps in fields and hedgerows.

A curious fad which had begun bothering playwrights and actors in the 1750s had now become a way of life among the upper classes and would soon spread through the country, to become a characteristic of the people. It began with the idea that it was bad form to show any sort of feeling in public: a carefully studied appearance of languid boredom took the place of laughter and clapping at the theatre – although the mob in the pit and gallery usually made up for the silence in the stalls and boxes.

This feigned languidness had become sufficiently popular for newspapers in the 1750s to advertise a pamphlet costing a shilling and called *The Folly of Enthusiasm*. In an age when the upper classes were frequently ill educated, languidness could hide its owner's ignorance on a subject, and it also disguised laziness. But the fashion continued to become an attitude, and two centuries later it is still 'bad form' to display feelings in public; this attitude is usually described as 'keeping a stiff upper lip'.

Outside London at the beginning of the war a labourer living in at a farm was paid £10 a year, while a woman was paid 6d a day for weeding. A schoolmaster would count himself lucky to be paid £1 a month while a maid received £5 a year and a charwoman usually 6d a day. Meat cost an average of 3½d a pound while tea, often smuggled, was about 10s a pound. Houses were lit by candles or cruses burning fish or animal oil.

Travel was both tedious and expensive. The stage wagons used by the majority of people took three weeks to reach London from Cornwall, and the prudent traveller made his will before starting out. The post-chaise, four-wheeled with two or four horses, the driver riding postilion, cost up to a shilling a mile. Roads between towns comprised gravel and pebble thrown on mud and the traveller prayed for dry weather – but not so dry that the coach wheels turned up clouds of dust.

France's declaration of war by no means took Britain by surprise. In April 1792 the National Convention had declared war against the

Emperor of Austria, following that in September with an attack on the King of Sardinia. The war against Britain and against the Netherlands followed on 1 February 1793 (although the news did not reach London until the 4th), and was followed by a declaration against Spain on 7 March.

On the day of the declaration against Britain, most of the Royal Navy's ships were still laid up out of commission or in a dockyard undergoing repairs, but work was going ahead preparing them. Five three-deckers were in commission while 16 more were still laid up or in dock. Twenty-one two-deckers were in commission and 71 laid up or being repaired – a total of 26 ships of the line ready for action with 87 not yet commissioned. Thirty-two fifth-rate frigates were in commission while 49 were laid up or under repair.

But the ships laid up since the last emergency, in 1791, had to be commissioned quickly; they needed officers and seamen, a vast amount of rigging and provisioning. They represented employment for men ranging from highly skilled petty officers who had been serving in merchant ships to young officers who had spent the last few years on half pay – men like Captain Horatio Nelson, who had been unemployed for five years and whose name was well down the captains in the Navy List. Naval commanders and captains in peacetime were little more than casual labour, with years spent on half pay. Like actors, it was sometimes more important to know influential people than to be extremely competent because an ounce of influence was usually worth a pound of skill.

Like most intelligent people in Britain, Nelson had seen war with France as inevitable and the previous autumn he had written to the Admiralty asking for a ship. Nothing happened for many weeks, but on 7 January he wrote to his wife Fanny that the First Lord of the Admiralty, Lord Chatham, had 'made many apologies for not having given me a ship before this time, and said, that if I chose to take a sixty-four [gun ship] to begin with, I should be removed into a seventy-four'.

By 26 January he knew that his command would be the *Agamemnon*, then at Chatham, and he told his brother she was a ship which he regarded as 'without exception one of the finest sixty-fours in the Service, and has the character of sailing most remarkably well'. The young post captain, only too well aware that his stock did not stand very high at the Admiralty – he had been over-zealous and upset local merchants while commanding the frigate *Boreas* in the

West Indies, though in the five years since then the official memory had apparently dimmed – was well pleased with his luck.

John Markham, second son of the Archbishop of York, was another young post captain who had been on the half-pay list for the past few years and who had applied to the Admiralty for a ship. Thirty-two years old, a bachelor and a competent officer, he had just spent Christmas at Bishopthorp, the Archbishop's residence in York, reunited with his favourite brother David, an Army officer recently invalided home from India after being badly wounded while serving under Lord Cornwallis in the siege of Bangalore. While John tried for a ship, David was waiting for promotion, and he became a major in the 20th Foot on 23 February.

Markham – known to the family as Jack – was given command of the *Blonde* frigate, which was laid up at Deptford, on the Thames. The most important person on board a man of war when she is being commissioned is the first lieutenant, and Markham was lucky that the Admiralty agreed to his request to have Anthony Ponsonby, a young lieutenant from Cumberland.

The third person through whose eyes we shall occasionally see the Royal Navy was a midshipman on the day the war began, James Gardner, and one of the few employed: he was serving on board the 98-gun three-decker *Queen*, fitting out at Portsmouth. Gardner, twenty-three years old, had spent the previous eleven years in the midshipmen's berth of several ships, collecting a store of experiences which would occupy half the autobiography he subsequently wrote. Born at Waterford, in Ireland, Gardner was the son of a commander in the Royal Navy.

Some of the people we shall meet had not been born on the day the war began; yet by the time it ended at least one of them would be commanding his own ship. One who was to be swept up by the press gang, Robert Hay, was four years old, born on a farm in Dunbartonshire. Within a few weeks of the war beginning the lease on the farm ran out and a new lease meant a rent that was nearly double. Hay's father sold up his farm implements and moved his family to a village in Renfrewshire, where his brother was running a bleaching business, and took a job as a boilerman.

Down the Thames at Greenwich a 58-year-old naval pensioner, William Spavens, was having to make a lonely and frightening decision. For more than thirty years he had been suffering from a leg injury and receiving a small pension, but towards the end of 1792 it had become very ulcerated and when he saw his doctor on 28 January 1793 it was realised that the shin bone had been eaten away. The surgeon of the Greenwich Hospital saw him, brought three other doctors to give their opinions, and on 14 February operated on Spavens, to see if an amputation could be avoided.

The war had been going on for two weeks when Spavens learned that he would have to have another operation, this time to amputate the lower part of the leg, and this was done on 28 May. For many years, since he was pensioned off from the Navy, Spavens had been making leather gloves and breeches at Louth, in Lincolnshire. His pension varied, averaging about £5 a year, but after the amputation it was increased to £6. Spavens had a wife and family to keep and, while he recovered from the amputation and the Royal Navy hurriedly commissioned its ships for the new war, Spavens began writing his story, which he called *The Seaman's Narrative*. Mr Richard Sheardown, the printer in Louth, was interested in the story and printed it in 1796 with a note on the title page, 'Sold for the Benefit of the Author', the price being 2s 6d 'sewed'. An almost unknown volume, it gives one of the finest pictures of life at sea on the lower deck.

William Richardson had been born in South Shields in 1768, the son of the master of a merchant ship. He was brought up with four brothers and two sisters by a doting mother who, he recorded, 'shifted me from one school to another whenever I took a fancy to be displeased with my schoolmaster, so that I was in a fair way of becoming a dunce'.

His father, coming home on leave, made the same discovery and sent him off to a boarding school where he learned, among other things, the theory of navigation. He was then apprenticed in 1781 for seven years to the master and owner of a merchant ship and in it he sailed to the Baltic several times, to the Barbary coast of North Africa, and to North America.

With his apprenticeship completed, jobs were hard to find, and Richardson served as a seaman in his father's ship, making thirteen voyages in 1789 from Shields to London, carrying coal. In 1790, tired of the coal dust, he joined a slaver fitting out in the Pool of London. He did one voyage in her, out to the Guinea coast, across the Atlantic to Jamaica and then back to London, when, off Beachy Head, Richardson and many others of the slaver's crew were pressed by the aptly named *Nemesis* frigate. He was soon paid off when the

Spanish crisis cooled down and joined a ship belonging to the Honourable East India Company.

He was shipwrecked near Calcutta just as news arrived that Britain and France were at war, and within a few weeks he had been pressed yet again. He claimed that he had been only three years at sea (he had served thirteen) and that he had neither money nor clothes, but the captain of the *Minerva* frigate was unimpressed; Richardson was rated an able seaman and, as he noted later, 'All my clothes were on my back, and with an old silver watch and one rupee . . . I had now, as it were, the world to begin again.'

Jeffery Raigersfield was a midshipman in the Navy as the war began. He was a serious, rather Teutonic young man of twenty-two, the son of John Luke, Baron de Raigersfield of the Holy Roman Empire. The Baron had come to England in 1756 as a member of the Austrian Embassy and decided to stay in the country, marrying an Englishwoman. His son Jeffery wanted to go to sea, and his father had enough influence to arrange it.

His story (like many similar it was written not for publication but for his family to read) shows a rather truculent young boy going to sea first in the *Mediator* in 1783 at the age of twelve, and seven years later taking a long leave to stay at an abbey in Tournai to learn French. The French attack on Austria soon brought him home to find a fleet fitting out at Spithead. His father had enough influence with Lord Howe, its commander-in-chief, to get young Raigersfield installed in the midshipmen's berth of the *Victory*.

Nelson fretting in Norfolk, Markham staying at Bishopthorp and Raigersfield learning French at Tournai are good examples of the unemployment experienced by naval officers in peacetime, who forfeited their half pay if they took a salaried job 'in the public service'. Some very competent officers were at this time serving in foreign navies. Russia, for instance, had many ships but her officers were so badly trained that a man rated incompetent would get rapid promotion, and the Tsar was delighted to have British captains.

Sidney Smith had received his commission as a lieutenant in 1781, became a commander in 1782, and in 1783 was 'made post' – the curious way in which the process of being made a captain is described. A few months later his ship was paid off, and, with England at peace, Smith was unemployed and went on to half pay, a phrase which was valid only if 9s was half of 25s.

In 1788, when war seemed likely between Sweden and Russia (and

British officer would be pitted against British officer), he served with distinction in the Swedish Navy and for his bravery he was given an English knighthood on his return to London. By 1793 he was serving in the Turkish Navy and was at Smyrna when he heard the news that France had declared war on England. He promptly bought a small lateen-rigged vessel, named her the *Swallow*, and set off down the Mediterranean from Turkey looking for the English Fleet and hoping to find some French prizes – and risking being shot by the French as a pirate if he was caught, because he did not have a letter of marque allowing the *Swallow* to operate as a privateer.

Telltale compass in captain's cabin

CHAPTER TWO

Behind the Screen Wall

As the war began, Europe was a continent where everything was on a small scale. London's population of 750,000 made it the largest of the capitals, Paris had 650,000 inhabitants, Vienna 200,000 (the same as Amsterdam) and Madrid 150,000.

The latest intelligence reaching the Admiralty as the new war began showed that at Brest, Rochefort and Toulon there were 21 French ships of the line ready for sea, 15 more fitting out and 21 'in good condition'. Another dozen were being built. Quite apart from preparing the ships, the French were busy renaming some of them with names more in keeping with the revolutionary spirit. The *Couronne* became the *Ça Ira* and the *Sceptre* was renamed *Convention*. The *Suffren* changed to *Redoutable* while the 110-gun *Bretagne* became the *Révolutionnaire*.

The Royal Navy was comparatively strong in the number of its ships, thanks to the war with France, Spain and America which had ended in 1783 and had led to the building of many more ships. Some of them were in better condition than they might have been because of the Nootka Sound crisis with Spain in 1790, which had led to the hurried repair and commissioning of many ships – a flurry and bustle which had also led to the pressing of William Richardson from the slaver off Beachy Head.

Although the great building programme of the 1780s had left Britain with a powerful Navy, as the new war began in 1793 most of its strength was on paper, probably impressing the leaders of the French Revolution in Paris but frightening many of its own admirals in London.

The reason was that the Nootka Sound alarm had shown a new generation of men what ten years' neglect could do to wooden ships: they had been laid up, swinging to buoys with rainwater lodging in the woodwork and rot spreading through massive timbers and hull planking alike, an impartial cancer flourishing because no one realised that its enemy was fresh air and its allies green wood and humidity.

The British Parliament added another million pounds to the Navy vote for 1793, allowing an extra 16,000 seamen and 4,000 marines, making a total of 45,000 men and an estimate of £4,003,984 1s 2d for one year.

These men were those who genuinely liked serving in the Royal Navy, seamen who had been working in merchant ships between the international crises. Only among officers and warrant officers was there still unemployment. At the beginning of the year, a month before the war began, there were 446 post captains, 163 commanders, 1,417 lieutenants and 297 masters. Yet fewer than 150 ships, commanded by captains or commanders, were in commission: fewer than 150 of the 609 captains and commanders, a quarter, were employed. Less than half the lieutenants had appointments in peacetime and many of the less senior ones were glad to serve as able seamen in merchant ships to eke out their half pay of 3s a day.

The mere hint of war sent admirals, captains, commanders and lieutenants to London where, a few hundred yards along Whitehall from the Houses of Parliament, the Admiralty building stood well back from the road. Built forty-eight years earlier of yellow brick, the building formed three sides of à hollow square, the fourth side being Whitehall itself.

Whitehall is wide but it was then one of the noisiest streets in London: soldiers with hoarse-voiced and bellowing sergeants marched to and from the Horse Guards a few yards away; carriages were always clattering along with the coachmen bellowing warnings of collisions; brewers' drays squeaked as they carried casks to their customers; hucksters, pedlars and journeymen shouted their wares and skills.

The noise had been too much for their lordships, particularly the First Lord, whose official residence was the part of the building nearest Parliament, and Robert Adam was commissioned to design a screen wall to shut out the noise but leave a large and high enough gateway and arch for carriages to make the swing into the cobbled courtyard. Now, facing each other across the top of the arch, Adam's two symbols – horses (land) with wings (air) and dolphin tails (the sea) still stand.

Inside the cobbled courtyard and opposite the gateway, four large columns guarded the main doors, inside which was the large, square entrance hall, high-ceilinged, with arched corridors leading left and right at the far end, and a large fireplace on the left wall. Three curious black leather armchairs, built with wide hoods and heavily padded, stood there for the use of the messengers and porters, who could put their feet into drawers which slid out from beneath the seats and combined with the hoods to protect them from draughts. The messengers and porters were famous as tyrants of the Admiralty, treating all but admirals with haughty disdain unless they received a large tip to augment their wages, which ranged from £40 to £60 a year.

A large six-sided candelabra hung from the ceiling in the centre of the hall, a three-anchor badge above each face and a crown on top. The second door on the left, just inside the main door, led into a small waiting-room, the most hated room in the whole Admiralty. A drawing by the cartoonist Cruikshank showed the following verse written on a wall:

> In sore affliction, tried by God's commune,
>   Of patience, Job, the great example stands,
> But in these days, a trial more severe
>   Had been Job's lot if God had sent him here.

Any officer applying to the First Lord for an appointment to a ship – or wishing to see him for any reason – had first to wait. Lieutenants, captains, admirals – all had vivid memories of that small waiting-room.

The Board Room, where the Lords Commissioners of the Admiralty met, is a large, rectangular room with three large windows on one wall. In 1793 they looked on to a stable. The Board Room is striking; panelled in dark wood, high-ceilinged, well proportioned, it has an atmosphere of being used for serious purposes, and few things have been changed. The ceiling is decorated with rose emblems, white and gilt; the fireplace, surrounded by mottled brown marble, carries the arms of Charles II. Above the fireplace there were long horizontal rollers on which charts were stowed like blinds, and they fitted within a large pearwood carving which formed a three-sided frieze. This, the work of Grinling Gibbons, was carved in 1695, and among the carvings are intricate working models of an astrolabe and a pelorus, a set of shot gauges and a tiny open pod of peas, Gibbons's own trade mark. The carvings and fireplace came from Wallingford House, which had been partly destroyed to make way for the Admiralty building.

In one corner of the room stands a tall grandfather clock, made in 1700 by Langley Bradley, the man who built the great clock of St Paul's cathedral. On another wall was a large dial which at first glance looked like a clock with a gilded pointer going across the dial, instead of two hands, but round the outside instead of hours from one to twelve were the thirty-two points of the compass, while the face of the dial was a map of Europe, stretching from the north coast of Spain up to the Baltic. The spelling of place names indicated that even in 1793 the map was old – Calais was 'Calice', the North Sea was the 'British Ocean', while the Scilly Islands were marked 'Silly I.'

The pointer was nearly always moving: it was linked by a complicated series of rods and cams to a wind vane on the roof and showed their Lordships the wind direction. Like the fireplace and its pearwood carvings, the wind dial was a legacy from Wallingford House and had been working since 1695, showing which way the wind was blowing and giving an indication whether the fleet – or the enemy – could sail.

A similar device was fitted to the house built on the corner of Hill Street and Berkeley Square by the ill-fated Admiral Byng, whose execution was contrived by Anson, the First Lord, and Anson's father-in-law, the Earl of Hardwicke. The house still stands but the wind vane is no more.

Today the chart rollers are no longer in existence. The wind dial is in their place over the fireplace while a large portrait of Nelson by Guzzardi hangs where the wind dial was once fitted. The Langley Bradley clock is in the same place, still showing the time. The fireplace and carvings remain untouched.

Although many decisions were made by 'the Board of Admiralty' it was rare for all the members to meet: much of a day's business was decided by the First Lord – usually a politician – or the 'senior or first professional lord', a naval officer. Four members might attend a meeting to make some important decision, and sign the minutes and other documents, many of which required a minimum of three signatures; but the day-to-day routine was dealt with by the First Lord or the 'professional lord', working with the Board Secretary, Evan Nepean. The Admiralty office was run with a remarkably small staff – less than sixty in 1801, ranging from seven Lords Commissioners to the housekeeper, three watchmen and the gardener.

The senior civil servant in the Admiralty, Nepean, attended their Lordships in the Board Room, sitting at the corner of the table on the First Lord's right with the second secretary on the left. His method of answering letters – one which had long been followed by the Secretary – was to fold over a bottom corner and write on it briefly what their Lordships had decided. An unsuccessful application would have a curt 'Rejected' noted on it, with the date, whereas a complaint from or against some officer on a distant station often had the phrase 'Request him to forward more details'.

Once the Board meeting was over – even though it was often little more than a discussion attended by two members and the Secretary – Nepean would go to his office and dictate full answers to one or other of his clerks, his letters usually beginning with a variation on the phrase 'I am directed by my Lords Commissioners of the Admiralty . . .', while dispatches from officers addressed to Nepean normally began with a formula based on 'Be pleased to inform their Lordships that . . .'.

The letters would then be signed by Nepean or, if necessary, one of the Lords – who made a point of calling in during the evening, before the messengers were due to leave, simply 'for signing'. Commissions and important orders for admirals were usually signed by three members, as though this was traditionally a quorum, otherwise the correspondence was addressed to or signed by Nepean, as Board Secretary.

The second secretary kept the minutes of Board meetings, writing the decisions down in a long, ledger-like volume marked 'Rough Minutes'. The notes for a whole meeting often comprised three lines of hasty scrawl, but usually a Board meeting was merely the official stamp for decisions already made by members meeting in one of the offices in the club-like atmosphere. This usually led to a franker assessment of difficulties, or the shortcomings of a particular officer, than a formal discussion. The Admiralty at this time had strong-minded First Lords – Spencer, Dundas (later Lord Melville) and St Vincent.

The actual chain of command that led to an admiral or captain on some distant station carrying out orders which may have originated with the Prime Minister and a Cabinet meeting was relatively simple.

If there was to be an important expedition and the decision to mount it was a political one, then the Cabinet would make it, usually meeting at Downing Street, the residence of the Prime Minister. The Secretary of State for Foreign Affairs would then pass the instructions on to the First Lord of the Admiralty. In fact it was rarely as formal as that.

Once the First Lord had received his instructions, the Board would meet to provide ships and men. Orders might have to go to the Navy Board, which was responsible to the Admiralty for the actual ships and ran the Navy Office at Somerset Place.

If there were enough ships immediately available, then orders were drawn up for the admiral commanding the relevant fleet. The main decision and the general sense of the instructions would be noted in the rough minutes. The actual orders were usually drafted by the First Lord or the senior 'professional lord', or by the two men together. Evan Nepean then had a fair copy made, another copy went into the 'Lords Letters, Admirals and Commanders in Chief' file, and a messenger left the Admiralty to deliver it.

If it was to one of the main ports or anchorages – Plymouth, Portsmouth, Deal, Sheerness, Harwich or Great Yarmouth – the messenger rode a regular route, changing horses which were waiting for him. Messengers for particular places left the Admiralty every evening at set times, while other messengers regularly left the ports and anchorages with letters for the Admiralty.

The tasks of the various lords of the Admiralty for many years depended on the whim of the particular First Lord and the energy or otherwise of the individual. The first man to organise and list the task was Lord Barham, formerly Sir Charles Middleton. He did so in May 1805.

He wrote that the First Lord would 'take upon himself the general superintendence and arrangement of the whole', while the 'senior or first professional lord' – a naval officer – would do the same when the First Lord was absent. This officer (later called the First Sea Lord) would deal with the day's correspondence 'but more that of the Ports and all secret services'. He was to draft all orders and letters necessary 'and pass to the Secretary for action'.

He was also – with the First Lord's approval – to control the movement of ships on home and foreign stations and give any necessary orders 'to the admirals, captains and commanding officers of ships on service'. His other tasks included distributing seamen and marines, equipping all ships, and promotions.

The second professional lord would deal with all the correspondence and papers of the Navy Board, the Transport, Victualling, Sick and Hurt Boards and Greenwich Hospital, while the third professional lord, the most junior of the naval officers on the Board, would – with the First Lord's approval – deal with the promotion of commission and warrant officers who were without ships because of shipwreck or seniority.

The civil lords, 'in order not to interrupt the professional lords', were to sign 'all the orders, Protection warrants and promiscuous papers daily issued from the office'. Lord Barham also outlined the Secretary's job: with the assistance of the second secretary he was to open all correspondence and hand over all that was not secret 'to the Reading Clerk for arrangement and distribution and abstract in the several books of reference'. He was to sign orders as they were written by the clerks from the minutes made by the Board members.

The second secretary was to be in charge of the Board's minute book and keep it up to date, examine reports from the signal stations and 'be in charge of the telegraph'. (The telegraph tower was erected on top of the Admiralty in January 1797, and began working on the 28th.)

The clerks were to be at their desks by ten o'clock. The 'confidential clerks' would prepare the orders and instructions on secret subjects from the Board's minutes. There were nine 'principal clerks', who had special duties. The first ran the office and looked after the cash; the second entered the Lords' letters in the letter books – the equivalent of carbon copies – and also letters to the Ordnance, Navy, Transport, Victualling and Sick and Hurt Boards. The third dealt with secret orders to admirals, captains and others, while the fourth handled discharges from the Navy, letters from admirals, and letters of marque for privateers. The other five dealt with the rest of the routine – letters to captains and lieutenants, admirals 'and other public officers'.

It was the custom of the Lords of the Admiralty to hold a reception, or levee, on a particular day in the week, and securing an invitation – and a chance to advance himself – was the ambition of almost every captain on half pay. One of them, Captain Glascock, wrote 'Leaves from a private log of a captain' in an otherwise serious narrative, *Naval Sketch Book*, to describe, in the abbreviated style used in a ship's log, an experience on levee day.

He was in his lodgings on 25 November. 'At eight, rose and rigged. – Suicidal day. – Prepared toast, "Thick and dry, for weighing". – *Mem*. Butter bad for bile. Levee-day – lashed cables – cleared hawse – brushed up boots and brains – piped to breakfast. – Glanced at paper – barren of news: naval appointments shy. Prepared to unmoor – unmoored. At *ten* weighed – made sail – stood for Admiralty. Entered hall. Noted name for Lordships' levee. – Bowed the list. *Mem*. Polite to porter, took him for peer. – Deed done – wore ship. Steered for Strand – altered course occasionally. – Killed time – heavy on hands . . .

'Wore round for Guards. Worked into Admiralty Bay. Telegraphed porter; [was] answered in the negative. – Name returned in "rejected addresses". – Mortified much – shammed indifference. – Long list – some consolation. – Laughed it off – lounged about . . .

'*One* p.m. – High water. – Hall full – crowded fleet – "short tacks" – long faces – longer claims . . . Two p.m. – Fresh breezes – official bustle – officious porters. – Bells ringing – clerks running . . .' For a few minutes his hopes are raised but the 'signals from aloft' are mistaken; he misses the levee.

Glascock was in fact putting a bold front on his unsuccessful sally into the Admiralty. Few officers visited the Admiralty or the Navy Board without paying some fee or another to one of the clerks. Much of the staffing in both these offices was on the basis that a clerk's regular salary paid by the Admiralty would be augmented by fees they charged the officers.

It was, quite simply, making the Navy's sea officers help pay for the civil administration and the cost of the sinecures by insisting that they had to have certain documents which could only be obtained from officials requiring fees. And the fees, considering the pay, were high. In peacetime an officer on half pay wishing to travel abroad had to get a leave of absence, for which a fee was charged. Every midshipman needing papers showing how long he had served was charged a fee before attempting his lieutenant's examination, and if he passed it cost him another fee to have his passing certificate registered.

Fees were paid – and went to clerks – by the owner of a privateer for the granting of a letter of marque, by every captain for getting his annual accounts passed at the Navy and Victualling Office, by every seaman in the merchant service as the price of a 'Protection', a piece of paper which made him free of the risk of being impressed.

However, the Admiralty never approached the College of Heralds who could put a man heavily in debt for fees if he had received a knighthood, baronetcy, barony or some such fee-fertile honour. The fees were payable before the rituals were completed, so all too often it was a case of debt before honour.

The officials in the Admiralty were paid on a system still universal among government departments: the seniors were paid too much, the juniors too little. Evan Nepean, the Board Secretary, received £4,000 a year (the First Lord was paid only £3,000). The second secretary had £2,000 while the next man, the chief clerk, received only £800. The six clerks under him were paid between £500 and £300, and the nine junior clerks between £250 and £150. Five 'extra clerks' received £90–£100 a year.

There were always plenty of sinecures available, too. Nepean, the most highly paid man in the Admiralty, was also clerk of the Admiralty Court in Jamaica, and the West Indies was a happy hunting-ground for men with friends or relatives in the Government – Percy Charles Wyndham was receiver in chancery at Jamaica, and held a similar job in Barbados, as far away from Jamaica as the Arctic Circle is from Gibraltar or San Francisco. His brother Charles had another sinecure in Jamaica, so that three successive names of officials in the Admiralty Court were P. C. Wyndham, Evan Nepean and C. W. Wyndham. H. W. Bentinck was Registrar of the Admiralty Court in Martinique, Vendue Master at Demerara, and Navigation Officer at Barbados, while his brother was Governor of St Vincent. These men spent most if not all of their time in England, receiving their full pay and, where necessary, paying a clerk to do any routine work required.

Men like Nepean were not venal; on the contrary, he was an honest and very efficient Secretary to the Board and Member of Parliament for Queenborough, near Sheerness in Kent (regarded as an Admiralty seat, along with places like Portsmouth, Rochester and Sandwich).

In an office like the Navy Board, however, where contracts were being given to merchants for just about everything from ships and timber to provisions, the scope for corruption was enormous, and the Comptroller, Sir Andrew Snape Hamond, took advantage of it, as will be seen later.

Politics were still the curse of the Navy. Only ten years earlier, in the previous war, the fall of Lord North's Government after the disaster in America led to Lord Rockingham's new Whig Government sacking Admiral Sir George Rodney as Commander-in-Chief in the Leeward Island station and sending out Admiral Pigot, a nonentity who was of the right politics.

Pigot was taken out to his new command by Captain Thomas Pasley, commanding the 50-gun *Jupiter*. Pasley kept his own private journal, and although he liked Pigot personally he made some illuminating comments, the first being the day after Admiral Pigot joined the ship for the voyage: 'Weather blustery and disagreeable. The Admiral and all his youngsters [i.e. midshipmen] most heartily sea sick, owing to his not having been to sea for nineteen years.'

When the *Jupiter* arrived in the West Indies, Pigot found that Rodney, the man he was to supersede, had just won the Battle of the Saints. Rodney had captured Admiral de Grasse in his flagship, the *Ville de Paris*, and seven other ships of the line. The *Jupiter* arrived in Port Royal to find 'the French ships taken – *Ville de Paris* (100), *Hector* (74), *Glorieux* (74), *Ardent* (64), *Jason* (64), *Caton* (64) . . . Such a Fleet . . . never was seen before in this western world . . . '

An admiral, like a captain, had one main chance of becoming rich, and this was from prize money. The commander-in-chief on a station received an eighth of all prize money won by his captains, and one who was more concerned with his pocket than the requirements of his station made sure that his favourite frigate captains were out cruising in places where they were likely to find prizes, a case where duty, private profit and patronage went hand in hand to the prize court, and the captains who found no favour with the admiral received all the convoy work, which was tedious and unrewarding.

Such an admiral did his best to get a lucrative station, and such an admiral was Sir Hyde Parker, later to be Nelson's senior at the Battle of Copenhagen, and such a station was Jamaica. The First Lord of the Admiralty, Earl Spencer, writing to him when Parker was being replaced after four years there, said: 'I trust you will not look upon your recall in any other light than as is meant, namely, as a change of service, which may naturally be looked for after so long a term as you have enjoyed of the most lucrative station in the service . . . I rejoice that your stay on the Jamaica Station has proved so advantageous. . . .'

The correspondence between the First Lord and the Admiral also showed that distance did not lessen the effectiveness of patronage:

usually the last sentence in a letter was enough. 'Give me leave to recommend to you for promotion on some future opportunity Lt Matthew St Clair of the *Lapwing*. I should also be glad to hear of Captain Barton of that ship having a larger frigate . . .' was a very typical reference from Spencer, this time to Admiral Harvey on the Leeward Islands station.

Spencer's letter to Hyde Parker commenting on the Admiral's recall ended: 'I am much obliged to you for attention to my recommendation of Lieut. Childs and of all the other persons whom I have recommended', and referring to Hyde Parker's successor he added, 'and I beg you would be so good as to give Lord Hugh Seymour a list of those which shall remain unaccomplished at the time of his relieving you'.

It was of course a two-way traffic: Parker requested commissions for young men in whom he was interested and who were serving in Europe, and other admirals did not hesitate to make their requests.

Yet patronage, properly used, did much to save the country in wartime by giving outstanding men rapid promotion. It is pointless speculating what would have happened had Nelson not eventually received rapid promotion, so that he was in a position to win his three great and decisive battles, the Nile, Copenhagen and Trafalgar, but without the influence of his uncle it is unlikely that he would ever have become a captain, and without the influence of Earl St Vincent — who used it simply because he recognised Nelson's brilliance — he would never had been given the command of the ships that led to the victory at the Nile. But for a junior Nelson's inspired action, bordering on disobedience, at the Battle of Cape St Vincent, there would probably have been no victory or earldom for Sir John Jervis.

The Admiralty's main problem was, of course, communications. Orders for admirals on the home station could be sent by messengers on horseback, using the regular messenger system. Orders for admirals at sea — blockading Brest, for instance — were taken from Plymouth or Portsmouth by frigates or cutters. To admirals in the West Indies the Admiralty could use the Post Office packet brigs for everything but the most urgent dispatches. There were never enough frigates, and sending one specially to, say, Jamaica meant losing it for many months.

The Post Office packet service, on the other hand, provided a regular and fast service to all the West Indian islands. A packet sailed every two weeks from Falmouth for the West Indies whatever the weather (providing she could carry a double-reefed topsail), averaging forty-five days to Jamaica after calling at several of the Windward and Leeward Islands. Port Royal, Jamaica, was the last port of call before sailing for Falmouth, usually a 35-day passage. Thus the commanders-in-chief at the Leeward Islands and at Jamaica would rely on receiving and sending dispatches every two weeks without losing any of their valuable frigates. Duplicates of all letters went by the next packet and third copies were often sent in a convoy.

The whole system of communications with the West Indies could, however, be halted if the French captured the packets, and there were periods when privateers had great success – at one time four homeward-bound packets were taken within four weeks. Not only were original letters lost but the duplicates were lost as well.

In the southern part of Britain, signal towers were built on the coast every few miles so that signals could be sent to or received from passing ships. For ships starting off down the Channel from the Thames, for instance, there were signal towers at the North Foreland, at East Hill, near Dover, Little Cornhill, Dover, Folkestone, Hythe, Dungeness, Heene, Fairlight, Beachy Head, Seaford, Hawke Hill (Brighton) and Shoreham. They continued with the same frequency as far as the Lizard, forty-eight signal stations which cost the Admiralty very little to run.

Each station was allowed a lieutenant (paid 7s 6d a day and his half pay), one midshipman at 2s a day and the pay of a fourth-rate, and two seamen at 2s a day. 'House, coals and candles' were provided.

Lieutenant Gardner, sent to command the station at Fairlight in January 1806, found that he had two dragoons, in addition to the seamen, to act as messengers. Invasion was feared, he wrote, and he had 'the strictest instructions to be on the look-out by night and day'. He denied that a signal station was an easy berth, declaring that 'I suffered more from anxiety at this station than ever I did on board a man-of-war'. Nature was also the worst enemy, particularly for a station perched high on a cliff – 'I have often been in dread for the safety of the house', particularly in a south-westerly gale, and he admitted that 'I'm astonished the house did not blow away'.

These signal stations, which were intended as look-outs as well, were in addition to the towers built across the country and in sight of each other, all the way from the Admiralty down to Portsmouth and, later, on to Plymouth. These were telegraph towers and used a system of blinds and shutters fitted on a large frame to pass simple messages.

Nine such towers were needed to reach Portsmouth. The first frame was built on the Admiralty roof, and had to be seen by men with telescopes at the next one, in Chelsea. After that they were at Putney, Cabbage Hill, Netley Heath, Hascombe, Blackdown, Beacon Hill, Portsdown and finally Portsmouth. Another twenty-one towers were needed to take a message on to Plymouth, going by way of Wickham, Blandford, Nettlecombe, Dalwood Common, Haldon, Knighton, Marley, Lee and Saltrum. It was the boast in Plymouth that a short message could be sent to the Admiralty and a reply received in fifteen minutes.

The difficulty and slowness of communications – whether laboriously by flags from a signal station perched on a headland, and communicating with a passing ship, or by orders being delivered to some distant admiral by frigate or Post Office packet brig – meant that commanding officers had much more responsibility on their shoulders.

The lieutenant commanding a small sloop, or a senior captain commanding a two-decker, or an admiral commanding a squadron or a station frequently met a situation where the uncertainties of war left him with a vital decision which he alone could make. Many dispatches from the West Indies marked in the Admiralty with 'R' (for received) and the date showed that, although the packet might take only thirty-five days to reach Falmouth from Port Royal, the letter had been written fifty or sixty days earlier; and even urgent dispatches sent by frigate depended on the vagaries of the winds: calms could last a week, a gale could add a fortnight to a crossing. 'I received yesterday your letter of 8th of October last,' Spencer told Parker on 5 December 1799, and almost exactly a year earlier he wrote that a letter of Parker's dated 10 August did not reach him until 21 October.

Nelson's greatness over the Battle of the Nile was less the actual fight than the earlier chase. The entire responsibility was his – he had a squadron and the enemy was somewhere in the Mediterranean. At this time Nelson's name was thirty-ninth of forty-two rear admirals in the Navy List, which in turn meant he was fourth most junior of the Navy's ninety-nine admirals. He missed Napoleon at Toulon, had nothing more than a hunch where he was going, raced diagonally across the Mediterranean to Alexandria, arrived there ahead of him without realising it, sailed back to Malta for news, and finally went back to Alexandria and found the French squadron. The point is that Napoleon could have gone anywhere – through the Strait of Gibraltar into the Atlantic, or to Turkey more than 2,000 miles to the east. Already one senior admiral had become a bitter enemy of Earl St Vincent because such a junior admiral as Nelson had been given the squadron to watch Napoleon. Nelson knew that one mistake meant professional ruin, and at no time could he ask a senior for advice or assistance. Several years later he chased the French fleet across the Atlantic and back before Trafalgar – a move his critics called a wild-goose chase and his friends the revelation of a shrewd strategic insight.

Decisions were left to 'the man on the spot' because there was no alternative, and most commanders-in-chief were very touchy about what they often saw as Admiralty interference in their own preserves. The penalties for being wrong varied only in degree – an admiral was recalled after a bad misjudgement and usually never employed again, though he received half pay and continued to be promoted by seniority as those above him died. The captain of a ship could be court-martialled on one of several charges – from 'failing to do his utmost', which usually implied cowardice, to disobeying orders, which often meant that he had attempted too much. But there was a good rule of thumb for all officers: if you succeed, no question is asked; if you fail, no answer will be sufficient.

In the way that it administered the Navy, the Admiralty was very much like a board of directors of a large company who make the broad and important decisions but leave others to fill in the details. The 'important decisions' were limited to three main areas – which men were to be in command of fleets and ships; how these fleets and ships were allocated; and what tasks the fleets, and sometimes individual ships, were to carry out.

The Admiralty laid down few instructions; the Navy was run on a day-to-day basis by the thirty-two Articles of War (comparable, the cynic might say, to the Ten Commandments, but strictly enforced), and a volume of 'Regulations and Instructions', which was notable for laying down the number of guns to be fired in various salutes, and such other ceremonial.

It is easier to say what was left to the officers than to say what the

Admiralty laid down. The admiral was given no instructions about strategy or tactics; all he had were the 'Fighting Instructions', which told him nothing about fighting and listed the penalties for failure as well as providing an admiral with justification for caution. The few books on naval tactics published during the previous fifty years were usually written by civilians. A volume which had a great effect on tactics was the work of a French priest, Père Hoste; two other Frenchmen, Morogues and Bourdé de Villehuet, had written more recently and their work was being translated; and a Scottish landowner, John Clerk, was writing a book on tactics that would interest Nelson.

The volume most commonly read by lieutenants and captains dreaming one day of hoisting their own flags and commanding a squadron or fleet was *A System of Naval Tactics*, published by David Steel, who sold charts, nautical instruments and manuals at the Navigation Warehouse in Little Tower Hill. The book, a slim, octavo-sized volume with diagrams, sold for 7s 6d and owed much to Morogues. One of Steel's most expensive items was one that makes the point: *The Elements and Practice of Rigging, Seamanship and Naval Tactics*, was in two volumes and cost four guineas, and Steel was making no idle boast when he said that in the volumes the subjects were 'more fully and correctly treated than ever before in the English language'.

As far as a ship was concerned, apart from a routine for the necessary paperwork, there was no drill laid down for the handling of the guns, no sail drill and no set uniform for anyone except officers and certain warrant officers. As soon as a captain took command of a ship he gave a copy of his own standing orders to the first lieutenant. The copy – often the size of a small book – described exactly how the captain wanted the ship run and was a reflection of his methods, quirks and prejudices. The officers, midshipmen, warrant officers and petty officers promptly threw away the copies they had made of the previous captain's standing orders and copied out the new ones, which were usually quite different.

The captain's orders usually specified the uniform to be worn by officers and petty officers on various occasions, and revealed a good deal about a commanding officer. Captain Richard Keats requested officers to 'pointedly distinguish' good men, and insisted that seamen were addressed by their own names. Altogether he laid down eighty-eight instructions, described in more detail later, aimed at the efficient running of the ship.

Even courts martial lacked Admiralty rules and were run on a curious mixture of tradition and common sense, handed down from captain to captain, as will be described later, and it was not until eight years after Trafalgar that a privately published two-volume book on naval courts martial established any sort of continuity in the way men were tried. The Admiralty simply stood by the thirty-two Articles of War – they were the rules, passed by Parliament, that officers and men broke at their peril – and a brief reference to courts martial in the Regulations and Instructions.

This apparently lackadaisical way of running a Navy which within a few years would be the largest the world had ever seen was curiously effective. Most of the great battles it fought were decisive, particularly where the admirals used their own tactics, notably Admiral Duncan at Camperdown and Nelson at the Nile, Copenhagen and Trafalgar. It would be naive to say that over the years the Admiralty was conscious that its admirals and captains were individualists because the majority of them were not, but the battles involving both fleets and individual ships that nearly two centuries later are still names to conjure with were for the most part fought by men who would have been stifled by regulations – whether a Nelson at the Nile and Copenhagen, or someone like the turbulent Thomas Cochrane, later Lord Dundonald, with his own incredible fight when his *Speedy* captured the Spanish *Gamo*. The Navy in many ways reflected the national character: the people of a country which functioned without a written constitution had, and still has, a deeply-rooted suspicion of regulations, preferring to follow tradition and habit.

The effect, though, because of patronage, luck or endeavour, was that with a few glaring exceptions the right men ended up in the right jobs. The ponderous Sir Hyde Parker spent four years in the West Indies, getting rich but also doing reasonably efficiently what was a tedious routine job. In the same period Commodore Nelson disobeyed all the rules at Cape St Vincent. However, the average politician's love of compromise nearly caused a disaster when the plodding, nervous Parker was put in command of the fleet sent against Copenhagen, with the mercurial Nelson as his second in command. The Government was saved the price of this absurdity and presented with a victory by what can only be described as a satisfactory private arrangement reached between the two admirals.

CHAPTER THREE

Acorn and Oak

Captain Cuthbert Collingwood, later to become an admiral and Nelson's second in command at Trafalgar, had his home at Morpeth, in Northumberland, and when he was there on half pay or on leave he loved to walk over the hills with his dog Bunce. He always started off with a handful of acorns in his pockets, and as he walked he would press an acorn into the soil whenever he saw a good place for an oak tree to grow.

Some of the oaks he planted are probably still growing more than a century and a half later ready to be cut to build ships of the line at a time when nuclear submarines are patrolling the seas, because Collingwood's purpose was to make sure that the Navy would never want for oaks to build the fighting ships upon which the country's safety depended. In turn, the oak trees being felled to build ships in Collingwood's day had sprouted when the buccaneer Sir Henry Morgan was still alive, James II was new to the throne, and St Paul's Cathedral was still being rebuilt after the Fire of London.

Forests of oaks and the building of ships had a close relationship: the shipyards were usually on rivers down which the timbers could be carried on hoys or barges, or close to ports to which it could be carried in merchant ships. By the beginning of the war, the shortage of oaks was beginning to be a great worry.

In 1618, the ships of the Navy had totalled 16,000 tons, and by 1806 the total was 776,000 tons, but in 1783, towards the end of the American war, the House of Commons had ordered a survey of the country's forests, so that the result could be compared with one made in 1608. Six forests were involved and they showed that whereas in 1608 there had been 234,000 loads of available timber 'fit for the Navy' there were only 50,000 in 1783. (A load comprised fifty cubic feet, while a ton of timber was about forty cubic feet. Thus

1,000 tons equalled 800 loads.) The amount available in the New Forest, for example, had dropped from 115,000 loads to 33,000, and in Sherwood Forest from 31,000 to 2,000.

The 1783 report revealed a frightening position: that the six major forests had timber enough for only twenty-five or thirty ships of the line. It had been estimated that the average annual need of the King's yards and the merchant yards (based on the years 1760–88) was 50,000 loads. But the situation was in fact far worse: by 1791 the actual annual consumption had risen to 167,000 loads for merchant ships alone, with the Navy needing 218,000 for new constructions and repairs.

The difference was made up by combing the country for more wood (but there was a limit to the amount of oak that could be hauled from small woods along poor roads to a distant river) and from abroad, much of it from Danzig, in the Baltic, and Holstein, one of the German provinces.

Shipbuilders regarded English oak as the finest; they declared that all else was prone to rot, and generally not the stuff to which an honest shipwright should take an adze. But given that there were shortages, then they preferred Italian oak; that from the Adriatic shores grew with fine curves, the so-called compass timber needed for the rounded frames of ships. After that, they would accept Danzig oak, and that from Holstein. Oak from Canada and America, although used in quantity for a few years, never found favour: it rotted far too soon, the shipbuilders claimed.

The quantity of timber and metal ware that went into a ship is best shown by following the construction of a ship of the line, and the *Bellerophon* is a good example. She was commanded at the Glorious First of June by a Scotsman who was severely wounded; at the Battle of the Nile by an Irishman who was badly wounded; and at Trafalgar by an Englishman who was killed, a Welshman taking over. To her, Napoleon Bonaparte surrendered himself in July 1815.

Better known to seamen as the Billy Ruff'n, she was a 74-gun ship, a third-rate under the Navy's system of rating a ship, when a first-rate ship had more than 100 guns (and a crew of 850 or more), a second-rate 90–98 guns, third 64–80, fourth 50–60, fifth 32–44, and sixth 20–30.

In practice, flagships were usually first- or second-rates and the majority of any fleet comprised third-rates ('seventy-fours'). There were few fourth-rates – by then they were not strong enough to stand in the line of battle and were too clumsy as frigates – while most frigates were fifth-rates.

By no means all the third-rates in commission had been built for the Royal Navy: in 1799, in the sixth year of the war, of the 130 third-rates in commission 29 had been captured between 1758 and 1798. The rest had been built since 1753 in various areas, and one of those ships, listed under Chatham, was the *Bellerophon*, which was in fact built by a small yard at Frindsbury, across the river Medway from Chatham. When the Admiralty decided to build her, the Navy Board awarded the contract to the firm of Graves and Nicholson. Eight ships had been built to the design, which was already twenty-three years old and by Sir Thomas Slade (who had also designed the *Victory*).

Graves and Nicholson had been anxious to get the contract, the largest so far placed with a private yard on the Medway. The draft of the *Bellerophon* showed that she would displace more than 1,600 tons, and be 138 feet long measured along the keel, and 168 feet along the gun deck, the two measurements of length commonly used. Her maximum beam would be an inch and a half short of forty-seven feet, and fitted out but not commissioned she would displace 1,613 tons. The agreed price (by the time she was commissioned she would cost £30,232 14s 4d) worked out at a little under £18 a ton.

Frindsbury is on the north side of the Medway, on a bend just beyond Upnor Castle, whose walls were damaged by roundshot from De Ruyter's ships when the Dutch sailed up the river in Pepys's day. Graves and Nicholson had to order the oak from the contractors, who regularly sent their buyers round to inspect the woods and forests and find suitable timber. Trees were felled, stripped of their bark and branches – except where they would make compass timber – and hauled by horses to Prentice's Wharf at Maidstone, where they were loaded on barges to be floated down the Medway to the yard's own dock. The *Bellerophon* would need at least 2,000 oak trees, and if the trees had been planted thirty feet apart she would clear fifty acres of forest. Her life had really begun about the time that Cromwell's Roundheads defeated the Royalists at Worcester and the future King Charles II fled to France: then the great oaks which were to build her were little more than saplings or sprouting acorns.

While the big trunks were being brought to Frindsbury, the yard's forge was hard at work. The ironwork – various kinds of fittings ranging from gudgeons and pintles for the rudder to the cranse iron for the bowsprit – would weigh a total of 100 tons, while more than 30 tons of copper bolts would hold the ship together, along with nearly 30,000 treenails, all had to be cut from selected wood.

However, before anyone put adze or saw to timber in the yard, the first task was to take Sir Thomas Slade's 1/48th scale plans (drawn on sheets of paper the size of a small kitchen table) and produce something that shipwrights could use. This was done by using the mould loft – a large floor almost as smooth and big as a ballroom – and drawing on it in chalk the full-size shapes of the keel, stem, stern, frames and all the hundreds of specially shaped pieces needed to build the ship.

From these chalked shapes on the floor the templates, or patterns, were made from thin wood and battens, much as a woman would lay out a dress pattern on the floor and decide to cut out the shape in brown paper, using that to transfer the pattern to the dress material. The wooden patterns were then nailed to the timber to be shaped.

Although many of the timbers were both thick and curved there was no way of bending it in this size, so naturally curved wood had to be found and shaped. Men from the Admiralty were constantly visiting all suitable forests and carving the government's broad-arrow symbol on trees which had these curves, either in the trunks or the boughs. Called 'compass timber' because the curves formed a radius, it was always in short supply; indeed, compass timber from an old ship which was being scrapped was often used again in a new one, so that in their ignorance the shipwrights often transferred the invisible spores of rot from an old ship straight into one whose keel was just laid.

On Graves and Nicholson's sloping ways, a series of five-foot high blocks were placed like railway sleepers, with enough space between them for men to work on the keel, which would be placed on top and form the backbone from which the curved ribs, called futtocks, would rise like the ribs of a body.

Each of these futtocks, forming nearly a quarter of a circle, was made up of several pieces of specially selected curved wood (compass timber) because no trees could grow at the correct curve in one complete piece. For the smaller curved pieces needed in the ship, wood could be put into a large kiln and boiled until it became pliable enough to bend.

Making up each rib to the right curve – and each differed slightly from the next one – tested the skill of the builder. It was built up from at least three pieces called the first, second and third futtocks. These ribs were fitted to the keel, and on top of them the keelson (pronounced kells'n) was fitted, running parallel with the keel and above it. A heavy bolt was fitted vertically through keel, futtock and keelson at every point where a futtock crossed the keel. The stem and the deadwood – the flat vertical section aft to which the rudder would be fitted – were built up, like a giant jigsaw puzzle, until the ship was standing on the ways, an enormous skeleton, and the planking started.

The construction was slow and the supervision fell on Nicholson, whose partner Graves died soon after the *Bellerophon* contract was signed. Wood was sawn in the sawyers' pits, futtocks were finally shaped by men using adzes – axes shaped like heavy short-handled hoes with which a skilled shipwright could shape wood, producing a surface looking as if it had been planed. Once the planks were ready, the whole *inside* of the ship was then planked, with the planks going over the inside of the futtocks. The *outside* of the futtocks was planked up in the normal way and another set of frames, called riders, were then fitted over the inner planking, so that in effect a ship was built within a ship, giving immense strength.

The planks were fastened with treenails, the long wooden pegs that acted like bolts or screws, each one of more than 30,000 being driven home by a mallet. The various decks were laid on beams crossing the ship and made up of two or three pieces of timber scarfed together, each beam being slightly rounded along the top to give the deck a camber, or 'round up', of six inches on the gun deck and an inch less for each deck above.

The hull and deck planking was caulked with oakum soaked in tar, and then some of the ironwork could be fitted. The months went by and the people of Frindsbury and Chatham opposite became used to the sight of the *Bellerophon* slowly rising up in Graves and Nicholson's yard. A large number of the local men worked there; almost everyone in Frindsbury had a link with the ship through a relative or friend employed on her.

After a year the planking had just begun; after a year and a half she looked like the hull of a ship, even to a layman's eye. In places her sides were nearly two feet thick, and already nearly 4,000 sheets of copper were ordered, ready to be nailed on her bottom in the dry dock later, to protect the underwater part of the hull from teredo and gribble, woodworms living in the sea and which in tropical waters can honeycomb a piece of wood within a few weeks. The sheets, weighing more than twelve tons, had been brought round from the Thames.

Slowly the total weight of the ship increased – the oakum hammered into hull and deck planking weighed nearly twelve tons while the pitch added another five. A dozen tons of tar was used to coat the outside of the hull. Whiting and white lead, used between joints, totalled more than six tons and finally, one of the last tasks before launching, the painting started. Four hundred gallons of linseed oil would be used, much of it poured into the wood as a preservative, but the three coats of paint called for in the contract would weigh four and a quarter tons.

Over at Cliffe, a few miles from Frindsbury, Mr Richard Chicheley was finishing off his carving of the figurehead of Bellerophon, lean and lithe, with a short red cloak, golden helmet with white plumes, javelin poised in his right hand, and seated on his horse Pegasus as though ready to do instant battle with a chimera. The Chicheley family had carved figureheads for many years. Finally the figurehead was mounted, the paintwork touched up, and the whole thing covered with canvas until launching day.

For many days the whole yard reeked of paint. The inside of the gun port lids were by tradition painted a dark red, the same as much of the ship's hull below decks, so that blood spilled in battle would not show so much. But it was mainly a tradition; in all the battles in the Navy's history, the casualties were never high enough to justify the choice of colour.

For the whole of September 1786, excitement was growing at Frindsbury: painters waited for coats to dry, inspectors from the Navy Board paid unexpected visits. The master shipwright at Chatham Dockyard – paid £200 a year, and having a first assistant, second assistant and third assistant, each paid £100 a year – was on board daily, being rowed over from the gun wharf on the Chatham side of the river.

It was rare for a woman to launch a ship and the Admiralty agreed that the Commissioner Resident at Chatham, Commissioner Proby, should launch the *Bellerophon*. Proby was in effect the uncrowned king of the Medway: the Deptford and Woolwich yards on the Thames were directly under the supervision of the Navy Board but Chatham had its own commissioner and a large staff – larger than that belonging to the only other commissioner nearer than Portsmouth, Sir Isaac Coffin at Sheerness.

The launching date was arranged for 6 October, a Saturday, which meant that all the hundreds of people living in villages nearby could attend the event of the year without losing a whole day's pay. By now the great bulk of the *Bellerophon*, with no masts fitted and no guns, was lying on the slightly inclined stocks. Her hull gleamed black from the coatings of tar; from the future waterline downwards the hull was bare except for tar, waiting for the sheathing. She was sitting on a frame called the cradle, which was specially built so that it would slide down the ways with the *Bellerophon*, keeping her upright until she was afloat, and then falling apart so that the pieces of wood could be pulled out of the way.

Strong timbers called shores, the lower ends stuck in the ground and the shores going up at an angle to press against the hull, prevented the ship and cradle sliding down into the water. On launching day, with the ways thickly coated with tallow, the shores would be removed one by one until only a few, called the dog shores, would remain to be knocked away at the last moment so that the ship's own weight would then take her sliding on the cradle down into the water.

Commissioner Proby planned a great day: the band of the Chatham Marines would be on board the *Bellerophon* and would play 'God Save Great George Our King', and then 'Off She Goes!' as the ship slid stern first into the water.

Flagpoles had been rigged where very soon masts would be stepped, and flags twenty feet long in the hoist were ready – the red Admiralty flag with its gold anchor fouled, a Union flag, the flag of the Navy Board (three gold anchors) and the ensign of the Commander-in-Chief at the Nore. The Commissioner's ten-oared barge, freshly painted, would wait at the King's Stairs and, as soon as the Commissioner arrived from his house, row him across the river to Frindsbury for the launching.

The landlord of the Crown Inn at Rochester, a short distance away, had received his instructions for the 'elegant dinner' to be served about 3 p.m., following the launching (which was timed for high water at 1.45 p.m.), and which would round off the day for all the local dignitaries, the mayors of the Medway towns, the Bishop of Rochester and representatives of the Admiralty and Navy Board.

Hundreds of people, from the Medway towns of Rochester, Chatham, Gillingham and Strood, from Hoo, Shorne and Chalk, Gad's Hill and All Hallows, had made their arrangements: they would travel by coach and by farm cart, on horseback and on foot, and they would toast the launching with their own ale and then settle down to a good meal of cold meats before returning home.

The weather, however, was doubtful: Thursday was fine – the kind of autumn day when the northern shore of the Medway between Hoo and Findsbury was a mass of red and gold from the leaves and trees, and duck and geese flew into the saltings, the marshes flooding at high water which ran from Hoo all the way to Sheerness and Queenborough, at the river entrance. On Friday, though, there was a strong gusty wind which soon brought low cloud and rain squalls from the west and which increased during the night until by Saturday morning it was blowing more than half a gale. The tarred hull glistened from the rain and the great flags were sodden, jerking in the stronger squalls.

But that afternoon when the official guests and the hundreds of sightseers arrived at the yard in time for the launching they found the *Bellerophon* already afloat, sitting on the water like a complacent black swan, waiting to have her masts put in, the flags flogging like torn sails and showering everyone who came near.

What had happened was that the high wind, buffeting the *Bellerophon*'s side, had made her shake and tremble, putting a great strain on the dog shores. Mr Nicholson and his senior men knew there was no chance of reinforcing the shores at this stage; the wind was increasing by the hour and very soon the dog shores began to creak and groan. It was obvious to Nicholson that at any moment they would collapse and the ship would start sliding down the ways, unnamed, unblessed – indeed, heartily cursed.

Then the shores began to collapse. Fortunately the tide had made enough so that the ship would float once clear of the ways. Supposing the ship should go into the water without a christening? Launching day was by far the most important in a ship's history – at least as far as her builder was concerned – and Mr Nicholson rushed to the platform built high in the air at the *Bellerophon*'s bow. The cover was off the figurehead and Bellerophon himself, in golden helmet, lithe, florid, of wet complexion, towered overhead, astride his horse Pegasus.

By now the whole ship was trembling badly and, as warning shouts came from his men, Mr Nicholson seized the traditional bottle of port which was waiting for Commissioner Proby, poured himself a glass after the custom of the times and, watched by the men whose work and skill had fashioned the great ship from trunks of oak, cried 'Success to His Majesty's ship *Bellerophon*' and drained the glass. Hastily recorking the bottle, he flung it against the bluff, apple-cheeked bows and the *Bellerophon* groaned and creaked as she slid down the ways into the muddy waters of the Medway.

As a fighting ship the *Bellerophon* was far from completed. Her new captain had been appointed, Captain Thomas Pasley, a 52-year-old Scot whom we shall meet later and who had recently spent a tiresome four years commanding frigates on convoy escort duty.

At the moment the *Bellerophon* was floating high in the water: her masts were yet to be stepped, the great yards had to be crossed, her bow looked stubby without its bowsprit and jibboom. All her guns, shot, powder and provisions had yet to be stowed, quite apart from the weight of all the rope needed for standing and running rigging.

The masts and yards and bowsprit weighed a total of more than sixty tons – the mainmast, the lowest section on which the topmast, topgallant and royal would fit, weighed fourteen tons. Twelve tons of spare masts and booms would be stowed.

The amount of rigging needed to support the three masts, bow-sprit, and jibboom amounted to twenty-six tons. This, called the standing rigging, was fitted when the masts were stepped, but the running rigging – in effect ropes which moved, hoisting or trim-ming sails and yards – weighed seventeen tons, while the total number of blocks (known on shore as pulleys) came to more than ten tons.

The sails would take up more than 10,000 yards of canvas, weigh-ing six tons. The spare set – which did not duplicate every sail – added more than three tons. The sails of warships were not the gleaming white clouds of canvas beloved of so many artists and poets; they were the normal colour of woven flax, described by one of Britain's marine artists as 'a warm tint of raw umber with a little raw sienna or perhaps a touch of yellow ochre'.

As soon as the wind died down the *Bellerophon* was taken from Frindsbury across the river to Chatham, towed over by men rowing in boats, and put in the dry dock to have the copper sheathing put on. Then she was taken out and secured alongside the sheerhulk, an old ship with a very strong single mast and sheers. These, two long and strong wooden legs fitted like a letter A without the cross bar, were hinged to the deck at the bottom and attached from the top to the mast by strong tackles. The sheers, leaning outwards from the hulk, could hold a mast suspended over a ship and lower it down into the appropriate hole in the deck on to the keelson. A mainmast, apart from weighing fourteen tons, is about 150 feet long, and a number of men were needed to hoist the mast up and then lower it slowly while the *Bellerophon* was moved back and forth, inch by inch, until the hole was directly beneath the mast, when it could be lowered right down and fixed in place by wooden wedges, and then the rigging fitted.

By now Captain Pasley and most of his officers had arrived, with more than half the 600 men who would make up the ship's company, and, once the lower masts had been put in by the sheerhulk, the *Bellerophon* was towed into the dockyard for the rest of the fitting out. The topmasts could be hoisted from on board, using tackles, followed by the topgallants.

Fitting out a new ship was the great test of a first lieutenant, who started off with a bare hull, empty below and above decks. Slowly equipment and provisions were brought on board – usually extracted from the dockyard by alternate threats and pleas – and gradually the *Bellerophon* sank lower, her waterline rising towards the edge of the copper sheathing.

The *Bellerophon* was intended to carry three kinds of guns. The twenty-eight on the lower deck, fourteen each side, fired a round shot weighing 32 lb and with a diameter of just over six inches. With a ten-pound charge of powder the maximum effective (but not accurate) range was about 3,000 yards, although captains preferred to fight at very much closer ranges. At a two-degree elevation and with a ten-pound charge, the 'first graze' for a 32-pounder was about 1,000 yards, but the more usual range for battle was under 100 yards.

A 32-pounder of the type used in the *Bellerophon* weighed $2\frac{1}{2}$ tons without its carriage. The twenty-eight 'long' 12-pounders, mounted on the middle deck, each weighed 34 hundredweight. On the poop, the highest deck and right aft, the *Bellerophon* had her lightest guns, eighteen 9-pounders: there they would not affect her stability so much, although each weighed 26 hundredweight. They had the same range as the 12-pounders, 1,800 yards. (Later she would also be fitted with eight carronades.)

All fighting ships were built with considerable tumble-home, the name given to the rounded sides, so that a section sliced from the *Bellerophon* would look like a wineglass, the tumble-home being the inward curve of the upper part.

The main reason for tumble-home was the great weight of the guns and the problems of stability. To keep a ship stable the greatest weights must be kept lowest. As much as possible was stowed below the waterline, where it acted as ballast, but there was no choice with the guns. The heavy 32-pounders were on the lowest deck and because of the wineglass shape were the furthest from the centre-line. The 12-pounders, although higher, were nearer the centre-line, where the heeling effect of their weight would be less. The 9-pounders were the closest in, so that there was a difference of several feet between the muzzles of the 32-pounders and the 9-pounders. Stowed well down below the *Bellerophon*'s waterline was shot for all the guns, totalling 80 tons, and 20 tons of gunpowder.

Masts, sails, guns and powder by no means accounted for all the weight: six anchor cables, massive and made of hemp, had to be brought on board and coiled down in the cable tier, 25 tons of weight. Five anchors added another 15 tons.

The ship's boats weighed nearly 10 tons, and then came the stores of the various petty and warrant officers – the bosun and carpenter accounted for 48 tons while the gunner, with his breeching and tackles for the guns, needed more than 20 tons.

With all these items stowed on board the *Bellerophon* was nearly down on her 'load line', the depth at which she was designed to float with everything on board. By now – thanks to her wineglass shape – it was taking nearly 18 tons to sink her an inch, but there was another 600 tons to come. Provisions, spirits and slops – the clothing sold by the purser – came to more than 200 tons, water 260 tons (more if there was room to stow it) and coals and wood, used for cooking, 50 tons. The men forming the *Bellerophon*'s ship's company, and their possessions, came to 65 tons. By now the *Bellerophon*'s displacement was more than 2,500 tons; she had taken on board as many tons as she weighed when she was launched at Frindsbury.

CHAPTER FOUR

Copying the Enemy

A ship of the line was truly a floating castle: inside her were a great number of guns, a magazine full of powder, a locker piled high with shot, and food and water to last her garrison of several hundred men for more than three months.

The British ships were well built and strong and their men fought bravely, but one skill eluded the Navy Board – the ability to design fast and weatherly ships. Most of the best ships in the Royal Navy in this war were those captured from the French or Spanish, or copied from them. However, the important thing was that the Admiralty was well aware of the deficiencies of its own designers and its attitude was simple enough – fast ships were needed, whether captured or copied.

Different nations produced different types of fighting ship. Often their needs varied, sometimes they had different geographical problems, occasionally they produced brilliant or uninspired or incompetent designers. Because of their shallow coasts, Dutch designers were given limits on the draught of their designs; Danish and Swedish designers usually had to make provisions for oars, or sweeps, in the smaller ships because, although tideless, the Skagerrak, Kattegat and Baltic could often be windless, and sometimes a current could run in the same direction for days on end so that ships had to be rowed against it.

That designing a sailing ship was an art rather than a science is best shown by the methods used. The designer usually received only the admiralty's or ministry of marine's basic requirements – the number of guns (from which the size of the crew was standard) and how many months' provisions she was to carry, with the powder and shot.

Without any knowledge of hydrodynamics or many of the natural laws that today are accepted as commonplace, the designer knew from experience that fundamentally a fat, squat hull could carry more than a slim one, but it would sail slower and would not go to windward so well. The slim hull would go to windward better but would heel more in a given wind – making problems for the men at the guns – and would not be able to carry so much sail or so many guns, men, provisions, shot and powder.

The designer of a ship of war had to be a master of compromise. From his own experience of past designs, or knowledge of the performance of specific ships, he had to produce the fastest and most weatherly hull possible that would carry the weight required and provide a stable gun platform. His only real tools were his experience and his eye. He usually began by making a model of the hull, his eye always seeking the fairest possible curve, smoothing away and rounding the model as much as he could to produce the best possible streamlined hull shape – although he did not know the phrase – that would result in a fast and weatherly ship.

The demands on him were thus many and contradictory. She had to be stable enough to carry sufficient sail to get her offshore and out of danger in a gale of wind – which meant that she had to have sufficient beam and draught. She had to be built strongly enough to survive mountainous seas and the enemy's broadsides, which meant thick and heavy scantlings. Speed meant a narrow hull; stability meant a beamy one; weatherliness – in this case the ability to carry sail in a high wind and get to windward – meant beam and draught for stability, and slimness for windward ability. Out of this mass of contradictions the designer produced his drawings or his model of a ship like the *Bellerophon*.

Yet the basic tonnages – guns, powder and shot – were almost the only figures that would change only slightly. The scores of tons of drinking water and hundreds of tons of food – the ship's company would slowly eat through that; towards the end of four months the *Bellerophon* would be many tons lighter, affecting the ship's trim and 'stiffness', her ability to stand up to the press of wind on her sails without heeling too much.

Depending on the period and place, his completed model (often several feet long: examples of 'shipyard models' are on display in many museums) or a set of drawings or both were approved and sent to the master shipwright at the shipyard. If he used only a model, then the lines plans were taken off – a process by which the wooden model was reduced to drawings which showed graphically how the ship appeared when cut into many slices, one set indicating the horizontal sections, another the vertical, a third the cross-section.

Designing was at this stage clearly a curious mixture of art and science: the science could be called experience, the art the indefinable creative ability that one man had to produce a ship that was better than that designed by a rival. French designers were not only producing fast and weatherly ships, but they designed strong ships as well. The Spanish, too, were building fine ships – due to the skill of a Catholic Irishman named Mullins.

As soon as a ship was captured from the enemy it was the custom to 'take off the lines'. The ship herself then sailed under the British flag, usually keeping her French name, and, if she proved a good ship, more were built like her.

For example, three frigates were captured from the French, the *Danae* in 1759 and her sister ship, the *Prudente*, in 1779, and the *Fortunée* in 1780. But before the *Fortunée* was captured the Admiralty had built a frigate called the *Minerva*, designed from the plans copied from the other two. More frigates were constructed to that design in the next two years, including the *Arethusa* built in Bristol, the *Phaeton* in Liverpool and the *Latona* on the Thames, and when the war with France began in 1793 they were reckoned among the finest frigates afloat.

Many other French designs were copied, usually with modifications. The 74-gun *Northumberland*, built in Deptford and launched in 1801, was a copy of the French *Impérieux*, while the 74-gun *Superb* was built in Northfleet, a copy of the *Pompée*.

In 1807, after the second attack on Copenhagen, when the Danish fleet surrendered, the 80-gun *Christian VII* was among the ships brought back to England. She was only three years old, built after Nelson's attack of 1801, but in the opinion of the British officers who sailed her and the Navy Board surveyors she was a very fine ship, although too small for the number and size of guns she carried. She was put into dry dock and her lines were taken off. Orders were given to build an identical ship, which was started at the King's yard at Deptford and was called the *Cambridge*, while the *Christian VII* went into service with the Royal Navy without change of name.

Of the twenty-seven British ships of the line that fought at Trafalgar (the *Bellerophon* among them) three had been captured from the

French. However, not all British ships sailing in the Royal Navy with French names had been captured: the 110-gun *Ville de Paris*, one of the biggest ships of the line in the Royal Navy, was built at Chatham in 1795, the 98-gun *Barfleur* was also a Chatham-built ship, the *Foudroyant* had been built in Plymouth and the *Alcide* at Deptford. There were many more – *Courageux, Belliqueux* and *Raisonable* among them. Ironically, the *America*, a 64-gun ship, was launched at Deptford in 1777.

The reason French names were given to British-built ships was usually that they were new ships replacing old ones of the same name captured in previous wars. The 24-gun *Bacchante*, captured in 1803, was broken up in 1809, and a new ship built in 1811 carried on the name. *Blanche* was a favourite name. A 32-gun frigate built in Bursledon in 1786, she was wrecked in 1799. A new *Blanche* was launched at Depford in 1801 and was captured by the French in 1805, the name going to a new 36-gun frigate the following year. She in turn was wrecked in 1807, when the name was given to a privateer captured by the *Powerful* in 1806 and bought by the Navy Board. She was broken up in 1814, and the same year the name was given to a frigate building at Chatham – the fifth ship to hold the name in twenty-eight years. The names were not always particularly attractive to the English eye or ear. The 26-gun *Belette* was taken from the French by the *Victory* at Toulon in 1793 and she was burnt in Corsica three years later. Her successor was built in 1805 and wrecked in the Baltic in 1812. She was followed by the third *Belette* the same year. (When the first *America* of 1777 was lost in 1800 she was replaced in 1809 by a second ship of the line built at Well's Yard in Blackwall, on the Thames.)

The Admiralty also rang the changes. When the French *Danae* – captured in 1759 and copied – was finally broken up the name was unused for a few years, until the 20-gun French *La Vaillante* was captured and, by a curious twist, her name was changed to *Danae*, and she later ended up back in French hands.

Sometimes when a French name was regarded as unsuitable another French name replaced it: the 74-gun *Peuple Souverain*, captured at the Battle of the Nile, became the *Guerrier*, while the *Tonnant* and *Conquérant*, which were with her, kept their names. The *Aquilon*'s name was changed to celebrate *Aboukir*, the more popular name at the time for Nelson's victory at the Nile, the Battle of Aboukir Bay. The *Spartiate* kept her name but the *Franklin* was changed to *Canopus*. The *Tonnant* and *Spartiate* both fought under the British flag at Trafalgar and the *Canopus* missed the battle only by chance.

There was occasionally a case of 'set a thief to catch a thief': the 24-gun French privateer *Bourdelais* was a new ship and considered one of the fastest privateers sailing out of the French ports. Various British frigates had tried to catch her, but she always escaped – until the 44-gun *Revolutionaire*, taken from the French in 1794, managed to capture her. It was a triumph for the French builder – the same man constructed both ships.

By 1799 the war had been in progress for six years, and there had been several great sea battles bringing victory to the British – the Glorious First of June against the French in 1794, Cape St Vincent in 1797 against the Spanish and Camperdown against the Dutch, and the Nile in 1798 against the French. The year 1799 is therefore a good time to look at just how Britain was getting on with her men of war.

The backbone of the Navy was its third-rate ships of the line (from 80 to 64 guns) and its frigates. It had 130 third-rates in commission, twenty-nine of them captured from the enemy between 1758 and 1798. Sixty-eight had been built on the Thames between 1755 and 1799, while nine had been built at Chatham, seven at Harwich, four in Portsmouth, two at East Cowes, three at Buckler's Hard (near Beaulieu) and eight in Plymouth.

There were 136 fifth-rate frigates in commission, forty-two of which had been captured between 1780 and 1799. Another forty-two had been built on the Thames, nine at Chatham, six in Bristol, ten at Bursledon, seven in Liverpool and others at Buckler's Hard, Mistley and East Cowes.

The building programme had of course swamped the King's yards so that the larger private yards had all the construction and repair work they could handle, but the smaller private yards were not being given orders as they had been between 1780 and 1785: then sixth-rates were being built by almost any yard bold enough to make a bid. Three 28-gun ships were built on the shore at Sandgate, near Hythe, in Kent; three were built at Dover, while Itchenor and Milford in Hampshire each managed a fifth-rate frigate, East Cowes launched two, Buckler's Hard six and Northiam one.

The effect of these building programmes was that there were few coastal areas from Harwich round to the western border of Hamp-shire which were not associated in a particular way with one ship or another: a 28-gun ship being built 'at the back o' the beach' at Sandgate, in Kent, was probably constructed by men whose families had been building fishing boats – often used for smuggling – for generations. The influence of the Royal Navy, at times tenuous, nevertheless was widespread; it was part of the atmosphere which made Britain a seafaring nation. Shipbuilders could be designing and building fast smugglers to evade the Revenue cutters; they could also be building ships of war.

Some of the most famous (although not necessarily the most powerful) men-of-war of Nelson's day were built in a private yard at Buckler's Hard, a small and picturesque village on the west branch of the Beaulieu River (then usually spelled Bewley, as it was pro-nounced), which flowed into the north side of the Solent. The *Agamemnon*, of which Captain Nelson was so proud, the 74-gun *Swiftsure*, which fought at Trafalgar, the *Euryalus* frigate, which first spotted the combined fleets of France and Spain leaving Cadiz for the battle – all three ships were built under the watchful eye of the master shipwright Henry Adams, the *Euryalus* costing £16 10s a ton, a total of £15,568 16s.

Buckler's Hard owed its position as a shipbuilding village to a curious collection of circumstances. The second Duke of Montague (not to be confused with the later second Lord Montague, who wrote a brief history) owned large estates which included Beaulieu and the nearby village of Buckler's Hard. He also owned St Vincent, in the West Indies, one of the major sugar-producing islands.

The Duke wanted to set up local industries and Buckler's Hard – originally called Buckle, after a family that had lived there for many generations, the 'Hard' referring to the hard gravel foreshore on the otherwise muddy bank of the Beaulieu River – seemed to the Duke an ideal place to build ships: thousands of oak trees grew on his estate all round, and only four miles away, at Sowley Pond, was an ironworks where a waterwheel worked the forge hammer.

The Duke made an offer to any suitable shipbuilder: he could have land for a quay for a rent of 6s 8d a year, and for every house he built for workmen and their families, the Duke would give him three loads of timber, almost four tons, free of charge.

It was an attractive offer and the firm of Wyatt & Company across Southampton Water at Bursledon decided to make the move. They loaded their long saws, adzes, planes and other tools in a small coasting vessel and moved to Buckler's Hard in 1743.

While some men began building the ways on which ships would be built and launched into the river, others started on the houses, leaving a wide space between the two rows for timber to be stacked for seasoning (one reason why the street is so wide today).

Wyatt's took with them their young overseer, Henry Adams, who supervised the construction of a large kiln in which wood could be boiled. With a representative of the Duke he went round the countryside marking oak trees for felling. Soon they had been cut and stacked between the two rows of houses – curved trunks and branches for the compass timbers, straight trunks to be sawn into planking by sawyers working two at a time at a saw so long that the man at one end stood in a pit, the trunk above him.

Wyatt's – which soon became in effect Henry Adams – secured an order to build a 14-gun ship called the *Surprise*; she was followed next year by the 18-gun *Scorpion* and then, once the Navy Board was sure of the competence of Henry Adams, the 50-gun *Woolwich*. Significantly the contracts for all three ships stipulated that Henry Adams (only thirty years old when the *Surprise* was laid down) was to be the overseer.

He lived in the end house on the north side, and the row of houses running each side of the great pile of timber and the ways sloping gently down to the river were the homes of all the rest of the men needed to build the ships. A shipwright's eldest son might be a treenail cutter, the next one a caulker, the third an apprentice. By now the Duke had named the village Montague Town, but the local people stuck to Buckler's Hard. Adams eventually took control of the yard and within a few years went into partnership with a London builder, Mr James Barnard, who owned the Grove Street shipyard in Deptford. Adams was soon supervising ships at both yards, the last built at Barnard's yard before the lease expired being the 74-gun *Northumberland*, launched in the summer of 1798 when Adams was seventy-five and reluctant to make the long journey to Deptford too frequently.

The great advantage of the Buckler's Hard yard was that it was near Portsmouth: once launched, a hull could be taken round to Portsmouth where there were sheerlegs for putting in the masts, while the dockyard had all the thousand and one items needed to fit out a ship.

In 1786, while the *Bellerophon* was being completed on the Medway, Henry Adams' yard was having a quiet time, and many small private shipyards round the coast, having launched their ships of war, were now with the peace looking for merchant ships and fishing craft to build. Although it was never to be repeated, the scale of building in private yards between 1777 and 1785 showed that as long as these yards were still in business the Navy need never be short of fifth- and sixth-rates.

Taking just the last five years, the names of the places which built these ships are interesting. In 1780, Mistley launched one and Bursledon one (four more were built on the Thames), while in 1781 Bursledon launched one and East Cowes one. In 1782 Bursledon launched one and Mistley one. By 1785 Sandgate was launching one (the *Hind*, 28, with the *Dido*, 28, completed the year before), Dover two, Bristol one (having launched five in the previous six years), Northiam one, Harwich one and Mistley one.

The prices of building began rising quickly after the French declared war in 1793, and those charged by Henry Adams give a good idea of the prevailing rates. The 32-gun *Cerebus* frigate cost £9,954 in 1794, a rate of £12 10s a ton. The 16-gun *Bittern* sloop cost £5,332 in 1796, a rate of £13 a ton. By 1797 the 38-gun *Boadicea* cost £16,885, or £15 10s a ton. Even a 24-gun storeship was costing £14 10s a ton by 1799, while a ship of the line, the 74-gun *Spencer*, launched in 1800, cost £20 a ton.

For all the romance in the building of the Royal Navy's ships, the waving flags and the sound of bands playing at the launching, a ship was often rotten as she slid down the ways, a beautiful woman already riddled with a fatal disease.

The reason was quite simply that wood rot was not understood: how it began and how it spread was as much of a mystery as how to prevent it. We have already seen that the shortage of compass timber often meant that some timber from an old ship was used in the building of a new, and although the wood looked sound it almost certainly contained the spores of rot – 'that little soft patch' which was considered unimportant but which carried what might be termed 'wood cancer' to new timber.

Seasoned wood was almost impossible to find by this stage in the war and green wood is, of course, much more prone to rot, quite apart from the fact that it shrinks as it dries out and, when used for building, leaves cracks or 'shakes' which hold water and breed the spores of rot. Ventilation to prevent rot was not understood and many ships were in any case built out in the open. During the year and a half or two years that she was being built, rain seeped into every part of a ship and started rot or spread rot already existing in reused compass timber.

All this meant that a new ship was soon in need of repairs, and older ships were at times hard put to it to stay seaworthy. The *Victory* cost £97,400 to build in 1753; but in the fifteen years between 1790 and 1805, the year of Trafalgar, repairing her cost £143,600. A report to the House of Commons in 1814, the year before the war ended, showed that twenty-three 74-gun ships cost £1,068,000 to build, but after from one to eight years at sea cost £1,148,000 to repair.

The *Astrea* frigate was built at East Cowes in 1781 and cost £7,855, but she needed 'small repairs' three years later costing £3,414 and more totalling £4,271 two years after that. So that the cost of the first five years' repairs, £7,685, was within £200 of her building price. She was then laid up for seven years but, with the war beginning, more repairs to the hull alone cost £5,347 and fitting her out another £5,677. Defects in 1794, 1795 and 1798 cost £539, £1,500 and £3,849. The copper sheathing was replaced for the third time in 1798 for £4,128. By then repairs had cost four times her original price. She was recoppered the very next year (when she was fitted out as a troopship) for £7,375, and was repaired and recoppered again in 1805 for £12,506.

To be fair to the East Cowes yard that built her, more than £20,000 of that money went on repairing or replacing the copper sheathing. As late as 1805 little was understood of the problems of electrolytic action. Putting copper sheathing anywhere near iron bolts or fittings under water was known to cause trouble – the iron rusted away. That had been reduced by using copper or bronze for fittings and fastenings wherever possible instead of iron, and putting the sheathing on the hull over tarred paper or tarred felt. In the late 1780s the effect of electrolysis, the process which was eating away the iron fastenings, was still so bad that the Admiralty began removing the sheathing when a ship was laid up for more than a few months and putting on new sheathing when she was commissioned.

The cost of ornamental carving was not reckoned in the total cost of building a ship; instead the Admiralty laid down a strict scale for various ships from a first- to a sixth-rate. This allowed £55 8s for the taffrail of a 110-gun ship, £30 18s for a 74, and £12 7s for a frigate, and set out prices for the taffrail boards (fitted each side of the bowsprit) and the quarterpieces. But any captain who ordered more, or who wanted extra gold leaf to pick out the carving, had to pay for it out of his own pocket.

Quite apart from going to war to safeguard naval supplies – much came from the Baltic – a successful battle sometimes yielded not only prize ships but marine stores. Gambier's attack on Copenhagen in 1807 led to the capture of sixteen ships of the line, while ninety-two transport ships were needed to bring back the timber, rope, canvas, masts, yards and powder taken from the dockyard and arsenal in the Danish capital.

The expedition to the Scheldt in 1809 led to the capture of a 74-gun Dutch ship, with a frigate and a brig being captured on the ways. The frigate and brig had to be destroyed but the timbers of the 74 were brought back to England and a ship built at Woolwich. She was launched in 1812 as the *Chatham*. A new 38-gun frigate was also captured at Flushing.

By 1795, after two years of war, when it became obvious, in the words of the man who long ago wrote the best history of British naval architecture, 'that French ships of war were superior, in point of sailing, to the English ships', the matter was raised in the House of Commons, 'where some of the naval members appeared unwilling to allow to the enemy that superiority on which other members strongly insisted'.

Although Parliament did not get at the truth of the matter – the Admiralty in fact controlled certain parliamentary seats so that it always had its defenders, particularly against attacks by independent naval officers elected in constituencies over which the Admiralty had no influence – the cause soon became obvious.

As some of the best French ships were captured and their lines were taken off, it became clear that the perfidious French were by then building larger ships. As a rule of thumb, the longer a ship is the faster she is, and when the 80-gun *Juste* and the 80-gun *Sans Pareil* were captured by Lord Howe at the Glorious First of June in 1794 it was found that although only 80-gun ships they were longer than some 100-gun ships in the Royal Navy. The third-rate 80-gun *Juste* was 193 feet on the gun deck; the first-rate, 100-gun *Victory* was 186 feet and the 98-gun *London* 176 feet. The latest British 80-gun ships were much shorter – the *Caesar*, built at Plymouth the year before, was 181 feet on the gun deck.

Then the ships taken at Toulon by Lord Hood in 1793 were measured, among them the 80-gun *Pompée*. She was 183 feet on the gun deck. Not only that, the lower masts of the third-rate 80-gun *Impétueux*, captured at the same time, were four feet higher than those normally fitted in a first-rate 98-gun British ship, and her topgallants were higher than usual.

Why had the Royal Navy just launched an 80-gun ship, the *Caesar*, which was only 181 feet on the gun deck when the French had built the *Juste* of 193 feet, which was so superior? The British designer, Mr Hunt, had no explanation; it was as if the French had won a no-trump game. The Admiralty, however, saw the lesson to be learned: new ships would be longer in relation to their beam than earlier. The fault, though, had not been entirely with the designers: the Admiralty had always insisted that ships had to be limited to a certain size, dependent on the number of guns they carried. The answer, though, seemed to be in building ships of a longer waterline length.

Within four years that answer seemed to be wrong. In 1797 the lines were taken off the four big Spanish ships captured at Cape St Vincent on St Valentine's Day. Two were 112-gun ships and two were 74s, and all four were superior sailers. But the 74s were not as long as the French – one was 179 feet and the other 176 feet on the gun deck, compared with the *Juste*'s 193 feet and the British *Caesar*'s 181 feet. But they were much *beamier* than British ships – 49 feet 7 inches and 48 feet 11 inches, compared with the *Bellerophon*'s 46 feet 10 inches. The *Leviathan*, which had been in the Glorious First of June and had been built at Chatham only seven years earlier, had a beam of 47 feet 6 inches.

There had long been a prejudice against beam, but now it seemed that it did not make for slower ships. Nor were the French and Spanish increasing the dimensions of only the ships of the line: two frigates captured in 1794 were much larger – and superb sailers. The *Pomone* carried 40 guns, had a length on the gun deck of 159 feet 2 inches, and a beam of 42 feet. By 1797 the *Endymion* was launched at Randall's yard in Rotherhithe, a copy of the *Pomone* except that she had eight inches more beam. Her captain, Sir

Thomas Williams, reported after her first cruise that she was a superb ship.

British designers were left puzzled. French ships were longer – and faster. Spanish ships were shorter, beamier – and faster. Now the French were producing longer *and* beamier ships which were faster. The fact was the old rules about length and beam were being overturned; frigates particularly would have to be larger.

The type of British man-of-war most likely to be seen at sea was the frigate, whether escorting a convoy in the North Sea, beating out towards Ushant with dispatches for the fleet blockading Brest, or cruising for enemy privateers off some islands in the West or East Indies. They were called the eyes of the fleet, but they were the maids of all work. Certainly an admiral commanding a squadron or fleet wanted them ranging ahead and round him, extending his view over the horizon. But out in the West Indies, for example, it was the frigate that patrolled the Spanish Main, and the islands of the Lesser and Greater Antilles, trying to stop any French or Spanish traffic.

Frigates were fifth-rate ships, carrying between 32 and 44 guns, and officially their complement was between 220 and 300 men. In wartime few frigates, whether large or small, ever had anywhere near a full complement: a 32-gun frigate with an official complement of 220 would have been lucky to have 160 men two years after the war began, and within a few years would have been content with 120.

A visitor to a frigate would climb up the battens fitted to the ship's side to find that she appeared to have three decks, yet a three-decker was the name for one of the larger ships of the line. The reason for the apparent contradiction was that in this context a 'deck' meant one that carried guns. The main deck of a frigate carried her main armament. A 32-gun frigate was likely to carry thirteen 12-pounders along one side and thirteen the other, with four 6-pounders on the quarterdeck and two 6-pounders on the focsle.

At the after end of the main deck were the captain's quarters. There was a cabin running the width of the ship and referred to as 'the great cabin'. In it a 12-pounder gun on each side took up a lot of the space. Forward of this were two small cabins, the 'coach' on one side, which was often used as a dining-room, and the 'bed place' on the other side.

The furnishings depended on the captain's taste and the length of his pocket. If he had a private income or had been lucky with prize money the great cabin would probably have comfortable armchairs and tasteful curtains which could be drawn across the stern lights, the windows stretching across the transom. There would also be a wine cooler – a bulky, lead-lined affair usually heavily made of mahogany – and silverware in racks along the sideboard, and decanters and glasses. The bed place contained what to a layman would seem to be a large but shallow open-topped box slung by ropes at each end so that it swung as the ship rolled. This was the cot; in effect a hammock with box sides, usually covered with material and well padded (and embroidered if the captain had a loving wife); however much the ship rolled the captain could be sure he would not be tipped out.

The captain was the only man to live, eat and sleep on the main deck. The rest of the ship's company lived on the lower deck. At the after end of the lower deck was the gunroom (called the wardroom in larger ships), a large cabin with a table down the middle and several tiny cabins forming one side and more the other – accommodation for the lieutenants, two marine officers, master, purser, and surgeon. Larger frigates had more cabins; the number varied. The cabins were far from substantial; they were 6 feet long and 5 feet wide, with headroom usually less than 5 feet 4 inches. The outside of each cabin was formed by panels fitted into grooves and had a swing door 22 inches wide with a sash of stone-ground glass. The 'bed place' or bunk was 2 feet 6 inches wide with lockers underneath. A cupboard, chair and stand for a handbasin usually completed the cabin's fittings. An officer's sword and telescope were often stowed in racks outside the cabin, where they could be snatched up in an emergency.

The captain's accommodation was made up in the same way, the bulkheads having hinges at the top so that they could be swung up parallel with the deckhead – the ceiling to a layman. The reason for these flimsy structures was that in battle the killers were usually splinters, not the actual round shot, and it was important to clear away anything that could produce splinters. Thus in time of battle every bulkhead in the captain's accommodation was either hinged up out of the way or taken down and stowed below the waterline, so that the main deck was entirely clear from one end to the other.

Forward of the gunroom there were more small cabins against the ship's side, the accommodation of the bosun, gunner, carpenter and captain's clerk. A large cabin formed the midshipmen's berth. None of the cabins on the lower deck had any natural light, apart from that which managed to get down the hatches and companionway. Immediately forward of the officers' and warrant officers' accommodation the marines slung their hammocks. They were intended to form a barrier between the officers aft and the seamen, who slung their hammocks further forward.

Although the captain lived officially in solitary state at the after end of the main deck, in fact there was often livestock at the forward end: the manger, right in the bow, was the place for poultry, pigs and even cattle, kept on board to provide fresh meat, eggs or milk for the officers, who had to pay for them. Just abaft the manger was the galley stove which heated up the great coppers in which the food was boiled. Even a glance along the main deck emphasised that a frigate, like any other ships of war, was primarily a floating gun platform. So many feet were needed for a gun to be loaded, be run out again, be fired and recoil. The men had to fit in the space that remained.

The lower deck, with the men sleeping in their hammocks, was packed and airless, but although the officers had more space they had much less air. The tiny boxes of cabins prevented any circulation, while the seamen's hammocks were slung near the main and fore hatches.

An average 32-gun frigate was about 130 feet long on the gun deck, with a beam of 35 feet. The lowest gun ports along the main deck were about 7 feet above the waterline. The ship was massively built; the frames, or futtocks, were about 11 inches square. The thickness of the hull planking varied between 3 and 5 inches, and when she had her full complement of men on board and water and provisions she drew an average of 17 feet.

The 'rooms' in the ship, as opposed to cabins, were used for storage. The bread room was lined with deal planking and fitted with bins to hold the oatmeal; the fish room (containing dried salt fish) and spirit room were lined with a thick layer of mortar and hair, and nailed over this were deal battens.

The most carefully guarded of all the storage places was of course the magazine and powder room. The passageway to it was lined with lead sheeting (which had to weigh 5 lb a square foot) and the floors were plastered with mortar, and over that was a lining of deal battens. The magazine itself was lined with a thick layer of copper sheeting, which served several purposes – keeping out rats which could chew holes in the flannel cartridges, keeping out damp, preventing powder getting into the grain of wood, and preventing any sparks. The door was hung with brass butt-hinges with copper screws, and fitted with a lock of brass and copper. There was no kind of metal that could cause a spark, and men were searched before they were allowed to enter. Men working inside wore flannel boots, and the only light came through a small glass window, outside of which a lantern was placed, guarded by a sentry.

The key to the magazine was the most carefully guarded in the ship. Even the gunner, without whom no one could enter the magazine, had to have the captain's permission to unlock the door. In action, 'fearnought' screens of thick flannel were unrolled across the passage to the magazine and soaked with water. Anyone going along the passage had to wriggle round the screens, which were intended to stop the flash from an explosion passing along the passage and reaching the powder.

The magazine was in fact a large box fitted into the ship so that it was lower than the deck: anyone entering it had to pass down several steps. The reason for this – the so-called hanging magazine – was that it could quickly be flooded in an emergency.

The powder, in copper-lined casks, was tranferred to cartridges, cylinders of thin flannel, as required. It was up to the gunner to have enough cartridges stowed in racks ready for the guns to last a stiff action but keeping as much powder as possible in the casks.

Lieutenant's cocked hat 1791

CHAPTER FIVE

The Captain Will . . .

In battle, no ship was any better than her captain. Like any other long war, the battle against France frequently provided surprises: some stalwart men who would obviously become heroes proved in action to be strangely backward; other men, quiet little fellows with no apparent thrust or with hearty and amiable souls like bishops, turned into butchers. But as always it was the captain who provided the lead.

The captain's role in peace or war has to be understood before one can consider the powers he had. In the course of a voyage a ship could spring a leak, be becalmed in unexpected currents, run aground in darkness, lose masts through rigging failure and then, helpless, be driven ashore. An anchor could drag, or she could lose the wind while tacking through a difficult channel and drift ashore. The master could make a mistake with the navigation, a young lieutenant on watch might give the wrong orders in a sudden squall so the masts went by the board – there were scores of ways in which a ship could be lost, and in every case the first thing that happened after such a loss was an official inquiry into the captain's activities, often followed by a court martial.

The captain could not watch and oversee everything, despite regulations, as anyone who has ever commanded a vessel at sea knows only too well; no captain could stay awake every minute; his task involved delegating authority.

Apart from the ship, he was ultimately responsible for the feeding, discipline, health and well-being of every one of his men. The purser had the task of obtaining and issuing provisions and clothing, the surgeon looked after the sick, but the real responsibility was the captain's. The lieutenants, master, and warrant and petty officers

had the task of enforcing discipline, but the captain had the responsibility. If half a dozen men or the whole ship's company mutinied,
the captain (if he survived) would face the Admiralty's wrath –
although the mutineers would be hunted down.

The captain had to be father and confessor, judge and jury, to his
men. He had more power over them than the King – for the King
could not order a man to be flogged. He could and did order them
into battle and thus had the power of life and death over everyone
on board. In return for all this responsibility he was by far the
highest-paid man on board, received by far the largest share of prize
money, had quarters larger than all the rest of the officers put
together, and by comparison had no work to do, apart from his
accounts and keeping a daily journal (which was all too often a
rewritten version of the master's log).

He could indulge in almost any whim; he could be a sadist –
mercifully there were very few – or a religious zealot; he could drink
heavily or make every drinker's life a misery.

The Admiralty, then, put virtually no restrictions on him – in
return for making him responsible for everything. Until 1806 the
Regulations said he could not order a man to be given more than a
dozen lashes, but captains awarded four and five dozen, noted it in
the log, and heard not a word of reproach from the Admiralty, who
read every ship's log. The restrictions on a captain's behaviour, then,
were those he applied to himself.

Yet the number of tyrannical captains in this war was very small.
The worst of them was Captain Hugh Pigot, commanding the *Hermione* frigate in the West Indies. He was murdered by a group of
mutineers who then ran away with the ship. Anyone who has read all
the available evidence on the case (it is extensive: see the author's *The
Black Ship*) can have no sympathy with Pigot, yet he was an exception: there were perhaps half a dozen others (out of hundreds) who
should never have been given command of a ship. Pigot is a good
example of the weak point in an otherwise effective system.

For all the talk of 'influence' and 'patronage' – and this book
indicates just how powerful both were – the Admiralty did not want
to lose ships, so no obviously stupid captain was appointed. But
occasionally an officer who was a competent seaman but had defects
in his character which should have barred him did in fact obtain
command because of influence: he or a relative, for instance, knew
an admiral or minister. This was the case with Pigot, son of the

admiral sent out to replace the triumphant Rodney and nephew of a peer who was a wealthy nabob.

Sometimes when a man who was perfectly balanced as a lieutenant was given command of a frigate and moved up from the casual *bonhomie* of the wardroom, he found himself overwhelmed by the loneliness represented by the great cabin. Unless he invited officers – which he could not do too frequently – he ate every meal alone; when he walked the quarterdeck the officers and men left the windward side clear for him. He was the captain; no one joked with him, no one chatted, always there was an invisible wall between him and his officers, a wall which represented discipline but one that shut out the captain. It was a wall which vanished the moment a captain tried to make himself popular, currying favour among his subordinates. From then on he was no longer the captain; he was an object of derision among the men he was supposed to lead.

The loneliness of command was something that a good leader accepted; but with an inadequate man it led to drinking or brooding and introversion; a healthy attitude towards the Church could become a religious mania; a normal strictness could warp itself into sadism. Obsessions seemed to be lying around waiting to be claimed – having the decks scrubbed half a dozen times, having the ship's company dressed in a particular way (at a time when there was no uniform). Some captains judged the ship's efficiency by the sail handling and gave not a damn about gunnery; others were more concerned in the number of broadsides that could be fired in a given time.

A successful captain fitted no pattern. One thinks of Nelson – small, narrow-chested, fretful, with a whining voice, and as a captain inclined to meddle in matters it would have been wiser to ignore (as the merchants in Antigua found when the young captain of the *Boreas* frigate started invoking the Navigation Laws against the Yankee traders). There was Collingwood, quiet, firm, thoughtful, who rarely flogged a man, but had a reputation for coldness. There was Sir John Jervis, later Earl St Vincent, a dour and ruthless disciplinarian. There was Thomas Cochrane, a daredevil captain who cared little for orders (if he was receiving them) and even less for the enemy, fighting actions which almost defied belief. In every case the men followed them through thick and thin. Edward Hamilton, commanding the *Surprise* frigate, was such a harsh disciplinarian that his ship's company were terrified of him – yet when it came to cutting out a frigate from a port on the Spanish Main defended by three castles and more than 200 guns they succeeded with casualties which are unbelievable unless one has examined the official Spanish figures and list of names in the archives. The *Surprise* had four men seriously wounded and seven slightly, and no one killed. The Spanish lost 119 killed and 291 taken prisoner (97 wounded). Hamilton received a knighthood for his bravery and was later court-martialled for cruelty to a seaman, with no one pointing out the contradiction of a man so planning a desperate operation that none of his men were killed – and yet being harsh.

There was, then, no pattern. One captain commanded his ship with a joke on his lips and a gentle hand on the rein; another rarely spoke and even more rarely smiled. Yet each commanded successfully. There was, however, one type of captain detested by both seamen and officers – the easygoing, slack captain. The men hated him because it left the way open for bullying officers; the officers hated him because it meant they received no backing in enforcing discipline.

Discipline was based only on the Articles of War, thirty-six numbered paragraphs, each of between fifty and one hundred and fifty words, which laid down in broad terms the rules and regulations and penalties. The Articles covered the shortcomings of admirals and captains rather more than seamen, and several gave death as the punishment, taking the penalty out of the hands of the court, once a man was found guilty. The Articles of War will be described more fully later.

The popular idea of diminutive, curly-haired and rosy-cheeked young midshipmen bravely fighting back fear amid the thunder of gunfire as the ship went into action and spending the time before and after battle being bullied and eating poor food was correct but only in the sense that every broken-down drunk lying sprawled in an alley was once a bouncing baby.

The midshipmen's berth in most ships of war, whether a frigate or a flagship, usually had a scattering of boys under fourteen years old, but the majority of them were between twenty and thirty, with some forty years old or more.

The first step in going to sea on the long voyage which a boy hoped would eventually reach a landmark when he hoisted his flag as an admiral began with a captain or admiral granting a favour by agreeing to take a particular boy to sea with him. Until 1794 the boy would be described in the ship's book as 'captain's servant'; after 1794 an Admiralty ruling named such boys 'young gentlemen intended for the sea service'.

This meant that as the war began most midshipmen had started off as 'captain's servants', but because of the obliqueness of bureaucracy this does *not* mean that they were servants of the captain. The captain had servants paid by the Admiralty and the number was already laid down by regulation. The captain was allowed four servants for every hundred men in the ship, while lieutenants, masters, pursers, surgeons, chaplain and cook were allowed one each. These were genuine servants – boys or men who polished boots and waited at table, washed shirts and ironed stocks.

However, the 'captain's servants', later listed in muster books as 'Volunteers' and referred to as 'young gentlemen', or the much older 'younkers', were in effect the captain's apprentices. From 1794 they were allowed £6 a year; before that they received nothing. These boys could be anyone ranging from the captain's son or nephew to the eager offspring of a friend. Some captains were not above taking along a tradesman's son in return for not being pressed over a large bill.

It cost the captain nothing: he did not promise to teach the boy seamanship or navigation – he could pick that up as he went along – and the boy's parents provided his clothing. What the captain gave the boy was 'sea time'. He could not be promoted until he had passed his examination for lieutenant, and he could not sit for the examination until he produced certificates showing his name had been on ships' books for at least six years, two of which had been spent as a midshipman or master's mate. This should, of course, mean he had been at sea at least six years, but until 1794 this was by no means the case.

A captain could put a boy's name in the muster book for a couple of years before the boy actually went to sea – thus gaining the valuable 'sea time'. After 1794, when pay was introduced for the volunteers, captains had to be more careful: having a boy's name on the muster book meant he had to be paid and, if he was not on board to receive his pay and the captain had it instead, fraud was involved. The Admiralty, not unreasonably, took a very stern view of 'false muster', cases of which are cited later.

The interesting point is that at no time did the Admiralty have a hand in choosing (or rejecting) the 'young gentlemen'. They might eventually become admirals, ending up commanding fleets or serving as sea lords, but as boys starting a sea career they were not chosen by the Admiralty: they went to sea in a haphazard manner, their only qualifications being their parents' association with a serving officer. A 'young gentleman' became a midshipman without selection or fanfare, or the blessing of their Lordships.

The regulations said quite flatly that no one under twenty (nineteen before the war ended) could be a lieutenant but these were the days of enterprise and ingenuity, before a person's life was well documented. A 'birth certificate' giving a particular date of birth was not hard to come by and was usually a chit signed by the local parson or forged. The examining board looked carefully at the certificates of service signed by individual captains and made sure they added up to at least six years; they looked at the birth certificate – or copy of it – and read whatever date of birth it said. If their professional questioning convinced them that the candidate would make a lieutenant, they noted on the passing certificate that the candidate 'appeared to be more than twenty years of age'.

Therefore it was quite possible that an eighteen-year-old boy who (before 1794) had his name down in a ship's muster books for more than six years, but who had served at sea as a volunteer or midshipman for only three, could go up and pass his examination, producing a forged birth certificate showing that he was twenty and genuine certificates of service which did not lie when they said his name had been 'borne on ships' books' for six years.

The most important point was, did the youth know his seamanship and navigation? If he did not, then he would be thrown out of the examination room and told to try again a few months later. The examining board (a group of captains or admirals) might not dig with bureaucratic diligence into a candidate's exact age or be too fussy over the six years, but it was very rare for them to pass a youth who did not know his stuff. As in all examinations, some candidates were lucky in not being asked questions on weak subjects, and boards undoubtedly passed some candidates who, although weak in mathematics or navigation, more than made up for it in seamanship, leadership and personality. Had there been a medical examination, youths like Nelson would never have been allowed to serve.

The examination for lieutenant was the most important hurdle to clear: once he had passed, a midshipman could be given a commission enabling him to serve in a ship as a lieutenant (although this was by no means automatic) and then in time be promoted to commander (to command a sixth-rate ship) or captain (fifth-rate or higher). But midshipmen's berths were full of youths and middle-aged men 'passed for lieutenant' for whom there was no vacancy or who lacked patronage.

Joining his first ship was a day that every midshipman remembered vividly. One officer, Frederic Chamier, wrote later: 'The uniform dazzled my imagination; in it I paraded Grosvenor Place by daylight in the morning, to the no small gratification of myself and the astonishment of the milkmaids and chimney sweeps.'

For him the choice of the sea was made by a process of elimination:

> My father declared none of his sons should idle away life in a red coat covered with gold lace, like the Duchess of Gloucester's footmen, as an officer in the Guards . . . My mother objected to any trade, in which was included bankers, lawyers, fiddlers &c; and consequently I was condemned to the sea, to which I had some pretensions, as my grandfather was an admiral, and my uncle a half-pay lieutenant. Another offer was made to send me to India; and, of two evils, I imagined I chose the least in giving my consent to become a defender of Albion, and a thing to fit a midshipman's coat upon.

Dressed in his new finery, dirk round his waist and cocked hat on his head, he visited his school to display them and then went off in his father's coach to join his ship at Sheerness, a boat taking him off to the 36-gun *Salsette* frigate. Another boat had taken out his gear and it was being hoisted as Chamier came alongside.

' "Hulloa!" said the first lieutenant (seeing my chest marked No. 6 – a large, lumbering thing, in which my father had stowed his linen for an India voyage some years back), "Hulloa – No. 6! Why, does this youngster fancy the ship was made for him? Here, Mr M'Queen", calling one of the master's mates, "strike this chest into the steerage for the present; but it must go into the hold afterwards." '

As it was hoisted away Chamier stood on deck with his father and the *Salsette*'s captain while the ship's midshipmen inspected him. Chamier's first sight of his new home came when he went down the hatchway to look at the main deck.

Ye gods, what a difference! I had anticipated a kind of elegant house with guns in the windows; an orderly set of men; in short, I expected to find a species of Grosvenor Place, floating around like Noah's Ark.

Here were the tars of England rolling about casks, without jackets, shoes or stockings. On one side provisions were received on board; at one port-hole coals, at another wood; dirty women, the objects of sailors' affections, with beer cans in hand, were everywhere conspicuous; the shrill whistle squeaked, and the voice of the boatswain and his mates rattled like thunder in my ears; the deck was dirty, slippery and wet; the smells abominable; the whole sight disgusting; and when I remarked the slovenly dress of the midshipmen, dressed in shabby round jackets, glazed hats, no gloves, and some without shoes, I forgot all the glory of Nelson, all the pride of the Navy, the terror of France, or the bulwark of Albion; and, for nearly the first time in my life, and I wish I could say it was the last, took the handkerchief from my pocket; covered my face and cried like the child I was.

Later he was taken to the midshipmen's berth.

It was noon, at which time the men and midshipmen dine, and consequently I found my companions at their scanty meal. A dirty tablecloth, which had the marks of the boys' fingers and the gentlemen's hands, covered the table. It had performed both offices of towel and tablecloth since Sunday.

A piece of half-roasted beef – the gravy chilled into a solid, some potatoes in their jackets, and biscuits in a japanned basket, with some very questionable beer, formed the comestibles.

The berth was about ten feet long by about eight broad; a fastened seat, under which were lockers, was built round the bulkhead; and the table, a fixture from sea lashings, was of that comfortable size that a man might reach across it without any particular elongation of the arm.

A dirty-looking lad, without shoes or stockings, dressed in a loose pair of inexpressibles, fitting tight round the hips, a checked shirt, with the sleeves turned up to the elbows – his face as black as a sweep's, and his hands as dirty as a coalheaver's, was leaning against the locker, and acted in the dignified capacity of midshipmen's boy.

With fourteen masters, Chamier noted, 'it had been held by good judges one of the most difficult points to determine which is the most worthy of compassion, the maid of a lady of easy virtue, a hackney coach-horse, a pedlar's donkey, or a midshipmen's boy'. Chamier reckoned it was the boy, who was in 'about as cursed a situation as the vengeance of man could suggest – a *galley* slave he is in every sense of the word'.

After describing his first meal, Chamier gives a picture of the berth:

Glass, a brittle material, and one which shows dirt both in the liquid and on its sides, was too expensive and too easily expended to be much used in the Navy. Cups answered their purpose and therefore cups were used. The soup-tureen, a heavy, lumbering piece of block-tin, pounded into shape, was, for the want of a ladle, emptied with an everlasting teacup; the knives were invariably black, both on the handles and on the blades; and the forks were wiped in the table-cloth by the persons about to use them, and who, to save eating more than was required of actual dirt, always plunged them through the table-cloth to clean between the prongs.

The table-cloth was changed on Saturdays.

The rest of the furniture was not much cleaner: now and then an empty bottle served as a candlestick; and I have known both a shoe and quadrant-case used as a soup plate . . . It was in a habitation like this, 'a prison', as Dr Johnson says, 'with the chance of being drowned,' that the sons of the highest noblemen were placed; and here, instead of the well-powdered lackey, the assiduous servant, or the eager attendant, he found but one almost shirtless boy to attend upon fourteen aspiring heroes – heroes who commanded by rights of years and strength, not by birth.

On his first night he discovered the sleeping arrangements were also simple: 'A hammock served as a bed, and so closely were we all stowed in the war that the side of one hammock always touched that of another; fourteen inches being declared quite sufficient space for one tired midshipman to sleep in.'

Frederic Chamier came from a reasonably wealthy family who lived in Clarges Street, Mayfair, with butler, footmen and a coach. Jeffery Raigersfield, the son of Baron de Raigersfield, was seven years old in 1778 when Captain Cornwallis (later Admiral the Hon. Sir William Cornwallis) entered his name on the books of the *Lion*, but he did not actually go to sea for another five years – he joined the 44-gun *Mediator* in April 1783 as captain's servant. He was lucky that his captain was Cuthbert Collingwood, and when he first boarded at the age of twelve (with five years' sea time) he noted that his messmates consisted of 'one mate, four grown up midshipmen, a younker who had been at sea, myself, and a blackguard boy, that served the mess as cook and all else besides'.

He soon noticed that his large chest of clothes, 'which included ten pounds that was in it, in halfpence and silver, cost my parents one hundred pounds', began to attract the attention of his messmates whenever he went to unlock it. To begin with it was so full that 'assistance was necessary to close the lid down before it could be locked up', but it was not long before he could close it without help, 'for I began to lose my clothes, and no one knew anything about them'.

A favourite leather cap that he wore during the day often vanished at night, but 'at last it struck me that the blackguard boy of the mess seemed very quick at finding it when I offered sixpence to the finder'. But his complaints about his losses did no good. 'Therefore, after a good crying when I was alone, I became more cautious when I went to my chest, and heedful of those around me.'

The *Mediator* was preparing to sail for the West Indies, he wrote, so 'the sea stock for the mess was laid in; it consisted of a few pounds of tea and brown sugar, a couple of sacks of potatoes, and about sixty pounds of beef taken up from the purser [i.e. bought], which was salted down and put into a small cask to serve as fresh provisions during the voyage'.

Raigersfield accepted his life without much complaint, and without comment noted that the biscuit served to the ship's company 'was so light that when you tapped it upon the table, it fell almost into dust, and thereout numerous insects, called weevils, crawled; they were bitter to the taste, and a sure indication that the biscuit had lost its nutritious particles; if, instead of these weevils, large white maggots with black heads made their appearance, then the biscuit was considered to be only in its first state of decay; these maggots were fat and cold to the taste, but not bitter.'

Raigersfield gives an interesting sidelight on flogging in the *Mediator* under Captain Collingwood's command: 'During upwards of the three years and a half that I was in this ship, I do not remember more than four or five men being punished at the gangway; and then so slightly that it scarcely deserved the name.'

Raigersfield went to sea some thirty years before Chamier, and with many fewer midshipmen, and without the wear and tear of twenty years of war, the conditions were better than in the *Salsette*'s midshipmen's berth.

'Our spoons and plates were pewter, a dozen knives and forks, two cooking kettles, a frying pan and a copper tea kettle, there were a dozen tumbler glasses, two decanters, and a dozen tea cups and saucers, of the old blue dragon fashion, with a tin teapot, some celery seeds and onions to make pea soup savoury, was all the stock midshipmen at that time thought of taking to sea.'

He wrote sorrowfully that 'as to the mess things that I brought on board in my chest, such as tea, sugar &c, they had been consumed long before for the common good, and my pewter washhand basin, the only visible remains of all my more than ample fitting out, was only mine when others were not using it'.

Soon after the ship sailed (carrying Commissioner Moutray and his family to Antigua, and thus the woman to whom a young Nelson first lost his heart) Raigersfield was seasick for some time, but as soon as he recovered 'I went to visit my chest, but found it nearly emptied of all superfluities, and excepting three or four shirts and a scanty portion of other necessities, little remaining of all the abundant stock my parents had so carefully got together for a three years' station'. Raigersfield had had the key all the time and it was locked when he went to it. 'My loss was deemed fancy by those around me, and I was not only laughed at but given to understand that unless I could prove my loss, my complaint would rather do me harm than good, and I wisely followed this advice . . .'

Eighteen years later another 'young gentleman', George Vernon Jackson, joined the *Trent* frigate in 1801 at the age of fourteen, but, as he noted in the first few lines of his autobiography, his name had been on the books of four successive ships for the previous six years.

Jackson's background was vastly different from that of Chamier and Raigersfield. His father had been a purser in the Navy, with five sons and four daughters. They were all living at Charlwood, in

Surrey, when the father asked Sir Edward Hamilton – knighted two years earlier for cutting out the *Hermione* (see page 64) – to take his eldest son to sea.

He joined the ship with £2 in his pocket and, perhaps forewarned by his father, was not so shocked by what he found in the midshipmen's berth of the *Trent* – 'here I enjoyed the usual entertainment bestowed upon fresh arrivals, and formed in consequence anything but an encouraging opinion of the career before me'.

Being a 'new boy', he was invited to dinner with Sir Edward, 'whom, from stories already related to me, I began to regard as something preternaturally awful'. Just before Jackson joined the ship a midshipman had been flogged and turned out of the ship, a fact which 'gave my associates a capital foundation for enlarging upon the captain's character'. Jackson, writing later as an admiral, commented, 'The memory of the dinner haunts me still after the lapse of sixty and odd years.'

Hamilton's severe manner was in this instance justified. Of dressing himself for the encounter, Jackson wrote:

> Everyone knows the economy with which a young boy's naval outfit is regulated . . . my uniform would have suited a shape twice my dimensions. We wore knee breeches then, and I can laugh now at the absurd picture I presented in a pair that nearly eclipsed me.
>
> Do what I would, there was no help for it; the upper part of the abominable things were close under my arms, and the legs hung dangling about within a few inches of my heels . . .

Pale-faced and, he admitted, much below the average height of boys of his age, he presented himself at the captain's cabin where Sir Edward 'in no wise reassured my failing nerves by exclaiming as his eyes fell upon my person, "Why, what the devil have we got here? He looks as if he had been swallowed and thrown up again." '

Dinner was an ordeal – refusing a glass of wine led to one storm from Sir Edward; a comment on grog and mistaking olives for 'green plums' provoked two more. Finally Jackson was able to leave – with Sir Edward saying: 'Look ye here, sir, go at once to the ship's tailor and have a fathom cut off those infernal tails of yours.'

Captain Glascock, writing of his first day afloat in a frigate as a 'young gentleman', said that when he arrived on deck the first person he saw was 'a vulgar-looking, squat, round-shouldered man, whose obliquity of vision exposed every being he looked at to a sort of cross fire, from eyes which appeared to have a roaming commission.

'A "voice like a boatswain" had been a phrase with my father, and the association was revived by the stentor-like tone of this strange-looking person, who was dressed in a blue white-edged coat which displayed here and there a few anchor-buttons of different dies; to which was added a buff, soup-spotted vest, a pair of tarred nankeen trousers, and an old battered broad-brimmed leathern hat. This homely habit, with diverse distinguishable daubings of pitch or white-wash on his back, naturally induced me to conclude he could be no other than the boatswain.' The young gentleman was wrong: he was the frigate's first lieutenant. And soon he was told he would eat in the gunroom on his first day. 'Dinner being at last announced by beat of drum, down flew the officers, helter-skelter, to the gunroom, the start being decidedly in favour of the Lieutenant of Marines, a light infantry-like figure of about fifteen-stone weight.'

He discovered that, two decks below, the gunroom was 'a dismal dungeon-like looking place, flanked on each side by a row of miserably cramped cribs, called cabins. Overhead there was certainly what, by some poetic-license, continued to be denominated a skylight; but, as to any light afforded, it might as well have been underfoot, most of the panes in its frame having been fractured, and unpainted patches of solid wood substituted for what had once been transparent glass.'

Glascock then went on to describe the other inhabitants of the gunroom, including a 'young gentleman' more than old enough to be his father.

'At the head of the table sat a pale, calculating, anxious-looking, middle-aged man, whose sole pretension to anything like uniform consisted in wearing a cross-anchor button on a plain blue coat.' That was the frigate's purser, while at the other end of the table sat the officer of marines, 'whose easy contented air and portly person formed a lively contrast with the meagre figure at the head'.

While Negro boys waited on the rest, the Marine officer was served by a Marine private, 'a bolt-upright, grim-looking Jolly, whose head and the beams above were perpetually in collision'. The three lieutenants, the master, surgeon and one 'young gentleman', 'a venerable mid, about forty', formed the rest of the diners.

James Gardner, who served in the 28-gun *Boreas*, made no bones about how he and some of his forebears first went to sea. 'My father, the late Captain Francis Geary Gardner, was appointed through the interest of Admiral Francis Geary (afterwards Sir Francis), and of my mother's uncle, Admiral William Parry, to be master of the *Boreas* . . . with the promise of Lord Sandwich (then First Lord of the Admiralty) to be promoted when opportunity offered; which promise his lordship performed by appointing him lieutenant of the *Conqueror*.' And young James went along with his father in the *Boreas* for a short cruise, being sent off to school when the ship went to the West Indies.

Gardner's autobiography is particularly interesting because at the end of each chapter he gives a description, in a few crisp words, of some of the people serving in any particular ship. His first three such verdicts concerned his father ('considered one of the first seamen in the Navy'), the gunner ('a very good man but had a very bad wife') and the surgeon's mate ('he could play a little on the flute, and used to annoy all hands by everlastingly playing the King's Minuet').

Gardner was lucky while serving in the *Boreas* and the *Conqueror* because, being with his father, 'I had nothing to do with the midshipmen, as I lived in the gunroom of the former and the wardroom of the latter'. His next ship was the 60-gun *Panther*, which he joined early in 1782 and whose peacetime midshipmen's berth he described:

In this ship our mess-place had canvas screens scrubbed white, wainscott tables, well polished, windsor chairs, and a pantry fitted in the wing to stow our crockery and dinner traps with safety. The holystones and organs [used for scrubbing the deck: see page 167] in requisition twice a week made our orlop deck as white as the boards of any crack drawing room, the strictest attention being paid to cleanliness; and everything had the appearance of Spartan simplicity.

We used to sit down to a piece of salt beef, with sauerkraut, and dine gloriously with our pint of black strap [wine], ready at all calls, and as fit for battle as for muster.

His next ship, the *Salisbury*, was 'the most hateful and disagreeable ship I ever had my foot on board of – so unlike the *Panther*'. At the age of fourteen, Gardner found there was 'mastheading upon every trifling occasion. The senior midshipmen (with the exception of a few) were tyrants; and petty tyrants are usually the worst.'

His verdicts on the eight midshipmen with whom he served ranged from 'a tyrannical fellow and member of the Hell-fire Club', 'a drunken Hun' and 'remember little of him, and that no good' to 'a very good fellow and good sailor, but fond of grog and boasting'.

Gardner was later to be a shipmate of the famous Billy Culmer, who was still a midshipman at the age of fifty-seven. Hard-drinking, scared of no man and a protégé of Lord Hood, Culmer let himself be talked into taking the examination for lieutenant a second time. Old enough to be the father of the captains examining him, he lost patience over a seamanship question about how to handle a ship in what he considered an impossible situation, told them it was humbug and that he would let the ship 'go on shore and be damned, and wish you were all on board her'. The examiners gave him a certificate, but after two commissions as lieutenant he died in 1802.

Grenade, Brown Bess, boarding axe

CHAPTER SIX

In the Steep Tub

Having survived the perils of the sea and the midshipmen's berth long enough to reach the age of twenty, the 'young gentleman' usually kept a weather eye open for the next examination for lieutenants, held at the Navy Board (abroad a commander-in-chief ordered his three senior captains to examine them), and, with his certificates of service (which were also reports on him by his captains), went before the examiners.

The captain's son, James Gardner, did not sit for the examination until he was twenty-five years old, by which time he had spent thirteen years as a midshipman. He went up to London to take the examination, and although extremely nervous he found that one of the commissioners was 'an intimate friend of my father', while another, Sir Samuel Marshall, the Deputy Controller of the Navy, was 'a particular friend of Admiral Parry, my mother's uncle'.

The questioning began, but finally he passed and he was told 'the certificates I produced ought to get me a commission without interest. On this hint I transmitted them the next day to Earl Spencer, the First Lord of the Admiralty'. With that he rejoined his ship at Portsmouth, but a few days later, calling at the commissioner's office to see if there was mail on the table, 'the first I observed was directed to Lieutenant J. A. Gardner, H.M. Ship *Victory*'. The letter said 'That Earl Spencer had received my memorial on the 11th, and that my appointment as lieutenant had passed the Board on the 12th January'.

Gardner now had his foot on the first rung of a very long ladder. As a midshipman, if he could not get a ship he starved, as far as the Admiralty was concerned; there was no half-pay for midshipmen. As a lieutenant, a man began in effect to have an official existence and his name went into the Sea Officers List, the forerunner of the Navy List. The publication usually consulted was brought out by a private printer, David Steel, and gave in order of seniority all the admirals, captains, commanders, lieutenants, masters and surgeons serving in the Navy.

Steel's list was in fact a small booklet called *Steel's Original and Correct List of the Royal Navy*, published 'at his Navigation Warehouse, No 1 Union Row, the Lower end of the Minories, Little Tower Hill,' brought up to date every month and costing sixpence. The 1799 edition, for example, corrected to January, was a 48-page booklet which listed all the ships in commission and their captains, pursers and stations, ranging in size from three-deckers to fire-ships; the distribution of all the ships – in port fitting out, guard ships, whether in the Channel, West Indies or on whatever service – and the totals in commission; the lists of serving officers and their pay; superannuated officers and their pay; the masters, physicians and surgeons; and the dates of sailing for all the Post Office packet brigs.

Marine officers were listed, with the lieutenants employed in the signal towers (forty-eight in all); the French and Dutch ships captured were named, with details, and the officers on the impress service were given, with their towns. It was an invaluable sixpen-north for the French Government, who were careful not to allow a similar document to be published in Paris.

The pensions were given in detail: fourteen admirals were receiving special pensions, ranging from £3,000 a year for Lord St Vincent, Lord Duncan and Lord Nelson (the victors of Cape St Vincent, Camperdown and the Nile) to 5s a day for Rear-Admiral William Dudington.

The rates of pay of captains was given as £1 a day in a first-rate; 16s in a second-rate, 13s in a third, 10s in a fourth, 8s in a fifth and 8s in a sixth. The half pay – in effect unemployment assistance – for captains was also based on seniority – the first thirty on the list had 10s a day, the next fifty 8s, and the rest 6s. (To receive half pay an officer had to take an oath every six months that he was 'not employed in the public service'. Nineteen captains were 'superannuated' at 10s a day, and fifty lieutenants were retired with the rank of commander at 6s a day (more important, perhaps, their widows would receive £45 a year).

The half pay for lieutenants was in the same descending order. The full pay for lieutenants varied, those 'under an admiral' (which meant in effect serving in a first- or second-rate) receiving 5s 6d a day and others 5s a day.

Steel printed a note that 'the necessary time of service previous to passing for a lieutenant is six years in all; viz. four years as a landman or able [seaman], in which time two years service as a [captain's] servant will be allowed, and two years as midshipman or master's mate, in all six years'.

The latest officers to be promoted to the next highest grade went to the bottom of that list. The names were given in seniority year by year; thus the twenty-fifth lieutenant under, say, the heading of 1796, was the twenty-fifth to be appointed lieutenant in that year. As lieutenants above him died or were made commanders or post captains, so his name would advance up the list, because new names under later years were being added below him. It was more a question of being pushed up from below than rising of one's own accord.

A man did not have to reach the top of the lieutenants' list to be promoted because for lieutenants promotion was not automatic: the jump to commander or post captain was by selection, not seniority. If a man reached the top of the lieutenants' list without being selected, he stayed there until he died; he never made the jump to the post list. Indeed, by the time a man's name reached the top of the lieutenant's list he was likely to be very old.

The first lieutenant named in the 1799 Navy List was G. H. Fortye, under '1744'. The next two were under 1747, the next two 1757, while there were fourteen for 1758. Fortye had thus been on the List for fifty-five years.

Once a lieutenant was on the list he needed something that would then get him the command of a sixth-rate ship (which would mean promotion to commander, originally 'master and commander'), or command of a fifth-rate ship, which was the post for a captain, so that this promotion was called 'being made post', while the title that went with it was 'post captain'.

There are two important points, the first of which is that 'the rank went with the job', and the second that 'captain' was also the universal name for the man who commanded a ship, whatever his rank. A lieutenant commanding a little sloop, for example, was 'the captain' just as one of the most senior post captains in the Navy List, commanding a 98-gun ship, was 'the captain'.

Remembering that, for command, rank went with the ship, the

system of rates becomes important. The lowest rate, sixth, was for ships of from 20 to 30 guns, and a sixth-rate was commanded by a commander. Ships smaller than a sixth-rate were commanded by lieutenants, but were not 'rated'. A lieutenant could not command a sixth-rate (except temporarily in an emergency) and a commander could not command anything less.

A fifth-rate (from 32 to 44 guns) was a 'post' ship, commanded by a post captain. It was therefore the next promotion for a commander, but the Admiralty would not write to a commander and tell him he had just been made a post captain: instead they gave him the command of a fifth-rate, which had to be commanded by a post captain, so the commander automatically became a post captain, a permanent promotion.

It was a one-way affair: if a commander 'made post' and given the command of a frigate was unlucky enough not to get command of another frigate when the commission was over, he could not revert to being a commander: instead he went on to half pay as a post captain, and if he lacked influence he might remain on half pay for the rest of his life – a high price to pay for being made post when, as a commander, he might have been employed for years.

Lieutenants could make the jump to post rank, avoiding commander, by being given command of a frigate. The first lieutenant of a flagship, for example, was in a very good position – providing he was in good standing with his admiral – for such a promotion. The death of the captain of a frigate in the West Indies almost certainly meant promotion for one of the Admiral's favourite lieutenants. A sickly station and the Admiral's smile was the surest way to promotion for those who cared to gamble on staying alive.

The promotion to post rank was another landmark in a naval officer's career; indeed, it was the critical one because in reaching it he had assured himself that, if he stayed alive long enough, he was bound to become an admiral. As one naval officer commented, 'Death is the life of promotion'.

Midshipman George Vernon Jackson, for instance, joined the Navy in 1801, became a lieutenant in 1812, received his first command in 1818 (after the war ended) and was put on half pay in 1828, at the age of thirty-one. From then on, even though he could not get employment, men above him in the Navy List died or were promoted. As a man reached the top of the captains' list, he was made a rear-admiral in the next set of promotions, as a vacancy occurred, changing over to the bottom of the rear-admirals' list and beginning the slow move up through the three stages of rear-admiral, three stages of vice-admiral, and two of admiral.

Jackson lived on; by the time he was seventy-five his name had reached the top of the captains' list and he was promoted rear-admiral (and his half pay went up accordingly). Five years later he was a vice-admiral and in 1875, at the age of eighty-eight and seventy-four years after joining the Navy, he became an admiral, having spent forty-seven years on half pay. He died the following year.

In a pamphlet written by 'A Post Captain' and addressed to Lord Melville, then the First Lord of the Admiralty, a bitter officer referring to a captain's half pay pointed out that there was income tax and widow's pension payments to be deducted, leaving a balance 'which I need not remark to your Lordship is not equal to the wages of some of your domestics, or that of many journeymen mechanics'.

Promotion itself was costly; the King was pleased to promote you, but the government was equally pleased to tax you for the honour, quite apart from ensuring an income for its sinecure holders. A young lieutenant receiving his first commission giving him command of a fifth-rate, and thus making him a post captain, could be proud of the piece of parchment which began in flowing handwriting 'By the Commissioners for Executing the Office of Lord High Admiral of the United Kingdom of Great Britain and Ireland &c . . .' and perhaps daunted by the phrase which said that he was to obey orders, and he 'will answer to the contrary at your peril'.

It was indeed an impressive document: the Admiralty Office Seal filled the top left-hand corner and the signatures of three members of the Board of Admiralty followed the writing – but in the bottom left-hand corner the cost was shown by a small blue seal bearing a crown and 'II shillings and VI pence'.

Nor was the government the only beneficiary of a promotion: the new uniform put a profit in the tailor's pocket. A commander's uniform, for example, cost him more than his first quarter's pay: the full dress coat and epaulette was from sixteen to twenty guineas; the undress coat and epaulette eight guineas. A gold laced hat cost another five guineas; sword and knot six guineas. Commanders and post captains with less than three years' seniority wore only one epaulette, an economy in bullion even if it gave a rather lopsided appearance.

The regulations covering the duties and responsibilities of a captain or commander were strict. As soon as he received his commission he had to go on board, send the Admiralty and Navy Board weekly accounts of the work being done ('or oftener if necessary'), and he had to stay on board: he could not sleep anywhere else ('he is not to live out of the ship') without the written permission of the Admiralty or commander-in-chief. (The same rule applied to admirals; when they arrived in a home port they had first to get Admiralty permission even to go up to the Admiralty.)

He had to take inventories of all the stores – a job usually left to the purser, gunner, bosun and carpenter, although he was responsible for any shortages and was often charged for them. His clerk had to keep an account of all stores and provisions brought on board and compare it with the indents 'in order to prevent any fraud or neglect'. The majority of his duties were concerned with preventing fraud, whether it involved provisions and stores or seamen and their pay.

His prime task was 'to get the ship mann'd', and he was ordered 'not to enter any but men of able bodies and fit for service'. He was to keep the established number of men 'and not to exceed his complement', but in wartime he often sailed with a quarter fewer. The details of every man (name, age, where born, rate, whether a volunteer or a pressed man) had to be entered in a muster book, and he was supposed to muster the men once a week – in effect having a roll-call. Every two months he had to send two copies of the muster book to the Navy Board.

This was very important because it was the only check on the identities of the men serving in a particular ship. Although the Admiralty appointed the commission officers and the Navy Board the warrant, all the petty officers and seamen were sent on board from other ships or brought in by press gangs, and the only record of their existence was the entry in the muster book. When the men of the *Hermione* frigate mutinied and ran away with the ship to the Spanish Main, the hunt for the men began at once, using the latest muster book (and most of the men were caught and brought to trial, the last ten years later).

The muster book also recorded the men who had left the ship by one of the only three possible ways, which were indicated in the muster book by the initials 'D', 'D.D.' or 'R'. 'D' stood for 'discharged' – to another ship or to a hospital; 'D.D.' meant 'Discharged Dead';

while 'R' stood for 'Run', the Navy's phrase for deserting. If men deserted in one of the ports of the United Kingdom, the captain had 'to send up to the Secretary of the Admiralty their names, description, place of abode and all the circumstances of their escape'.

The complete instructions for a captain were a curious mixture ranging from 'he is not to make use of the ship's sails for covering boats, or for awnings' to 'he is to demand all seamen (His Majesty's subjects) from on board any foreign ship he may meet with, obliging their masters to pay them their wages to that day'. The last two of the sixty-one instructions said, 'He is responsible for the whole conduct and good government of the ship . . . He is also answerable for the faults of his clerk.' More important, he could not receive his pay 'without the proper certificates, and must make good all damages sustained by his neglect or irregularity'.

Other regulations covered different aspects of commanding a ship. A captain appointed to command a convoy – the senior officer of the escort, in other words – was forbidden to receive presents from anyone. It was a regulation usually ignored because the masters of merchant ships were in the habit (providing it had been a successful voyage) of giving the commander of the escort a piece of silver, a tray or teapot, or some such 'token of their esteem'. The regulations said that the captain was not to 'receive any gratification, nor to suffer any one else in the ship so to do'.

The fourth regulation in the section headed 'Of convoys' was intended to stop escorts leaving the convoy and going off on their own to chase prizes. A captain was 'not to chase out of sight of his convoy, but be watchful to defend them from attack or surprise; and, if distressed, to afford them all necessary assistance'. This regulation was well known to the masters of the merchant ships, who frequently sailed with very small crews, calling on the escort for men to help weigh anchor, or for a carpenter and his mates to patch a leak.

If the master misbehaved – deliberately sailed under reduced canvas at night, for example – there was little a captain could do, under the regulations, which said that 'If the master of a ship shall misbehave himself, by delaying the convoy, abandoning the same, or disobey the established instructions, the commander [of the convoy] is to report him, with a narration of the fact, to the Secretary of the Admiralty, by the first opportunity.'

Captains knew from bitter experience that this was a waste of time: an Admiralty complaint to a shipowner had no effect for the simple reason that the master was sailing under reduced canvas at night or with too small a crew because the shipowner had warned him to save money. The unscrupulous shipowner relied on the Royal Navy, justifying his behaviour by the taxes he paid. Knowing the regulations did little to help him, the naval captain had a few tricks available, and they are described later.

Captains and lieutenants came under the Admiralty; they were commission officers (the 'ed' was not added to commission for many years) who were given Admiralty commissions. Warrant officers, however, with a few exceptions (the master at arms and schoolmaster) received their warrants from the Navy Board and were divided into two types. The first were warrant officers 'of wardroom rank' – the master, purser, surgeon and chaplain – who thus lived with the commission officers. The other warrant officers – the main ones being the gunner, bosun and carpenter, although the sailmaker, cook, master at arms and many others were appointed by warrant – did not use the wardroom (the gunroom in a frigate).

There was one major difference between a commission officer and a warrant officer: the commission officer was appointed to the ship for one particular commission, and at the end of it he was once again unemployed. A warrant officer, though, stayed with the ship, even though it may be laid up – when his wife and children often moved on board.

Promotion for a warrant officer meant being transferred to a larger ship, when he received more pay for a higher rate, but the general rule was, once a warrant officer always a warrant officer.

Of all the warrant officers, the gunner was the one who had most influence on the 'young gentlemen'. In anything larger than a frigate the youngsters lived in the gunroom, ruled by the gunner; in a frigate they were aft in whatever berth the shipbuilder had devised.

The petty officers were the only ones in a ship appointed by the captain: the Admiralty sent him his lieutenants and, with the Navy Board, his warrant officers.

The master had the most wide-ranging instructions. 'He is, under the command of the captain, to have the charge of navigating the ship.' He was also responsible for stowing the ship, rigging and trim, as well as navigation and charts. He had to watch all provisions and stores taken on board and had to tell the captain of any that 'appears in any respect defective'. Taking on ballast was his responsibility, and he also had to make sure that everything was stowed properly in the ship, both to make the best use of all available space and have the ship floating on her marks. A ship down by the bow was hard to handle; a ship down by the stern would usually be slower.

The masters of the King's ships were for many years the Admiralty's only source of hydrographic information about changes along a coastline or reef, and each master was 'duly to observe the appearances of coasts; and if he discovers any new shoals or rocks under water, to note them down in his journal, with the bearing and depth of water'.

He had 'to keep the hawse clear while the ship is at anchor, and see that she is not girt with her cables'. He also had to provide his own navigation instruments, including a quadrant or sextant, which was an expensive item, as well as 'maps and books of navigation'. A master's pay depended on the size of his ship, ranging from £9 2s a month in a first-rate to £4 in a sixth-rate or smaller. A brass sextant with telescope, in a mahogany case, cost between ten and fourteen guineas, while an ebony one could be bought for six or seven guineas. A quadrant cost up to nine guineas. A case of instruments 'for navigation or drawing in general' cost up to £6, dividers 7s 6d and parallel rules up to £2. The master was, in the larger ships, the next highest-paid to the captain. In a first-rate the captain was paid £28 a month, the master £9 2s, and a lieutenant £7 (£5 12s in third-rates and smaller). Lieutenants might have commissions while masters had only warrants, but a wise captain took care that he had a good master, and a wise first lieutenant took care not to run foul of him.

The next man of importance in the Instructions was the bosun, who was in charge of the actual rigging (although the master was responsible for the way it was set up), cables, anchors, sails and boats. With so much rope and canvas in a bosun's care there was more than a temptation to sell pieces of the lighter canvas to seamen wanting to make new clothes, but the Regulations warned that 'he is not to cut up any cordage or canvas without an order in writing from the captain and under the inspection of the master'.

The bosun was in many ways the most important man in the ship as far as the crew was concerned: 'He and his mates are to assist and relieve the watch, see that the men attend upon the deck, and that the working of the ship be performed with as little confusion as may be.' The bosun and his mates passed their orders to the accompaniment of the shrill notes of the bosun's call, wrongly called on shore a 'bosun's whistle'.

Using his call a bosun and his mates could in effect make different types of signals, or calls, to the ship's company. By blowing into the call and then 'throttling' with his palm and cupped fingers a man could produce a note almost an octave above the first one. By varying the throttling a skilled bosun's mate could produce about eight notes. He could blow in three different ways – at a steady pressure, which produced a clear note; at a rapidly varying pressure, which sounded a trill; and with a vibrating pressure. The range of sounds is best described by the seamen's nickname for bosun's mates – 'Spithead Nightingales'.

The calls passed orders in three different ways. The first was when a distinctive call was played that had a meaning everyone on board understood without it being shouted. The second type drew every man's attention to an order the bosun's mate would call out as soon as he had finished 'the pipe', as the tune was called. The third was a call intended as a salute.

There were in fact 'pipes' and 'calls'. Among the calls were, for instance, the order 'Call all hands' or 'Call the starboard watch', while pipes included 'Pipe down'. The bosun's mate, about to deliver a long order, would play the appropriate call or pipe, shout 'D'ye hear there!' and then shout the order.

In handling the ship the bosun's call could pass orders very quickly and unmistakably. Haul, hoist, let go, belay, turn up – all these and many more had their own distinctive calls, the tunes often matching the action. 'Pipe still', for example, the order for every man on deck to stand to attention ('still'), usually as a salute to a passing ship, was a steady high note lasting five seconds. It was also a warning intended to avoid an accident.

The bosun's call was in effect a badge of office, but bosun's mates carried – until an Admiralty order banned them halfway through the war – another which was hated and feared by the seamen, a rattan cane known as a 'starter'. Some captains, even before the Admiralty order, forbade their use; others encouraged it. The canes were used to hurry men along, or for swift punishment.

Captain Richard Keats, commanding the *Superb* in 1803, noted in his captain's orders, 'The Boatswain and his mates comformable to the old custom of the service are to carry rattans but they are to be used with discretion.'

The gunner, armourer, and gunsmith were usually put together in the same set of regulations, although the last two were carried only in flagships. The gunner was the king of the powder room, or magazine, but a king strictly governed by a constitution drawn up by the Admiralty.

The gunner was the one man whose carelessness could destroy the ship in a moment, and the Regulations showed that the Admiralty was well aware of it: there were twenty-six instructions for the lieutenant, thirty-eight for the master, eleven for the bosun, but thirty-three for the gunner. They ranged from not swabbing a gun with water 'when it grows hot, for fear of splitting' to coating guns with a mixture of tar and warm tallow if they had to be carried in the hold. The boxes of 'grape shot and hand-grenadoes' were to be kept in a dry place, and he was not to load the guns with 'unfit mixtures, which do greatly endanger their splitting'.

His role as the senior of the gunroom in ships that had wardrooms was acknowledged in the 26th instruction – 'he is to keep good order in the gunroom, and suffer none to lie there but such as have a right, or whom the captain shall direct . . .' The last instruction said: 'No person shall be warranted as gunner before he has passed an examination before a mathematical master, and three able gunners of the Navy, and from them procure a certificate of his qualification.'

The carpenter's fourteen instructions told him to take care of the ship and her masts and inspect them daily, look after his stores, make sure the pumps worked, and in battle repair damage and plug shot holes.

The next man was the purser, the ship's business man, who will be dealt with later, and then the surgeon. When he was given his warrant the surgeon had to provide himself with 'instruments and a chest of medicines, according to the Rules of the Navy', and they had to be inspected and approved by the physicians of the Sick and Wounded, or the physician of Greenwich Hospital, as well as the governor of the Surgeons' Company. When they gave him certificates agreeing that his instruments were suitable and his medicines 'fit for use', he could join a ship, but once on board he was to watch his medicine chest – 'all such medicines or drugs as shall be found in the chest, not fit for use, must be destroyed'.

One of his instructions (out of a total of thirty-seven in the 1806 edition) said that he had to get 'a competent number' of printed sick or 'smart' tickets from the Sick and Hurt Board, because every man sent on shore to the hospital had to have a sick ticket. The remaining instructions were straightforward: he was to visit his patients at least twice a day, consult with the physician of the squadron over 'cases that are difficult', and be ready with his mates in time of battle, 'having all things at hand necessary for stopping of blood and dressing of wounds'.

The master at arms was appointed by a warrant from the Admiralty; one of the few warrant officers not responsible to the Navy Board. He was in effect the ship's chief of police. He was responsible for all the sentries, and was supposed to exercise the petty officers and men 'daily by turns' with muskets and pistols, 'having a proper allowance of powder and shot for that purpose'. He was also responsible for seeing that the galley fire and candles were 'put out in proper season'. His assistants were the ship's corporals, and all of them were under orders 'to acquaint the officer of the watch with all irregularities in the ship' that they saw.

Before a schoolmaster could get his warrant from the Admiralty he had to be examined by the Master, Warden and Assistants of Trinity House, as well as producing certificates concerning his sobriety and good behaviour. He was 'duly to employ his time in instructing the Volunteers in writing, arithmetic, and navigation, and in whatever may contribute to render them proficients'.

Drumming spherical trigonometry into unwilling heads of midshipmen was a thankless task for which he was paid (in a third-rate) £1 17s 6d a month, with a £20 bonus at the end of a year providing his captain gave him a certificate. His basic pay, though, was within 2s 6d the same (in a third-rate) as a bosun's mate, quartermaster, trumpeter and sailmaker. He also collected so much a month from each of his pupils, who were not restricted to the 'young gentlemen' – 'he is likewise to teach the other youths of the ship, according to such orders as he shall receive from the captain'.

The last of the men covered by the Instructions was the cook, an important member of the ship's company whose only real task was to watch water boil. A cook had to have a warrant from the Commissioners of the Navy, and to get that he had to prove he was a Greenwich pensioner. Eight instructions covered his role in serving the King. The second said that he was 'to have charge of the steep-tub and the meat put into it, and he is to be held responsible for any part of it which shall be lost through his want of care'. The meat, beef or pork, was months and sometimes years old by the time it was taken out of the cask, preserved by salt which was caked on the outside and impregnated it. Before it could be eaten the meat had to be soaked in water (steeped) for at least twenty-four hours. The cook's responsibility was in making sure that, if twenty-five chunks of salt beef were put in the steep tub, the same twenty-five chunks were taken out again. In merchant ships the meat was sometimes put in a net bag and towed over the stern, the rush of water working more effectively to wash out the salt. Foreign ships sometimes did the same thing, but used a metal container like a crude birdcage.

The fourth instruction concerned cooking the meat and the other food: he was to see 'that all the provisions are very carefully and cleanly boiled; and that they are served out to the men according to the established practice of the Navy'. This would seem to require some skill in cooking, but it did not. The meat was cooked simply by boiling it in the great copper heated by the galley fire: there was no roasting or grilling. In fact this was no hardship; the meat needed prolonged boiling to get rid of more salt and to soften it so that it could be chewed. All other food was issued to each mess, so that, if the issue of flour and currants was going to be used for a plum duff, the man elected mess cook for the week mixed the pudding, put it in a cloth bag, fixed on the metal tally giving the mess number, and took it to the cook, who threw it into the copper, and later hooked it out – and the dozens of others – and gave them back to the mess cooks.

Having read the Instructions, a Greenwich pensioner was equipped to be a cook in one of the King's ships. In fact the job was usually given to an old petty officer who had lost a limb. He was paid £1 5s a month in a first-rate and a shilling less in a sixth-rate. He was not bothered with killing the livestock often carried on board: that was a task for the cook's assistant, whose main skill was usually plucking a fowl for the wardroom or captain, or cutting a sheep's throat.

For all that, the cook was usually one of the affluent members of the ship's company because of the slush, the fat that floated to the top when the meat was boiled. The Regulations and Instructions forbade the cook from 'giving the skimmings of the coppers . . . to the men, either to mix with their pudding or use in any other manner as scarcely anything more unwholesome or more likely to produce the scurvy can be eaten'. It was a regulation invariably ignored because few cooks would pitch the slush over the side.

The salt meat issued to ships was supplied to the Navy Board by private contractors, and they were no more honest than any contractor supplying a government department staffed by men who considered corruption to be an unfair arrangement only when someone else received a bribe.

The Regulations said that 'no unusual pieces are to put up with the meat, such as leg bones, shins of oxen, cheeks of hogs, ox hearts &c'. However, the contractor supplied casks containing a particular weight of meat. The actual number of pieces was stencilled on the outside, but the only check made by the Navy Board was to weigh the cask, so few contractors were above using a heavy hand with the salt: every pound of salt saved a pound of meat. The Navy Board's check, apart from weighing the cask, was solely the rule of thumb that 450 pieces of beef or 900 pieces of pork made one tun.

The logs of the ships told a different story; the opening of a new cask of meat was noted down, and a typical entry was: 'Opened cask of beef marked 161 pieces, contained 157 pieces.'

The contractor found it profitable to sell the fattiest meat to the Navy Board, so when a mess was issued with its piece of meat, steeped but not cooked, a quarter might be bone and a quarter fat. After the mess tally was fixed on, it was boiled, and much of the fat floated to the top of the water in the copper, unappetising fist-sized lumps of yellowish sludge. By the time the meat was cooked it might weigh a quarter less, but the cook would have a bucket full of the slush. He had in fact been skimming money off the water, because the seamen were only too anxious to buy the slush to spread on their bread, the name given to the coarse biscuit – the source of so many stories about weevils.

Pensions were paid to the various types of officers and, in certain cases, to their widows. The widow of an officer killed in action received a full year's pay, and orphans a third of that, unless they were married, in which case they received nothing. If the officer was not married, his mother could claim a widow's share – providing she too was a widow and more than fifty years old.

In one of the few comparatively generous regulations, it was made clear that 'this bounty' covered men killed in tenders, boats or on shore, as well as those on board a ship, and included 'those that are slain in fight with pirates, or in an encounter with the ships of friends by mistake'. Men who died of wounds 'are all esteemed as persons slain'.

A commission officer whose wounds resulted in the loss of an eye or limb, or the total loss of the use of a limb, received a full year's pay and could charge his medical expenses, providing he had a certificate from the Surgeons' Company in London and they agreed the expenses were 'reasonable'. The 'young gentlemen' received the same treatment as captains and lieutenants.

Warrant and petty officers and seamen received pensions from the Chatham Chest, a curious fund to which every British seaman contributed (although the government gave nothing), but a man 'hurt, maimed or disabled' had to produce a certificate 'expressing the nature of the hurt' and signed by the captain, senior lieutenant, master and surgeon.

For those who stayed alive and intact, there was half pay for all commission officers and pensions for the others. Bosuns, gunners, carpenters, pursers and cooks, who were employed all the time, had to serve fifteen years. Masters and surgeons 'whose employments are not constant', needed eight years of sea time before qualifying.

However, it was not a question of serving fifteen or eight years and then receiving a pension: they had to have a minimum of that much service to qualify for a pension if the physicians of the Sick and Wounded and the Surgeons' Company reported the man's 'incapacity to serve his Majesty'.

Yet the pension, when it arrived, was generous: in the case of bosuns, gunners, carpenters, pursers and cooks (the men with continuous service) it was equal to their pay in the ship of the highest rate in which they had ever served. Masters received half their pay and surgeons had the same as masters.

Captains and lieutenants often did not do so well: 'Commission officers worn out or disabled in the Service, are considered as their cases may deserve and as his Majesty shall think fit.' In other words, they had to petition the King.

We have seen how providing they had proper commissions, warrants or certificates from the Admiralty, Navy Board, Sick and Hurt Board or Trinity House, and the appropriate influence or luck – everyone down to the cook arrived on board a ship, leaving the chaplain and the seamen (a percentage of whom would then be rated petty officers by the captain) yet to join.

The chaplain occupied an odd position in the ship; indeed, only fifth-rates and higher had to carry one, but there were never enough to go round so it was rare to find them in anything less than a 74-gun ship. Since they had a choice, parsons generally preferred comfort and were rarely if ever found in frigates. On the whole, various churches left the Navy to sing its hymns and psalms in its own way, an unfortunate shunning of a great number of men who were both superstitious and religious. Within a year of the war ending, with more than 700 ships in commission, there were less than sixty chaplains.

The chaplain needed an Admiralty warrant (although their Lordships did not regard chaplains as warrant officers) and they were paid 19s a month, the same as an ordinary and 5s less than an able seaman. However, a chaplain received a bonus of 4d a month for every soul on board, and some chaplains doubled as schoolmasters, receiving the tuition fees as an extra (though not the monthly pay of £1 17s 6d).

More than almost anyone else in the ship, the chaplain depended on the attitude of the captain. If the captain made a fuss of him and frequently had him to dine, then the other officers followed suit. If the captain ignored him, then the chaplain sank to the level of the schoolmaster. If the chaplain asked the Admiralty to be allowed to serve in a particular ship, the captain could not refuse him, although there was no regulation governing the welcome to be given such a tactless ecclesiastic.

Most chaplains were remote from the men, although Robert Hay's comments from the lower deck reflect his Scottish background. He was serving as a seaman in the *Culloden* in 1804 when she was the flagship of Rear-Admiral Sir Edward Pellew and the Revd John Dunsterville joined the ship. 'He was of small stature, plump round face, his eyes peculiarly large but not expressive, his hair bushy and black as a raven and his complexion dark. He was somewhat cold, stiff, reserved and formal in his manners. Towards inferiors he carried a repelling aspect no way calculated to gain esteem or confidence.

'In all his transactions, which indeed were very few, with any of the seamen, he was quite upright and faithfully observed his promises, but he was exceedingly hard withal.'

Commenting that Episcopalians spent more time reading prayers and lessons than the Presbyterians, so there was less time for the sermon, Hay wrote that 'Mr Dunsterville, besides reading prayers on Sunday, would, when the weather permitted, deliver a sermon, but he was never under the necessity of composing any, for he brought aboard two or three dozen written ones, which were more than sufficient for the whole passage.'

William Richardson, on board the *Regulus* in 1809, was luckier with his chaplain. 'Divine service performed and an excellent sermon was preached by the Rev Mr Jones, touching on several remarkable instances of divine favour . . . how the winds favoured us in going into Aix roads and how they shifted to bring us safe out again.'

Speaking trumpet and telescope

CHAPTER SEVEN

The Press Gang

In wartime, one of the King's ships was in effect a great wooden hopper into which was fed men. They did not have to be educated, or men who wanted to go to sea: they needed to have all their limbs and most of their wits.

The figures for the size of the Navy in the first few years of the war are revealing. At the beginning of the year the war began, Parliament increased the size of the Navy to 45,000 (out of a total population in 1801 of about 9 million). This was increased to 85,000 (72,885 seamen, 12,115 marines) in 1794, then in 1799 to 120,000 (100,000 seamen, 20,000 marines), and by 1800 to 110,000 seamen and 20,000 marines.

The strength of the Navy, its nucleus, was its volunteers; not for nothing came the expression: 'Better one volunteer than three pressed men.' Captains were responsible for manning their ships. Before the war it was usually done by something approaching showmanship: a successful captain relied on his reputation, had a printer strike off some bold posters which were pasted up in likely towns, and equipped a ship's band – or hired some musicians – who went to towns with an officer to persuade young men to volunteer.

It all cost money and the captain had to pay – for the transport and accommodation of officers and men traipsing the countryside drumming up volunteers, and for the posters. But some of the posters were masterpieces – one surviving at the National Maritime Museum was put out by Lord Cochrane, wanting men for the 36-gun *Pallas* frigate.

It was headed 'God Save the King', followed by 'Doublons. Spanish Dollarbag consigned to Boney', and began: 'My lads, the rest of the GALLEONS with the TREASURE from LE PLATA, are waiting half-loaded at CARTAGENA.' The flying *Pallas* was waiting at

Plymouth 'for an expedition, as soon as some more good hands are on board'. Telling the men to rendezvous at the White Flag, Cochrane warned, 'none need apply but SEAMEN, or stout hands, able to rouse about the field pieces, and carry a hundredweight of pewter without stopping at least a MILE'. The final flourish, in large type, was: 'BONEY'S CORONATION is postponed for want of COBBS', and no one needed reminding that a cobb, or cob, was the sailor's slang for a Spanish dollar piece.

In wartime a captain could rely on getting some men from the Impress Service, the widespread system which operated the press gangs. But this source never supplied enough: he had to get men from wherever possible. Few had Cochrane's reputation and most sailed with many fewer men than the complement. Once a man volunteered, he received conduct money – in effect a bounty – and two months' wages in advance. This was not a burst of generosity on the part of the Navy: the man needed to buy warm clothes, hammock and blanket – known as slops – from the purser. In this way anyone joining a ship soon had a sea-going kit, and the Regulations said of volunteers, 'At their coming on board they may be supplied by slop clothes, but the value thereof must be deducted out of the said two months advance.'

The whole question of pay was a complicated one, but the men were often paid a year or more late. The Admiralty recognised this and, although it did not press Parliament to provide more money or otherwise ensure that the men were paid promptly, it did make certain regulations to safeguard the men. Ships were not paid while abroad, but as soon as the ship arrived back in England and her books were deposited with any Commissioner of the Navy, the men were paid within two months – but the last six months' pay was always held.

There were plenty of unscrupulous moneylenders and traders who would help an impoverished seaman in return for a letter of attorney: having a man's power of attorney was as good as an Admiralty promise to pay a set sum of money. For this reason a later Admiralty regulation said: 'No letter of attorney is valid, unless made revocable, and attested by the captain or commander and another of the signing officers of the ship. . . . Captains are to discourage seamen from selling their wages; and not to attest letters of attorney, if the same appear granted in consideration of money given for the purchase of wages.'

Knowing that a ship might not be paid for a year or more, an able seaman could sign an order on wages due which he could give to his wife or parents so that they could draw the money at the nearest Navy Pay Office. An order could not exceed £7 and had to be witnessed and signed by the commanding officer, who also had to provide a certificate, which had to be inspected by the Pay Office in London. This seemed a laborious process but the intention was to protect the seaman. The limit of £7 was an insurance by the Admiralty because a seaman's monthly pay was £1 4s. There was always a 'land shark' ready to offer him, say, £10 in return for a letter of attorney which would enable the shark to draw the man's annual pay. And unless the power of attorney was revocable the unscrupulous shark would keep on drawing – probably without ever seeing the man again. The Admiralty put a stop to this by saying, in effect, that it would not pay any money on the strength of a letter of credit unless it was revocable.

The Admiralty safeguarded both seamen and marines against arrest for debt: none could be taken out of the service unless the debt was more than £20 and contracted before joining the Navy. This last provision limited the Navy's role as a debtors' haven.

In wartime, with dozens of ships being commissioned and the high death rate from sickness on certain foreign stations, apart from the normal mortality, there was never a chance that the Navy could be manned by volunteers. Obviously the Impress Service would have to supply the extra men – at least, that is how it appeared to the authorities at first. But with 25,000 extra men voted for the Navy before the war began, 45,000 voted a few weeks later, 85,000 within a year, and as many as 100,000 by 1795, the Impress Service could not supply enough men.

The Impress Service, or the system of pressing men for the King's service, was not new; nor was taking a bribe to let a man go free – indeed Falstaff, in the days of Henry IV, admits:

> If I be not ashamed of my soldiers, I am a soused gurnet. I have misused the king's press damnably. I have got, in exchange of a hundred and fifty soldiers, three hundred and odd pounds. I press me none but good householders; yeomen's sons; inquire me out contracted bachelors, such as had been ask'd twice on the banns; such a commodity of warm slaves as had as lieve hear the devil as a drum; such as fear the report of a caliver worse than a

struck fowl or a hurt wild-duck. I press'd me none but such toasts-and-butter, with hearts in their bellies no bigger than pins'-heads, and they have bought out their services; and now my whole charge consists of ancients, corporals, lieutenants, gentle-men of companies, slaves as ragged as Lazarus in the painted cloth, where the glutton's dogs lick'd his sores; and such as, indeed, were never soldiers, but discarded unjust servingmen, younger sons to younger brothers, revolted tapsters, and ostlers trade-fall'n; the cankers of a calm world and a long peace; ten times more dishonourable ragged than an old faced ancient: and such have I, to fill up the rooms of them that have bought out their services, that you would think that I had a hundred and fifty tatter'd prodigals lately come from swine-keeping, from eating draff and husks. A mad fellow met me on the way, and told me I had unloaded all the gibbets, and press'd the dead bodies. No eye hath seen such scarecrows. I'll not march through Coventry with them, that's flat: nay, and the villains march wide betwixt the legs, as if they had gyves on; for indeed, I had the most of them out of prison. There's but a shirt and a half in all my company; and the half-shirt is two napkins tack'd together and thrown over the shoulders like a herald's coat without sleeves; and the shirt, to say the truth, stolen from my host at Saint Albans, or the red-nose innkeeper of Daventry. But that's all one; they'll find linen enough on every hedge.

The Impress Service, poorly organised at the beginning of the war, was limited to seizing men who were seamen – a word given its broadest interpretation – and was in competition with the militia ballot, into which, in theory, every man's name was put. Until 1757, the owners of property were responsible for supplying men and arms, but this was then changed so that each county was required to provide a certain number of men – the Quota system, described later in more detail.

The press gang, pressing seamen, the Impress Service – all lead to the question: what did 'press' really mean? In the early days a recruiting officer, whether for the Army or Navy, was always ready with 'the King's shilling'. If he could transfer that shilling from his own pocket into the possession of a civilian, he could claim that the civilian had entered into a contract with the King to serve him, however unwilling the civilian might be. The shilling was transferred in curious ways, a favourite one being by putting it into an unsuspecting man's tankard of ale so that when he next reached out to gulp his drink he took possession of the shilling. A wise landlord, not anxious to see his best customers hauled off to fight the King's enemies in distant parts, provided glass-bottomed tankards, so that the wary drinker could peer into it to see if a shilling was lurking at the bottom, ready to change him from a toper to a trooper as the recruiting sergeant's hand tapped his shoulder. The recruiter did not have to be in uniform; indeed, he and his mates were usually dressed in civilian clothes, cheery fellows, apparently celebrating some improbable event and encouraging any likely young recruit to join in.

The word 'press' was a corruption, in regular use by this war. The organisation at the ports was called the 'Impress Service', and the group of men under an officer was called a press gang, but the words were originally 'prest' and 'imprest'. The word 'imprest', noun or verb, means money paid in advance to some person or pay for State or government business, and comes from the latin *praestare*, to be a surety for something, and the old French *prest*, a loan or advance. Thus a man paid the King's shilling became an imprest, or prest, man, and in an age when spelling was not standardised eventually became 'pressed'.

The origins of the naval press gang, lost in the past, are probably bound up in feudalism. Long before England had a standing Navy, the Cinque Ports had to provide ships for the country's defence. The original Cinque Ports – Sandwich, Dover, Hythe, Romney and Hastings (though Richard I (1157–99) added Rye and Winchelsea, perhaps to show foreigners that they should never underestimate the English by assuming that cinque meant five) – had considerable powers: under a warden, they had their own criminal and civil codes, were exempt from various taxes, had special parliamentary representation and could pass their own local laws.

In return for all this they had to provide a fleet of ships of war when needed and anyway pay its expenses for fifteen days a year. These rights and obligations continued until the Navy grew under the Tudors, when the Cinque Ports declined in importance.

Finding ships meant finding men, and the Cinque Ports were not the only ones who had this task. The King, in defending the kingdom, called on ships and men, and the first on record as ordering their seizure with almost monotonous frequency was King John, who seems the first of the monarchs to have 'put it in writing'. Finding the Welsh a little tardy in coming forward, his warrant of 1208 warned them: 'Know ye for certain that if ye act contrary to this, we will cause you and the masters of your vessels to be hanged, and all your goods seized for our use.'

It soon became clear that the seaman virtually had no rights: he was certainly not covered by the Magna Carta. John signed this on 15 June 1215 and on 14 April 1216 ordered twenty-two seaports to arrest all the ships and crews lying in their waters and send them round to the Thames. It is significant that the barons, having just forced John to sign a document ensuring the liberty of all his subjects, not only raised no objections about the freedom of ship-masters and seamen, but arrested the ships. More important, John's successors did the same thing: every time a King considered Eng-land threatened (or wanted to threaten or go to war with another nation), press warrants were issued. No men, as Magna Carta guaranteed, were denied liberty – except seamen and, as Falstaff records, soldiers.

The only thing that happened was that as the decades went by the penalties became less: hanging a man because he would not allow himself to be pressed did not help get a ship to sea, a fact which eventually dawned on the King's advisers. By 1623 the seaman was commanded 'dutifully and reverently' to take the King's shilling, although it was tacitly understood that any reluctance would prob-ably result in a bang on the head from a press-gang cudgel. By the time of the Civil War the unfortunate sailor was being tugged two ways, as both Roundhead and Royalist sides issued press warrants.

One of the legends of Britain's past as a maritime nation has been that having a large merchant marine meant that the Navy had a large reserve of seamen. This is quite wrong; in wartime as many merchant ships are needed as in peacetime. But two things hap-pened. Merchant ships provided a very convenient target for the press gangs – they could take any men they wanted (except officers and apprentices) providing they left enough men on board to 'navi-gate the ship', a phrase open to wide interpretation, particularly if the pressing happened off somewhere like Deal to a ship inward bound to London: special 'ticket' men, exempt from pressing, were available in the Downs, the big anchorage inside the Goodwin Sands, to take a ship round to the Thames. The second effect was of course to drive up the wages of merchant seamen, increasing the difference with the Royal Navy's rates. Shipowners could always offer more money – albeit grumbling the while and increasing freight rates – and likely seamen would do their best to sign on in a merchant ship rather than fall foul of the press. Many merchant ships built tiny secret hiding places where two or three valued men could try to evade the sharp-eyed press gang. Hiding in the cargo generally was too dangerous; a cutlass was usually thrust into the spaces between sacks or crates.

William Richardson was pressed for the second time in very unusual circumstances. He had been serving in India on board a leaky old ship which, the second night after sailing out of the Ganges, ran into a rough head sea and sank. Thirteen of the crew and passengers escaped in one boat, but they had only two oars. Men baled with their hats and caps. Boats on a passage were often used as coops for livestock and 'in the boats were many live ducks'. With the heavy seas trying to broach the boat they baled – and eventually found someone had forgotten to put the bung in. At breakfast time they were sighted by another ship and rescued and by the next day were back in Calcutta, where Richardson called at his former lodging and was able to borrow two rupees and find accommodation. He wrote:

The next day, as I was sitting near the door, and it open, and smoking a cheroot while brooding over my hard fate, a guard of soldiers came along, and the sergeant seeing me, came and said that I was to go along with him. I asked him what for: that I was no deserter from an Indiaman, which I supposed he was looking after. He replied that his orders were to take every English seaman that he could meet with, and at this time he had upwards of twenty that he had taken, and one of them was the chief mate of a country [coasting] ship which I knew. . . .

The reason for this pressing, a thing seldom known here, was that the *Woodcot* Indiaman was lying here in want of seamen, having on board stores and ammunition and 150 artillerymen to sail for Pondicherry, a French place our Army was besieging; so we were all taken to Fort William and put into prison for the night, and after that sent on board the *Woodcot*.

Using the Honourable East India Company's own soldiers (the

only ones serving in India at this time) to press men for a ship belonging to the Company was illegal, but there was no one to argue about it and the John Company and Navy authorities would no doubt claim that the *Woodcot*'s cargo of stores and troops made her a transport ship.

It also put Richardson in another category. In his last ship, he was paid sixteen rupees a month, and she was 'swarming with rats' that 'cared but little for us and would even get up to the tops in search of food'. Yet rats had been only half the story – the ship 'was swarming with ants, cockroaches, centipedes and scorpions; we could not move a cask after a wet day, or an old sail, without some of the latter crawling out'.

Costs in Calcutta at this time, 1793, were not high: twelve ducks or fowls were one rupee. Eighty pounds of sugar cost one rupee, which was also the price of four pairs of heavy shoes. One rupee would also buy 1,000 cheroots. A seaman's light clothes for a six-month voyage came to seven or eight rupees. A rupee was then worth about 2s 3d.

His new ship, the *Woodcot*, was larger and much more comfortable, but he was a pressed man. With the south-west monsoon blowing he knew the ship would have to anchor several times in the 150 miles of twisting river, waiting for wind shifts, before they reached the mouth, 'so I made up my mind, should the opportunity offer while at anchor in the night, to swim on shore in defiance of tigers, alligators or anything else, and run my chance'.

The *Woodcot* finally arrived in Madras Roads, where Richardson and twenty-two other pressed men were transferred to the *Minerva* frigate, which was flying the flag of Rear-Admiral Cornwallis, brother of the Governor. Cornwallis and the *Minerva*'s captain inspected the twenty-three, chose three and sent the other twenty on shore, free men, 'to shift as well as they could'.

Richardson ended his description of his life so far with: 'And thus ended my services of near thirteen years in the merchant's [i.e. mercantile marine], a period of poverty, hardship, dangers and disappointments such as few, I believe, have experienced during that time.'

Despite his misgivings, Richardson enjoyed his service in the *Minerva* and was in her when she returned to England. He was transferred to the *Prompte* frigate and served in her for five years, being made acting gunner in September 1795, although he spent more than a year in home waters before being given leave to set foot on English soil for the first time in three years. As a result, he was able to visit Shields, his home town, where he discovered that his four brothers were all serving in the Royal Navy.

He found Shields 'not that merry place we had hitherto known it; everyone looked gloomy and sad on account of nearly all the young men being pressed and taken away'. Soon Richardson was a gunner (and thus a warrant officer) and he served until two years after the war ended. By 1819 the Admiralty, having far too many gunners, decided to superannuate a hundred of them, including Richardson, who found to his delight that twenty-three years service as a gunner gave him a pension of £65 a year 'and for which I am satisfied'.

Richardson had been lucky and sensible. At the age of fifty he was retired with a pension. Had he stayed in the merchant navy for those twenty-six years, it is unlikely he would have saved enough pay to yield him a similar pension, small as it was.

The first time Richardson had been pressed, in 1791 during the 'Spanish armament', was a very much more routine affair, although it was in peacetime, when the fleet was hurriedly mobilised because of the fear of war. He had been serving in *The Spy*, a slaver, as fourth mate at £2 5s a month, sailing for the Guinea Coast in May 1790, and taking a cargo of slaves to Jamaica, where *The Spy* shipped sugar, rum and mahogany, sailing in March 1791 for London. He wrote:

Off Beachy Head, we were brought to by the *Nemesis* frigate, Captain Ball, who pressed all our men except for four Germans (sugar bakers whom the captain had shipped in London to do the drudgery of the ship). Some of the poor fellows shed tears on being pressed after so long a voyage and so near home. The frigate sent an officer and a party of her men to take us into the Downs and bore up with us, where we both came to an anchor.

Next day an officer came on board with our men to get their clothes and notes for their wages; and our captain had the impudence to deduct from each man £3 for the loss of the two female slaves that got overboard and were destroyed by the sharks at Bonny.

However ruthless they might be in other respects, there was one aspect of pressing about which Royal Navy officers were punctilious, and that was making sure that seamen taken from merchant ships received all the pay due to them up to the moment of pressing. The chicanery of many merchant ship captains was well known: the instance described by Richardson is one of many. The seamen rejected their captain's claim, saying that it was not their fault that the slaves were lost, and with the Royal Navy officer supporting them the captain was obliged to give notes for the full wages, 'but this shows what a fraudulent fellow he was'.

Once the ship arrived at Deal, the *Nemesis* took her men 'and we got ticket men from Deal, (called so by having tickets to keep them from being pressed), and when we got to Gravesend our captain left us and went to London, leaving the pilot and me in charge of the ship'. Richardson and the pilot, using the ticket men, took the ship on to London, where Richardson heard that his father had died.

Two days later Richardson was busy on deck getting derricks ready to unload the cargo when a boat came alongside 'and the officer told me to get my things ready to put into her and go along with him. I told him I had charge of the ship, and he must be answerable for what happened. He said he knew that, but I must go.' He was taken to the *Enterprise* receiving ship, lying off Tower Stairs, where 'they let me know that the doctor of our ship had informed against me by telling them that I was only acting as chief mate, and had no protection, which was true'.

He was transferred first to a tender which took him to the *Otter*, then to the 74-gun *Marlborough*, and finally to the *Nemesis*, 'where I got among my old shipmates again'.

Richardson's first impressions of the Royal Navy are particularly interesting because he was twenty-three years old and had just finished a round trip as a mate in a slaver, and so would have been a good seaman and certainly not squeamish.

At Spithead he was transferred to the 98-gun *London*, where his station was in the maintop. 'Her lofty masts and square yards appeared wonderful to me, and I wondered how they were able to manage them; but I soon got accustomed to that, for we had plenty of exercise with them.'

He wrote that 'although the usage was good in general on board the *London*, yet I did not altogether like their manner of discipline'. One example he gave was that in weighing anchor when the ratings had to run along the deck with the fall (the tail of a heavy purchase, or pulley), 'boatswain's mates were placed on each side, who kept thrashing away with their rattans on our backs, making no difference between those that pulled hard and those that did not'.

Richardson does not add that this kind of stupid behaviour, by no means limited to his period, was more the fault of Captain Westcott, the *London*'s commanding officer, than the system.

Four months later, with the crisis over, the *London* and many other ships were paid off and Richardson was once again a free man. He was paid £4 10s for four months' duty, 9¾d a day. Yet perhaps the most significant comment on his service in the *London* is shown by his reference to the bosun, the one man in the ship who could make a rating's life a misery: 'We subscribed two shilling apiece to buy Mr Cooper, the boatswain, a silver call with chain and plate, with a suitable inscription on it for his kindness to the ship's company, and a silver pint pot for his wife.' Cooper obviously more than made up for the brutality of his mates if all the ratings in the ship gave up two and a half days' pay to buy him a present.

As a captain had written to the Admiralty many years earlier, 'One man out of a merchant ship is better than three the lieutenants get in town.' If impressing men from a merchant ship as they sighted the English coast after a long voyage seems harsh, the treatment of cartel ships shows better than anything how desperate was the Navy for men. After several years of war, both sides had accumulated a large number of prisoners, who were an expense in accommodation, food, and the troops needed to guard them. The British kept the French in floating hulks and in some new prisons specially built for the purpose, among them Dartmoor.

Occasionally prisoners were exchanged on a strict one-for-one basis, and the only French subject living in England as a representative of the French Government was M. Otto, the agent for the exchange of prisoners. As soon as the French Government was ready, Otto informed the Board of Transport in London and a cartel ship would sail from England for Cherbourg or Le Havre under a flag of truce with an agreed number of French prisoners, who would be released – in return for appropriate receipts – and a similar number of freed Britons would be taken on board.

The exchange was occasional because the British captured many more prisoners than the French – it has been estimated at about five Frenchmen to one Briton. Because cartel ships were few and far between, Royal Navy frigates patrolling the Channel kept an eye on them, and the press gangs covering the English ports to which they were returning also left a sharp lookout. The result was that the moment she sighted a returning cartel ship carrying freed Britons a

British ship of war sent an officer over to press as many men as she needed. Usually a dozen or so men were sufficient, so the cartel, carrying perhaps 200 former prisoners, could get back to England without being stripped – although there the Impress Service waited.

The cartel ships were hired merchantmen – it was part of the arrangement with the French that a ship of war was not used – and the officers and seamen were sympathetic to the former prisoners, doing whatever was possible to land them at a place where no press gang was likely to be waiting. One cartel evaded a waiting 14-gun brig and ran up the river into Rye on a moonlit night at the beginning of March 1800 to let 300 exchanged prisoners bolt on shore and disappear long before a press gang could arrive – the nearest headquarters of the Impress Service were at Folkestone one way and Littlehampton the other. A report to the Admiralty told their Lordships that the cartel ship had managed to get in and set free her men despite a battery and a guard on the wooden breakwater.

The Impress Service, described below, was in competition for men with the Quota Acts. The Navy was so short of men within a year of the war beginning that Pitt brought in two Quota Acts in 1795 which laid down that each county had to produce a quota of men, depending on its population and the number of its seaports. Yorkshire, the largest, had to produce 1,081, while Rutland, the smallest, was down for 23. London had to find 5,704 men.

To begin with, the counties offered money to volunteers, and the inland counties began with an advantage because the press gangs had not yet roamed their streets. But it was a foolish or patriotic man who volunteered as a Quota man in return for a cash bounty (starting at £5 but doubling or trebling within a year). If he went into the Royal Navy, he was certain to serve in a ship – most probably without leave – until the war ended. If he signed on as a merchant seaman he would be paid much more and could leave a ship at the end of each voyage, although he had to dodge the press gangs.

The response of the yeomen of England to the Quota system caused no queues to form at town halls; in fact the county authorities, in consultation with the justices of the peace, were soon reducing the sentences of men already in jail providing they would 'volunteer' for the Quota, and transgressors about to be sentenced were given the option: go to sea or go to jail.

In this way a poacher caught by a squire's gamekeeper with a brace of partridge in his bag found himself standing before a table set on the deck of one of the King's ships, giving the few details about himself that the captain's clerk needed to enter in the muster book. The Quota system did benefit one class of people – debtors. At this time a person could be imprisoned for debt, but one way of avoiding a creditor was to volunteer for the Navy, which would not give up a man for a debt of less than £20. So, providing a man owed less than that – or he could convince his captain it was less – the Navy defended him against all creditors.

The Quota system was something of a charter for landowners sick to death of regular poachers and for justices of the peace who were tired of regularly sentencing the same pimps, panders and vagrants. Now the Navy was a bottomless pit into which such men could be dropped. There was no discussion of the fact that a poacher sentenced to a month who became a Quota man instead was in fact being sentenced to ten years in the Navy.

A picture is often painted of the Quota system flooding the Navy with scoundrels, but there is no evidence that this happened, apart from isolated cases. At worse, it brought typhus to healthy ships with men from city jails. A healthy poacher might make the local landowner raise his eyebrows, but usually he coveted a landowner's rabbits because there was no work for him and poaching was the only way of providing meat to eat. Some of the best Home Guards in country districts during the Second World War were poachers – especially because for the first year, when the Germans were expected nightly, they had to provide their own weapons and ammunition.

By bringing in the two Quota Acts, Pitt had in fact given Britain its first look at conscription. It was a mild affair – London with its population of 750,000 had to find only 5,700 men, and they had to be within the age limits which the press gang was supposed to observe, eighteen and fifty-five. In the twentieth century it is fashionable to regard the Quota Acts and the system of pressing men for the Navy as rude assaults on the freedom of the individual. The fact is that only a small proportion of the men of England served in either the Navy or the Army. By comparison, conscription in the Second World War swept up every able-bodied man unless he could prove his civilian job was 'essential war work'. Young bachelors and the fathers of large families were called up – and before long women without children were drafted to factories, the women's services and agricultural work. Every one of a family of five sons, for example, would be called up, and the only safeguard was eventually brought in by Mr Churchill, who ordered that brothers should not serve together in the same unit.

Cat-o'-nine tails and handcuffs

CHAPTER EIGHT

The Perils of Marriage

The press gangs were, in theory, limited in the men they could seize. To begin with, the government claimed that any man 'using the sea' could be pressed, and various legal authorities over the years backed this up. The claim that a freeholder should be exempt was dismissed by Lord Thurlow while Attorney-General: 'I see no reason why men using the sea . . . should be exempted only because they are free-holders. . . . It is a qualification easily attained.' Sir William Blackstone said that pressing was based on the Crown's right to press everyone, and he was followed by Charles Yorke, the Solicitor-General in 1757, and Lord Mansfield.

So the Admiralty, maintaining that every British subject was liable for service, gradually accepted certain exemptions. A foreigner was exempted – officially. He could volunteer to serve in the Royal Navy (and many did, for reasons given later) but by a law of 1740 could not be pressed. However, the Admiralty soon gnawed at the law and the foreigner paid a heavy price eventually if he had anything to do with the British – if he served in a British merchant ship for two years, he became liable for pressing. Marriage could prove fatal, ending his freedom and possibly his life, because if he married a British woman he became a British subject by naturalisation, as far as the Admiralty was concerned, and the men interrupting his honeymoon were likely to be the press gang. A good example of the unexpected perils of matrimony was a seaman arriving in Bristol in 1806 in a ship from the West Indies. He was promptly pressed but, successfully claiming that he was a foreigner, he was discharged by the Navy. He celebrated his freedom by proposing to a Bristol girl and marrying her, and within three weeks of the wedding he was back in the Navy with 'pressed' against his name in the muster book, and this time the Admiralty refused his claim to be a foreigner.

A genuine foreigner who was pressed could always get his freedom, providing he could get his consul to apply for his release. Because a foreigner could rarely speak English and in any case was unlikely to be able to get on shore to see a consul, usually he stayed in the Royal Navy. If he was fortunate enough to be released, he was given a certificate of discharge, signed by the captain of his ship, certifying that the man had been discharged from the ship 'by order of the Right Honourable the Lords Commissioners of the Admiralty, by reason of his being a subject of ———; and by order of their Lordships had this certificate given him, to prevent his being impressed'. A note beneath the signature said: 'On the back of this certificate must be put a description of the man's person.' This was detailed, because the Admiralty did not intend that he should sell such a valuable document.

A high proportion of foreigners serving in the Royal Navy in wartime were doing so because they had volunteered, and the reason is not hard to find. Many of the men of the ports in the Baltic and Mediterranean could only make a living by serving in merchant ships. Places like Genoa, Leghorn, Civita Vecchia, Narvik, Oslo (then known as Christiania), Hamburg, Cuxhaven, Odense, Copenhagen and Malmö were thriving ports in peacetime and the bases of large merchant fleets. In wartime, with trade cut back or halted (because of the French occupation of Genoa, Leghorn and Civita Vecchia, for instance), there were no cargoes for ships and no work for seamen. If they were not to starve they had to serve under foreign flags, and this usually meant in British ships. If they served in a merchant ship they risked being accused of treason by the French if they were captured, so most chose the Royal Navy, where the chances of being taken prisoner were much less.

It is interesting to examine at random the muster books of Royal Navy ships. The small schooner *Pickle*, for example, brought back to England the dispatch describing Nelson's death and the victory of Cape Trafalgar on 21 October 1805. It was a bad voyage, with heavy weather and the fear of French privateers, but the ship's company were mustered on 28 October. She had an official complement of forty, but only thirty-three men appeared in the muster list, and their nationalities were: seventeen English, nine Irish, one Scottish, one Welsh, one Channel Islander, two Americans and two Norwegians.

The muster book shows that one American, Thomas Bascomb of New York, pressed in December 1804 in Plymouth, was discharged the following April in Bermuda. The ship's second master was an American serving quite happily in the Royal Navy, George Almy, from Newport. Of the English on board, incidentally, five came from the West Country, two each from Kent and Sussex, and one from London.

A few weeks before the fleet under Sir Hyde Parker and Nelson sailed for Denmark and the Battle of Copenhagen in 1801, the Admiralty ordered that all Danes, Norwegians and Swedes on board should be transferred to other ships.

The ship from which Nelson was to command the battle, the 74-gun *Elephant*, had only fourteen foreigners on board, and seven of them were Americans. All were listed as volunteers, two of them being senior petty officers and the rest able seamen. The 74-gun *Ganges* had the most foreigners in her ship's company, which numbered less than the 700 allowed. Four Danes, two Swedes and a Norwegian were transferred by Admiralty order before leaving England, leaving behind twenty-seven other foreigners. These included fifteen Americans, two from Holland, India, and Goeree (an island off Senegal), and one each from Prussia, Martinique, Portugal, Hamburg, Hanover and 'Africa'.

The third ship in the fleet, chosen at random because she was in the thick of the battle, was the 74-gun *Monarch*. She had a complement of nearly 700, and not one of them was a foreigner. Thus in three ships with a total complement of about 2,000 men, only forty-one were foreigners, plus the seven Scandinavians transferred before the ship sailed.

At Trafalgar, Nelson's flagship, the *Victory*, had seventy-one foreigners on board four days before Trafalgar. The Britons on board comprised 441 English, 64 Scots, 63 Irish, 18 Welsh, 3 Shetlanders, 2 Channel Islanders, and 1 Manxman. The 71 foreigners comprised 22 Americans, 7 Dutch, 6 Swedes, 4 Italians, 4 Maltese, 3 Frenchmen (volunteers and probably royalists), 3 Norwegians, 3 Germans, 2 Swiss, 2 Portuguese, 2 Danes, 2 Indians, 1 Russian, 1 from 'Africa' and 9 from the West Indian islands.

The pressing of Americans by the Royal Navy caused disagreements between the two countries and was one of the major factors leading to the war of 1812. Like most disagreements there were two sides to the question. The American view was quite straightforward

– she was now an independent nation and her people owed neither debt nor allegiance to Britain. The Royal Navy had no claim on American seamen, and to safeguard them the American Government, through its notaries, or commissioners of oaths (and later Customs officers), issued them with a Protection.

This was an impressive document headed with the Republic's arms and 'United States of America' printed right across the top. The wording varied slightly, depending on the notary's name and the state, and later it was adapted for use by Customs officers. A typical one, issued on 11 December 1795 to Daniel Robertson, said that 'I, John Keefe, a public notary in and for the state of New York . . . do hereby certify that Daniel Robertson, mariner . . . personally appeared before me, and being duly sworn according to the law, deposed that he is a citizen of the United States of America and a native of the State of Delaware, five feet ten and a half inches high and aged about twenty-four years, and I do further certify that the said Daniel Robertson being a citizen of the United States of America and liable to be called in the service of his country is to be respected accordingly at all times by sea and land.' The document was then signed and sealed by Keefe and, because he was illiterate, Daniel Robertson added his mark.

As far as the United States was concerned, Daniel Robertson now had a document affording him the freedom of the seas; if the Royal Navy sent a press gang on board the ship in which he was serving, even though she might be British, Robertson need only show his Protection to be immune from the press.

Seen from an American point of view, this seemed reasonable: here was one of the notaries 'in and for the state of New York' certifying in effect that Daniel Robertson was a native of the state of Delaware, 5 feet 10½ inches high and 'about twenty-four'. After 1796 a Customs officer could have issued a similar document.

The American Minister Plenipotentiary in London was frequently called upon to leave his residence in Cumberland Place to call on the Secretary of State to make a protest, while the consuls – in London (at Finsbury Square), Bristol, Falmouth and Liverpool, with a vice-consul at Poole – were frequently forwarding requests for named seamen to be released.

The British Government took an entirely different view, which was based on various factors – emotional and legalistic. The first concerned nationality. The British Government then held that a man born a British subject remained British: he could not renounce his nationality (and thus his obligations) simply by going to another country and living there.

It was prepared to accept that when a British colony revolted and achieved its independence its inhabitants took on a new nationality, but in 1793, at the beginning of the war, there was not an American subject over the age of twenty-three (apart from immigrants) who had not been born a British subject. And, almost as important, how did a man *prove* anything?

The British Government could, and the Royal Navy certainly would, point to Daniel Robertson and his Protection as being a good example of the uselessness of American Protections. A British Protection, like the discharge given to a foreign seaman, bore 'a description of this man's person', and it was detailed. Robertson's US Protection gave only two identifying details, his height and his apparent age, a vague enough fact. They argued that it gave no details of the colour of his hair, type of complexion, build, and so on. A British Protection, in other words, gave a complete physical identification of its owner, a description which would fit perhaps one man in a hundred, so that it could not easily be sold to someone else, or stolen and used by another man. In contrast, an American Protection could be used by anyone of approximately that height and 'apparent' age.

That was far from being the main British objection to a Protection. There was no way of proving that a man was an American subject. With the country only officially in existence for twenty-three years, there was no such thing as a real American accent; nor could a genuine American citizen produce a birth certificate because it did not exist.

The only thing an American citizen could do was what the Protection required him to do – go before a notary and depose that his name was so and so and he was born in such a state. The notary could run the rule over him and insert the height and he had to accept the man's word for his age. But no documents were produced; Daniel Robertson did not have to produce a certificate from the minister of his parish, nor a letter from a local leading citizen.

In other words, a Daniel Robertson – or any other name the man chose to use – of Stepney, London, could arrive in New York on board a British merchant ship, and go before Mr Keefe or one of his fellow notaries and swear that he was an American citizen born in, say, Delaware, and Mr Keefe had to accept the deposition and grant a Protection. Indeed, it is extremely unlikely that Mr Keefe suffered from an excess of Anglophilia; he would be well disposed towards anyone applying for a Protection. In any case he was not certifying that Daniel Robertson was American-born; he was certifying that Robertson had deposed that he was.

The fact that a Daniel Robertson could so easily get a US Protection was, the British Government argued, far from being the worst part of the system, even though the Protection merely certified that Robertson deposed that he was an American. There was nothing to prevent Daniel Robertson calling at all the other notaries in New York and collecting a Protection from each of them – there was no central register recording who had received Protections; the only record was that kept by each notary, who was required to note any depositions taken or certificates issued to anyone about any subject. A few days in New York could yield Daniel Robertson a score of Protections, and if the British ship he was serving in was calling at other American ports along the eastern seaboard he could call at notaries in each of them and acquire even more Protections.

If Daniel Robertson was in fact a Cockney from Stepney instead of a Jonathan from Delaware ('Jonathan' by now being the English nickname for an American person or ship), he had not only a legal but fraudulent Protection of himself, but he had a pocketful of American Protections to sell to any other Britons of his height and age who had the wish to leave the King's service – and the necessary £5 or more, which by the third year of the war was the minimum price for a black-market US Protection.

The British Government cared not at all that a fraudulent Daniel Robertson made a considerable profit from his visits to American notaries; it was much more concerned that, if Robertson had a couple of dozen spare Protections, the Royal Navy was about to lose a couple of dozen men.

There was, incidentally, no fear that the US consuls in London, Bristol and Falmouth, and the vice-consul at Poole, would become suspicious when one Daniel Robertson after another sought their assistance in getting their discharge from the Royal Navy: the original man would not of course give the same name to each notary. What he had to sell was a handful of Protections referring to a man of the same height and roughly the same age as himself – that would be the only similarity, and the result would be that within a few months the Royal Navy would lose a number of men of similar age and heig............ each man would be issued with a certificate signed b........... saving that he was a discharged foreigner – and givi......... detailed physical description of the man.

As far......... British Government was concerned, then, there was a defect i......... method of issuing .... Protections, which meant in effe......... a Royal Navy lieutenant in charge of a boarding party used h......... discretion. A seaman claiming .... e from New York, for in......... might be......... some sea......... ng questions about the p......... lieutenant had ever been there, and if his answers were unsatisfactory his Protection would be assumed to have been obta......... fraudulently.

T......... ease by which any man could fraudulently obtain a genuine Am......... documents which backed up a fraudulent claim to American nationality, ... the British view that a man born in Britain re......... ned British .... could sign .... a separate peace with th......... enemy by claiming .... were the two main legal o......... .

The third objection was emotional whether seen from the American or the British point of view. The War of Independence had ended only sixteen years earlier and was therefore fresh in everyone's mind. The war had lasted eight years and cost the new republic £15 million, while the cost to Britain had been a £115 million increase in the national debt and the loss of half a continent.

The material factors were of less consequence than the fact that the revolting colonists had accepted the help of France; the French had helped fight the British on land and at sea. Now Britain was fighting a republican France. The royalist France of Louis XVI which had helped the former British colonists get their freedom and establish themselves as independent Americans no longer existed; Louis had been executed, the mob had stormed the Bastille. America was very slow to understand that the new France was concerned with enslaving countries – it had begun at once with Holland – not freeing them; within half a dozen years the French occupied most of Europe, setting up an iron tree of liberty in every town as the army and tax collectors began to reduce the inhabitants to submission.

By 1799, less than a third of the way through the war, Britain stood alone against France and Spain. France had, by comparison, limitless manpower, having been the first nation to introduce universal conscription. The only way that Britain could fight back was at sea – and for that she needed seamen. She did not claim that she could seize foreigners and force them to serve in her ships, but she did insist that her own people could not escape their obligations by fraudulently obtaining Protections and then claiming to be foreigners.

The United States, being a new and thriving nation (her exports to Britain increased from £8,800,000 in 1793 to £14,500,000 by 1801), needed both new citizens and prime seamen. Few difficulties were put in the way of British seamen when they went before an American notary, or bought a Protection. Britain was determined to fight to prevent the French Empire spreading from the Arctic Ocean to the Indian Ocean; the Americans were determined to fight off what they considered to be renewed British interference in American affairs. Its leaders were not concerned that France had occupied the Netherlands, Belgium, Switzerland, Germany, the Rhineland, most of the states in Italy, and Poland.

Although it did not accept the claim of the United States for immunity for every man claiming to be American, Britain was very careful to avoid provocative acts. Her ambassador, Mr Robert Liston, was more than anxious to ensure that relationships were good.

Writing from Philadelphia to Lord Grenville, the Secretary of State, in August 1796 on 'the quality of an American citizen', he noted that 'It seems natural that the British Government should wish to confine the term to natives of America and those who were settled in the territory of the United States at the period of the establishment of their independence, while the Congress on the other hand appear desirous of extending their protection to persons who may have been naturalised by the laws of any of the individual states' or by earlier Acts of Congress.

By one of these, passed in 1790, aliens were entitled to claim citizenship after a residence of two years, while by another Act in 1795 they could claim it after five years' residence 'within the limits and under the jurisdiction of the United States'. This included service in American ships.

Liston assured Lord Grenville that 'the present administrators, though not satisfied at the propriety of these acts, have thought themselves bound to take measures for carrying them into execution, as appears by the enclosed circular letter from the department of the Treasury to the Collectors of Customs'. This was a result of an

Act just passed by Congress 'for the relief and Protection of American seamen'.

Liston told Grenville that he had discussed it with the American Secretary of State: 'On my mentioning . . . the little probablity there was that the British Government would admit the principles laid down in the Act . . . he acknowledged the difficulties that stood in the way of an amicable agreement between us.' This Act allowed seamen to get Protections from a Customs officer. The new type of Protection, signed only by a Customs agent, gave no more details and did not require any oath to be taken.

On the same day that he wrote about the new Act, Liston was complaining to Lord Grenville about the behaviour of a British naval officer towards the master of an American ship:

> It is with great concern I observe that the complaint of acts of injustice and insult committed by our officers against American citizens continue and increase, and that the pains taken by certain factions in this country to propagate and exaggerate the account of every unfriendly transaction have but too much effect in irritating the minds of the people against the British nation and government.
>
> A deep impression has in particular been made upon persons of all ranks by the enclosed statement of an outrage offered to Mr William Jesup, master of the American ship *Mercury* . . . which has been published in every newspaper in the United States.

The law exempted boys under the age of eighteen and men over fifty-five from the press gang, but the Admiralty was not bothered by that. 'It is incumbent on those who claim to be exempted to prove the facts,' ruled its law officers, and in an age before universal birth certificates the age limits were merely words. A boy or man was as old as he appeared in the eyes of the regulating captain (the title of the captain in command of a particular depot), and appearances depended on demand. Mr Alexander Stephens, a clerk in the Navy's Transport Office, complained in May 1813 that his thirteen-year-old son George had been taken up by the press gang.

Apprentices had to step warily. Those serving at sea could not in theory be pressed during the first three years after signing their indentures (which were usually for seven years), and if they were their masters could – if they wished, and few could be bothered – sue the Admiralty for damages or claim them under a writ of Habeas Corpus. There was, however, one loophole in the three-year rule – it only applied if the apprentice had not served at sea before signing the indentures. This usually meant that the lieutenant in charge of a press gang seized any boy that looked more than eighteen years old, claiming he had previously 'used the sea' and anyway was over the age limit. The apprentice on land was protected, if that was the right word, by the age limit, not by his indentures as such.

Merchant seamen were exempt for the first two years they spent at sea. This was laid down by the law of 1740 which, in theory, settled the whole impressment question. The aim of the law was to avoid merchant ships, and thus the nation's trade, being cripped by raids from press gangs. Again, the Admiralty could usually ignore it because a man could rarely if ever prove that he had been at sea less than two years. Even if he could show from the ship's books that he had been on board only a year, he could not prove that he had never previously served in another ship.

The Admiralty was forced to exempt certain officers and warrant officers, men who had spent years learning their jobs and who were vital to a ship. Masters, mates, bosuns and carpenters were exempt – providing they had an affidavit sworn before a justice of the peace and describing their qualifications. But no acting mate, bosun or carpenter was protected, as William Richardson had discovered (see page 102).

Yet masters and mates had to be wary: if one of their ship's company proved to be a deserter from the Royal Navy it was useless to claim (probably correctly) that they did not know. 'Harbouring a deserter from the fleet' made their protections and affidavits useless: the penalty was impressment.

No mate or apprentice liked being lent to another ship that was short-handed. Even though the ship might belong to the same owner, if the press gang caught him he could be pressed: his Protection was valid only if he was serving on board the ship in which he had signed on.

However, no man was really protected, even though he might have the required affidavit – also called a Protection – in his pocket ready to show the press gang, unless he stayed at sea. The moment he set foot on land (unless he could prove he was on 'ship's business') he could be pressed, and usually was. The exception was that a mate remaining with a ship could register his name at the impress office (usually called 'the Rendezvous'), but he had to get there in the first place without the gang catching him.

A merchant ship going into port to unload even a part of her cargo therefore exposed her master, mates, bosun, carpenter and seamen to danger, and it was a brave or careless man that stepped on shore unless he could prove he was on 'ship's duty'. Being given a few hours' leave was not enough – William Tassell, mate of the *Elizabeth* in the port of Lynn, in Norfolk, was given leave by his captain to stay on shore until 8 p.m. but when the press gang visited the local inn at 10 p.m. they found Tassell still drinking and pressed him. Tassell argued in vain that his captain did not object to him being two hours late; the Admiralty backed the regulating captain and kept Tassell in the Royal Navy. Tassell was probably unlucky in choosing Lynn, which, although small, boasted a captain as its regulating officer, at 20s a day, whereas most other ports of the same size had lieutenants at 5s a day, with 2s 9d a day subsistence.

Robert Hay had joined the Royal Navy in 1803 as a boy of thirteen, and was twenty-one years old and serving in the *Amethyst* frigate when she was wrecked in a storm in Plymouth Harbour. About thirty men were drowned as her boats smashed up in the heavy seas, but Hay managed to escape on a floating hatch cover, and when he found himself safe on land on a pitch dark night he decided to desert.

He found a 'safe' lodging-house in Plymouth but, with an old shipmate, a fellow Scot, decided it was too dangerous to visit his home in Scotland. The shipmate 'offered to purchase me woman's clothes and take me for his wife, or gentleman's clothes and take me as his master, or to travel with me by night and conceal ourselves by day'. Hay decided against it and signed on in a merchant ship, the *Edward*, bound for Jamaica.

He gives a good description of the plight of any merchant ship approaching a British port at the end of a voyage, knowing the press gang would be waiting to welcome them. As the ship approached Jamaica they began making stow holes, but the nature of the cargo prevented them making more than two. 'What with carpenter's warrants, apprentices' indentures and so forth, all on board were protected from the press but four,' wrote Hay, and he was one of the four. They drew lots for the two stow holes and Hay was one of the losers, which meant that he and the second man had to be on deck when the gang arrived.

My exposed partner dressed himself in greasy clothes, blackened his face with grease and soot, with intention of passing for ship's cook. I, on the other hand, with the assistance of some landsman's clothes, dressed myself like a footman, assumed an air of flippancy, and intended to pass for ship's steward. The cook is usually the most useless man on board, and the steward is in general no seaman. By assuming these characters we imagined the press officers would not think us worth removal.

In fact the ship put into Old Harbour, passing Port Royal, 'that hot bed of the press', at night, so neither disguise nor stow holes were tested. Within a short time Hay, who had been doing some woodwork, was made carpenter when the original man quit the ship, accepting £7 a month.

The *Edward* was the slowest ship in the convoy of more than seventy returning to England, and by the time she was sailing up the Bristol Channel Hay reflected that 'unless the press is very hot, a carpenter's warrant is generally considered a sufficient protection from it, but I had no warrant to show. The captain . . . did not wish to be at the expense of having one drawn up at Jamaica.'

As soon as the pilot came on board to take the *Edward* up the Severn he told how a press boat the previous day had been damaged going alongside a merchant ship, which had sent her carpenter on board to make repairs. No sooner had the carpenter finished than he was pressed, the lieutenant saying he was just the sort of handy fellow the Navy needed.

Hay 'resolved to put more faith in my stow hole' than in either the verbal agreement with the *Edward*'s captain making him carpenter or the press gang's mercy. As the gang came on board at night, Hay fled below 'and in a twinkling found myself beneath two tiers of sugar hogsheads, trembling like an aspen leaf'. Hay's fear was, of course, as much his fate if recognised as a deserter from the *Amethyst* as serving in the Royal Navy.

He was lucky to have chosen a stow hole so far down – the gang searched the hold, and 'thrust their cutlasses down to the hilt among the interstices of the sugar hogsheads. Happily I was more than a cutlass length down.' The gang in fact took the only two unprotected men they could find on board, although Hay had a very difficult time getting on shore without being detected.

After various adventures and within a day or two of his twenty-second birthday, Hay 'purchased a long coat, breeches and other corresponding vestments, and assuming as much as possible the looks and gait of a landsman, set out on foot for Bath, thence to take coach for London'.

The purchase of breeches points out one sartorial difference between a seaman and a landman: trousers were garments worn by seamen; nearly everyone else wore breeches. Trousers (more usually spelt 'trowsers') had wide bottoms which could be rolled up to avoid them getting wet when decks were scrubbed or seas were breaking on board. Breeches were worn only by officers.

Hay was successful in reaching London and, having 'gained a sight of the vessels' masts, had in imagination procured a passage, allotted the time for reaching Leith, and was considering within my own mind in what manner I should conduct my introductory visit to my friends.

'In the midst of this agreeable reverie I was when crossing Tower Hill accosted by a person in seaman's dress who tapped me on the shoulder, inquiring in a familiar and technical strain, "What ship?"'

'I assumed an air of gravity and surprise and told him I presumed he was under some mistake as I was not connected with shipping. The fellow, however, was too well acquainted with his business to be thus easily put off. He gave a whistle and in a moment I was in the hands of six or eight ruffians who I immediately dreaded and soon found to be a press gang.'

Hay was taken before a lieutenant, still protesting he had nothing to do with the sea, but the palms of his hands showed he was used to hard work and were 'perhaps a little discoloured with tar'. He was soon being persuaded to join the Navy, being told by an officer: 'Take my advice, my lad . . . and enter the service cheerfully, you will then have a bounty and be in a fair way for promotion.' Hay refused to volunteer and was sent below 'with these words thundered in my ear, "A pressed man to go below." '

The Navy's habit of offering every pressed man the chance of 'volunteering' was simply a way of giving them a chance of receiving the bounty, but it means that muster books are useless in subsequently determining how many of a ship's company were pressed. Only stubborn men like Hay were marked down as 'press'd' in the 'Whether Vol. or press'd' column, and it was an expensive gesture, costing him the £5 bounty.

The story of Robert Hay has a happy ending: sent to the *Ceres* at the Nore, he and a shipmate made a daring escape, swimming to the shore one night using bladders. By 30 October 1811 he arrived back at his home in Paisley, Dunbartonshire, 'after an absence of eight years and three months'.

One of the most important workers in the country was the harvester, a man who went from farm to farm, providing the extra labour needed at harvest time, whether it was getting up the potatoes, cutting and stooking the grain, haymaking or fruit-picking. The harvester always carried a certificate with him, his 'Protection', signed by the minister and churchwardens of his home village and stating that he was indeed a harvester. As such the press gang could not touch him.

Although there were few categories as lucky as harvesters who had almost automatic Protections, a few men 'using the sea' were given Protections – men working ferries in difficult places, for instance, boatmen in anchorages like Spithead who were needed to handle the small cutters taking officers out to ships, and pilots recognised by Trinity House. 'Gentlemen' were generally ignored by the press gangs, although the only qualification was that of dress. A 'gentleman' dressed in old clothes and wandering far from home was likely to be taken up.

The sea, as far as the Admiralty was concerned, covered most of the country in one way or another. A man operating a ferry across a river a hundred miles inland, the hand on a wherry carrying a cargo of hay along one of the inland waterways in Norfolk, a man fishing from a boat in sight of Windsor Castle, a man hunting mussels, whelks and oysters as the tide went down – all were liable to be pressed, although certain groups, such as the nearly 600 men working the trows on the Severn and Wye, had (thanks to the Association of Severn Traders) managed to get protections.

Fishermen working at sea had partial protection until 1801 – up to then the master, one apprentice, one seaman and one landman were exempted in every sea-going fishing vessel. After 1801, in an attempt to save the fishing industry, anyone whose full-time occupation was fishing was protected – and that included men working at curing and selling the fish as well.

There were several types of Protections, ranging from those issued by the Admiralty to the ones given by Trinity House to its pilots, but there were two universal rules concerning them. First, each had to describe its owner accurately and in detail, and, second, it had to be carried all the time and 'produced upon demand'.

An Admiralty Protection was headed, 'By the Commissioners for Executing the Office of Lord High Admiral of Great Britain . . . and of all of His Majesty's Plantations' and said:

> You are hereby required and directed not to impress into His Majesty's service —— providing his name, age and description be inserted in the margin hereof, and that he does not belong to any of His Majesty's ships.
>
> And in case the Protection shall be found about any other person producing the same on his own account, then the officer who finds it is hereby strictly charged and required to impress the said person and immediately to send the Protection to us.
>
> And we do hereby direct that this Protection for securing the forementioned person, and him only, from the press, shall continue in force for three months.

The Protection, signed and dated, was addressed 'To all Commanders and officers of His Majesty's ships, and all others whom it doth or may concern.'

The lieutenants or midshipmen in charge of press gangs were sharp-eyed and ruthless in the interpretation of the two rules, that a Protection must always be carried and must describe its owner. The beard or moustache a man grew when his Protection described him as clean-shaven was more than enough to turn him into a sailor, and the man who accidentally left his Protection at home was liable to spend many years in the Royal Navy before he opened his front door again. A brown-haired man whose hair turned white, a fair-haired man who started going bald, a bearded man who wanted to shave – all had to be careful of their Protections, except that the majority of them knew nothing about such things; often the first they knew of the danger of the discrepancy between the description and the fact was the lieutenant of a gang signalling to his men.

Very occasionally – rarely more than once a year – there was a sudden crisis requiring ships to be manned in a great hurry, and the Admiralty gave the order to 'press from all Protections'. The order usually concerned a particular area – Portsmouth and Plymouth, for instance, or the Medway towns and the Thames – and it meant just what it said: the press gangs went out and seized the necessary number of men, whether or not they had Protections. Once the particular fleet or squadron concerned had enough men, Protections were honoured once again.

The idea that a press gang was simply a group of seamen under a lieutenant or midshipman sent on shore to find a dozen or so men to fit out a ship's company is not incorrect but gives no idea of the Impress Service.

The Impress Service was an organisation covering every port in Great Britain in one way or another. Each major port had a captain in charge (paid £1 a day) while each smaller port had a lieutenant, who was paid 5s a day, with 2s 9d 'subsistence'. In 1799, six years after the war began, twenty-nine captains were at work, ranging from the American-born Jahleel Brenton in Edinburgh to Benjamin Hulke at Dover, and from Sylverius Moriarty at Cork to Thomas Hawker in Bristol. Under them were sixty lieutenants. Some were based at the same place as their captains; others spread the net more widely. 'London and the River Thames' had two captains and seven lieutenants. Yarmouth (Norfolk), Poole, Dover, Appledore (Devon) and Liverpool were among the places that needed a captain and two lieutenants; Bristol, Falmouth, Lynn, Southampton and Swansea each had a captain and a lieutenant. But Deal, Exmouth, Faversham, Gosport, Harwich and Littlehampton were among several ports that had only a lieutenant.

In each of these places – nearly fifty ports, and the countryside round them – the press gangs were at work. Their victims rarely had the tiny satisfaction of having been seized by brave tars who had fought for their country in a sturdy ship of the line and were led by an officer resting from one desperate cruise before the Admiralty sent him off on another.

The officers, with very few exceptions (Jahleel Brenton was one), were men for whom there was no other employment. Captains otherwise on half pay (Sylverius Moriarty in Cork was the last of the 'first fifty on the List' receiving 10s a day) were glad to be employed in the Impress Service; half-pay lieutenants who had long since given up hope of being made post were only too glad to join and live comfortably at the Admiralty's expense. Setting up the Impress Service in a port or town was a job of no great difficulty. The senior officer, whether captain or lieutenant, was called the Regulating (or Examining) Officer, and the house chosen as the headquarters was known as the Rendezvous. If the regulating officer was a lieutenant he might have one midshipman under him and three or four gangs of men.

Having rented the Rendezvous, the regulating officer then hired some tough men as 'gangers' – the men who would form the press gang. In exceptional cases they were seamen drafted from a ship; usually they were the bullies of the town, hired on the strict understanding that they would not be pressed; local toughs who were quick enough to spot the safest way of getting immunity.

The regulating officer then sent out the gangs. Some were led by lieutenants, others by midshipmen. Where no officer was available, the most intelligent man in a gang was put in charge. A gang did not just remain in the town: its presence very quickly became known and wise men vanished, to stay with relatives or friends in some distant place, or those that had to stay made sure they did not walk the streets without knowing that 'the gangers' were elsewhere.

The gangs roamed the surrounding villages and towns and were paid for travelling. An officer could claim 3d a mile and each ganger 1d a mile 'road money'. The gangs covered considerable distances – the lieutenant at Ilfracombe claimed for 1,776 miles in 1795 (a daily average of nearly thirty miles) and the captain at Swansea 1,561 miles, although with every mile representing 3d or 1d the word 'mile' might have been an intention rather than a measurement.

The midshipmen in charge of gangs were far from being the curly-haired, rosy-cheeked boys so favoured in Victorian prints; most were mature men, gangers with some education. Once the gangers had seized a man – a group if they were far from their base – they took him off to the Rendezvous, a building whose rooms had sound locks. There the man was held until the regulating officer could inspect him and (unless he was obviously a cripple or half-witted) certify him as fit for service. If the man claimed he was ruptured or suffering some other physical defect, the regulating officer would send for the local surgeon, who was usually only too anxious to examine the gangers' haul for the shilling a man offered by the Admiralty.

Sometimes the gang did not have to look for a victim: a merchant seaman or anyone 'using the sea' and liable to be pressed knew he was at the mercy of anyone who took it into his (or her) head to inform the press where he was. Such a tip was usually worth a pound reward. In a village or town ' 'forming the press' was a way of paying off old scores; a rival for a young woman's hand, a jealous mistress, an angry wife – all could rely on the press solving their problems. A labourer trimming a hedge, a drover taking a flock of sheep to market, a tinker wheeling his barrow to the next village and crying out for knives to grind, a huckster with a leather satchel over his shoulder containing his wares – many of them played the game of hunt-the-sailor, which involved keeping a weather eye open for a man wearing trousers or looking uncomfortable in breeches and coat, a man who walked with a roll and seemed to have blisters on his heels through being unused to wearing shoes.

Robert Hay, as a deserter hiding in a house at North Corner in Plymouth, not one hundred yards from the beach, watched through the window. 'Watermen's skiffs, merchantmen's yawls, warships' launches, pinnaces, cutters, gigs etc were every moment landing. Porters were trudging along under their ponderous burdens, women of pleasure flirting about in all directions, watching for their prey.' And he described how 'the jolly tar himself was seen with his white demity trousers fringed at the bottom, his fine scarlet waistcoat bound with black ribbon, his dark blue broadcloth jacket studded with pearl buttons, his black silk neckcloth thrown carelessly about his sunburnt neck. An elegant hat of straw, indicative of his recent return from a foreign station, cocked on one side; a head of hair reaching to his waistband; a smart switch made from the backbone of a shark under one arm, his doxy under the other, a huge chew of tobacco in his cheek, and a good throat season of double stingo [very strong ale] recently deposited within his belt by way of fending off care.'

Hay then gave the other side of the coin: the seaman he described belonged to a ship of war; the man serving in a merchant ship never dared to step out like that: 'Few days elapsed without my being doomed to witness the kidnapping operations of the press gang. This gang greatly damps all the enjoyment which sailors experience ashore.'

Seamen from merchant ships scarcely dared show their faces before it was dark. 'After the shades of night had fallen, and after getting their courage excited by a glass or two of good Jamaica [rum], they would sometimes sally out to take a ramble, but generally as their spirits and courage rose their prudence and watchfulness forsook them. Many, very many, instead of finding themselves in the morning in the arms of Polly would find themselves in the press room of a receiving ship in the more rough and unceremonious hands of a corporal of Marines.'

The gangers' pay varied – when the Navy was particularly short of men, it could reach 10s a week or more, but a ganger's official pay was all too often a small part of his income. The Impress Service gave impoverished and often unscupulous captains, lieutenants and gangers immense power over most of their fellow men. Any of them could in effect point to a man in the street or drinking a mug of ale and send him to sea, where he would serve into the distant future. Such a man taken to the Rendezvous put little or no extra money into a ganger's pocket. At one time he would share a shilling with his colleagues, and once it went as high as ten shillings. But the man about to be carried off might have a prosperous small business; he could offer the gangers a bribe – as Falstaff had found – to walk away without seeing him. £10 – which would mean £2 for each ganger – was a small price to pay for freedom, and often it was paid.

A sturdy butcher seeing the gang and a lieutenant pausing outside his shop once a week would be wise to provide a parcel of meat for the regulating officer, and the grocer and baker might add to the provisions as a wise insurance to make sure they stayed in business.

Commander David Shuckforth had been one of the Navy's most senior lieutenants (his name was seventeenth in the fifty lieutenants retired with the rank of commander and a pension of 6s a day) but until then he was a lieutenant of the Impress Service at Chester. When he heard of his promotion on retirement, which also ended his appointment with the Impress Service, he wrote a letter to his successor warning him of the regulating officer, 'Capt P':

> I have been with him six months here and if it had not been that he is leaving the place I would have wrote to the Board of Admiralty to have been removed from under his command. . . .
>
> Be very careful not to introduce him to any family that you have a regard for, for although he is near seventy years of age, he is the greatest debauchee you ever met with – a man of no religion, a man who is capable of any meanness, arbitrary and tyrannical in his disposition.
>
> This city has been several times just on the point of writing against him to the Board of Admiralty. He has a wife and children grown up to man's estate. The woman he brings over with him is Bird the builder's daughter. To conclude, there is not a house in Chester that he can go into but his own and the Rendezvous.

One can assume Bird the builder's labourers were safe from the gangers.

The vigorous 'Capt P' left Chester and went to Waterford, where he was to be the new regulating officer. His reputation preceded him and as soon as the owner arrived the local fish wives set about wrecking his house. His lieutenants complained about him to the Admiralty, who ordered an inquiry. This lasted ten days, because of the number of charges against him, and most of them were proved, bringing a long and venal career to an end.

The Admiralty was well aware what could go on with Impress Officers and their gangs – indeed, as if their Lordships had read Falstaff, the officers' warrant ordered them to take care 'not to demand or receive any money, gratuity, reward or any other consideration whatsoever for the sparing, exchanging or discharging any person or persons impressed or to be impressed'. But neither the man paying out to avoid impressment, nor the ganger or regulating officer accepting a present, was likely to make a fuss.

There were exceptions, though: the owners of fishing cobles working out of King's Lynn, in Norfolk, sent a petition to the Admiralty dated 8 March 1809, less than four years after Trafalgar, complaining that as the cobles came in with their catch the midshipman leading the local press gang 'had the insolence to demand three of the best fish for the regulating captain, the lieutenant and himself'.

A press gang, whether belonging to the Impress Service or from a particular ship, was part of the life of the times and some men regarded it as others might a bad illness. William Spavens was returning to England in a merchant ship just before the previous war began:

> On our return we did not come through the Downs and wished to shun Yarmouth Road to avoid the press; but the wind veering and blowing a strong gale, we were forced in, and soon after boarded by a boat belonging to the *Augusta*'s tender, and two of our crew were impressed; and when we reached Hull I shared the same fate, and was hauled on board the *John and Joyce*, tender to the *Culloden*.
>
> During my confinement, a scheme was formed by the impressed men, to take the ship from the crew, and run her on shore

to regain their liberty; but the plot being discovered, Lt Kirby sent notice of it to Capt Smelt, the regulating captain on shore, to send him a reinforcement, which he no sooner received than he doubled the guards, giving them positive orders to fire amongst us if we attempted to mutiny.

Spavens was soon a member of a press gang himself. He was serving in the *Vengeance* frigate, sent to Ireland 'to procure men for the service'. The *Vengeance* had two cutters and a wherry to attend her. The wherry, with an officer and twenty men on board, sailed out along the coast from Dublin Bay towards the high land of Wicklow, 'and when we perceived a ship coming in, we concealed ourselves, and let only the wherry men be seen, who were pilots for the bar and polebeg'.

The sailors on board the incoming ship were wide awake. One day, Spavens writes, the *Dublin* arrived from New York and 'we steered under her lee, asking if they wanted a pilot. The captain said they did, and told us to come alongside; but the men having some suspicion of our design bid us keep off, or they would fire upon us.'

The *Vengeance* fired guns to bring her to, and then sent a cutter with an officer and boarding party. The *Dublin*'s men would only allow the officer up the ladder, so the *Vengeance* arranged for two cutters, the yawl and wherry to try to board her as soon as it was dark.

This was done, but the *Dublin*'s men were, Spavens reported, at close quarters — they had barricaded themselves below, lashing down the hatches. 'We scuttled [made holes in] their decks with axes and fired down amongst them, while they kept firing up at us where they saw the light appear. After having shot one of our men through the head, and another through both his thighs, they submitted and we got sixteen brave fellows.'

Liverpool was a tough neighbourhood and before the Impress Service was established there pressing 'had been deemed impracticable'. However, some of the local citizens mentioned this to the *Vengeance*'s captain, who regarded it as a challenge. One night he sent in a cutter 'with some officers and a suitable reinforcement of men'.

Spavens described how they 'soon picked up sixteen men, but only one of them being a seaman, him we detained and the rest we set at liberty'.

The next day, 25 July, was Liverpool's fixed fair, so, 'mustering a gang of eighty men, we went ashore; and after picking up several stragglers, we surprised the *Lion*'s crew in the Customs house just as they were about renewing their protections.

'We secured seventeen of them, and guarding them along the streets, several hundreds of old men, women and boys flocked after us, well provided with stones and brickbats, and commenced a general attack; but not wishing to hurt them, we fired our pistols over their heads, in order to deter them from further outrage; but the women proved very daring, and followed us down to low water mark, being almost up to the knees in mud.

'We also pressed sixteen men out of the *Nancy* and fourteen out of the *Jenny*; the latter (being determined to preserve their liberty if possible) had confined their captain and chief mate in order to fight their way through; and the cook had got a pot full of boiling tallow to scald us with as we got up alongside; but the wind being foul and not having a pilot, and the second mate not daring to take charge of her in the river, they submitted to their fate.' The *Ingram*, arriving from Tortola, in the West Indies, lost twenty-six men to the gang, and several of them were flogged on board the *Lion* for firing into the press gang's boats.

The men pressed by gangs sent out from ships were obviously taken straight out to these ships, but those caught by the Impress Service and locked up in the various Rendezvous were taken to the nearest receiving ship, which could be anything from an old frigate to a hulk, and there locked up in the press room.

Despite having the gangmen of the Impress Service roaming the countryside, drinking in the alehouses and swinging their clubs along the quiet lanes (usually only the gangs from ships regularly carried cutlasses), the King's ships were always short of men. The complement of each ship was laid down by the Admiralty and a captain would consider himself lucky if he had three-quarters of his complement. Captain Glascock, writing ten years after the end of the war and with considerable detachment, commented that in wartime 'the very best disciplined ships, to the regret and dread of every officer who has a respect for his ship's company, are fain to recruit their crews from the hulks and jails of the Kingdom. The influx of such a tide of corruption must overwhelm all discipline, were not the mounds of authority strongly reinforced by increased vigilance and severity.'

He quotes a letter from the captain of the *Princess Royal* with the

Channel Fleet off Brest which said: 'I am upwards of seventy men short of complement; and I was obliged to take sixty convicts to fill up the number I have.'

By contrast, when fifty convicts were sent on board the 74-gun *Bellona*, the captain assembled them on the quarterdeck and described the need for good behaviour and obedience in a ship of war. Referring to 'the unhappy circumstances' under which they had been brought on board, he assured them that he would begin by regarding them 'as men without fault' but that any of them who subsequently committed an offence in the *Bellona* would get double the punishment. This had such a good effect, according to a contemporary account, that only one of the fifty men received punishment during the next four years.

The receiving ships, in which the men taken by the Impress Service were kept until they were transferred to ships in commission and needing men, were floating prisons. Midshipman Jeffery Raigersfield was serving in the *Vestal* frigate when she went to the Nore, 'and soon after myself, with a party of men, was sent on board to take the charge of a three-decker line of battleship that was lying here to receive pressed men; all her guns were out, and she had stumps stepped for masts.

'There were above eleven hundred men on board, the sweepings of all London, tailors, barbers, watermen, livery servants, waiters &c, and such a motley group I never before beheld so compactly lodged.'

A seaman 'compactly lodged' saw it differently, and one of the most vivid descriptions by a pressed seaman describes how 'a hot and pestilential effluvia rose and enveloped me. I looked through a heavy wooden grating across which was a strong iron bar with a huge padlock attached to it; and I saw that which threw me back almost fainting with horror . . . a crowded mass of disgusting and fearful heads, with eyes all glaring upwards from that horrible den; and heaps of filthy limbs, trunks and heads, bundled and scattered, scrambling, laughing, cursing, screaming and fighting at one moment.'

Robert Hay was a great deal luckier when he was sent on board the *Resolu* at Plymouth in August 1803. She was 'a kind of examination ship appointed to receive and cleanse all the newly raised levies that arrived in this port. After being thoroughly washed in a number of cisterns which were fitted around the sides of this vessel we were examined while in a state of nudity before a committee of surgeons. Those who had any appearance of disease or uncleanness were kept on board for cure or purification. The rest . . . were sent on board the *Salvador del Mundo*, which at that time lay guard ship in the harbour.'

The main reasons why pressed men were closely guarded from the moment they were picked up by the gangers until they were taken on board the ship in which they would eventually serve was that they were not subject to the Articles of War until their names had been entered in a ship's muster book and they had been rated – noted down as landmen, ordinary seamen or able seamen. It was impracticable to muster them in receiving ships so, from the time they were taken to the Rendezvous until they were mustered in their ships, they came under civil law.

Cutlass (hilt on left), *officer's sword* (hilt on right) *and midshipman's dirk*

CHAPTER NINE

The Real Enemy

In the Seven Years' War (1756–63), the Royal Navy lost 133,700 men by disease and desertion, but only 1,512 were killed in battle. In the Revolutionary and Napoleonic Wars, which lasted with a short break for twenty-two years, the Royal Navy lost 1,875 killed in the six major and four minor battles fought by its fleets and four by its squadrons, compared with more than 72,000 who died from disease or accident on board and another 13,600 who died in ships lost by accident or weather.

By 1799, in the sixth year of the war, when the Navy's strength was voted at 100,000 seamen and 20,000 marines, it had 634 surgeons, according to the Navy List published by Steel at the beginning of the year, and 646 ships in commission, with seventeen receiving ships in service.

This total of ships shows how in 1799 the Admiralty's effort was spread across the world. Two hundred and seventy-three ships (including thirty-two ships of the line and sixty-nine frigates) were in port and refitting, forty-eight were guard, hospital and prison ships, 119 were in home waters, and eighty-one in the West Indies. There were fifteen along the American coast and at Newfoundland, thirty-nine on the Cape of Good Hope station, sixty-nine at Portugal, Gibraltar and the Mediterranean, and two on the West African coast. Of this total of 646 ships, though, only about 400 carried surgeons; the rest had surgeons' mates.

A surgeon was paid £5 a month, plus 2d per man per month for the ship he served in and £5 for every hundred men he treated for venereal disease. There was also a payment to surgeons made yearly 'or as often as they pass their accounts' called the 'Queen Anne's Free Gift to Surgeons', which depended on the size of the ships in which they served, ranging from £62 4s 5d in a first-rate to £25 16s 10d in a sixth. The gift was also made to surgeons' mates, who usually served in cutters and tenders – they received £18 18s 10d.

Half pay for surgeons depended on their seniority – the first twenty, providing they had served nine years, received a generous 5s a day, and the next hundred with seven years' service had 3s, with the scale dropping to 2s 6d. The pay of surgeons' mates varied; a 'first mate' serving in a ship of the line who had his own set of instruments received £5 a month, the same as a surgeon but without the considerable extras. Second mates had £3 10s 3d a month; third, fourth and fifth had £3, and in ships where there was no surgeon a sliding scale of between £5 and £4.

Before being employed, a surgeon or a surgeon's mate had to pass 'an examination in surgery, at Surgeons' Hall, Lincoln's Inn Fields'. The Regulations laid down that a prospective surgeon or surgeon's mate had to apply to the Navy Commissioners of the Sick and Hurt at Somerset House for a letter to the Surgeons' Company. He then had to pass a second examination by the Surgeons' Company, and if successful he had to face a third one, by the Commissioners, who if satisfied then appointed him to a ship.

With a continual shortage of surgeons, the Commissioners were not very fussy and all too often a ship's surgeon was a disapointed man who could not make a living on land. James Gardner, in his opinions of his shipmates, found the surgeon of the *Salisbury* 'crabbed as the devil', while the surgeon's assistant in the *Orestes* was 'proud as the devil' and Thomas Trotter of the *Edgar* was 'a most excellent fellow with first rate abilities, an able writer and poet'. (Trotter, a former physician of the Fleet, did a great deal to improve the practice of medicine in the Navy.) The *Edgar*'s three assistant surgeons (the title after 1805 given to surgeons' mates) were described in order as being 'not very orthodox', 'much the gentleman', and 'drank like a fish'. In the *Brunswick* the surgeon was skilful 'but crabbed as the devil at times'. The ship's master was known as 'Pot Guts' while the surgeon was known as 'Bottle Belly', and 'used to eat very hearty and seemed to devour everything with his eyes on the table'.

The difference between a naval physician and a naval surgeon was considerable. The 1799 Navy List gives only three physicians of the fleets (Harness – who gave his name to a type of cask – Blair and Trotter, the man admired by James Gardner). The historians of

Medicine and the Navy wrote: 'In the eighteenth century the physician was a gentleman, bound by an ethical code which did not even permit him to sue a defaulting patient for his legitimate fees, whereas the surgeon and the apothecary were regarded merely as craftsmen.' They point out that a physician had a medical degree, whereas the surgeon's qualifications were nominal, although changes made in 1805 meant that a physician had to serve as a ship's surgeon for five years before being appointed to a fleet or hospital.

All through the centuries the seaman's great enemy had not been rumbling broadsides ripping his ship to pieces with roundshot and grape, langridge and bar shot; nor had the great killer been storms and hurricanes and uncharted rocks. A musket ball, the shot and nails and scraps of metal fired from a privateer's musketoon, the slash of a cutlass or the jab of a pike – in war these took a negligible toll of men's lives compared with at first scurvy (a vile disease which, within a century, was to become almost unknown) and now typhus and yellow fever.

Scurvy killed more in war simply because there were more men at sea. Convoys sometimes arrived in England from the West Indies with the ships almost unmanageable because of men helpless and dying from disease. Yellow fever in the West Indies did its best to kill off the survivors. But typhus was by now the main enemy because of the vast number of men brought into the Navy by the Quota Act and the press gangs.

In 1806 William Turnbull, 'Fellow of the Medical Societies of London and Edinburgh, a Member of the Royal College of Surgeons . . . and formerly a surgeon in His Majesty's Navy', published his 412-page volume *The Naval Surgeon*, which covered every aspect of his work at sea. It is particularly revealing now in showing what was not known at that time.

Describing scurvy and correctly noting that it was caused by the seaman's diet, he pointed out that on land it was common in areas where the people 'derive their principle nourishment from fish, which, although not salted above six months, imparts nevertheless to those people, evident symptoms of scorbutic diathesis'.

He and his colleagues were, of course, mistaken in their view of what caused scurvy, but they knew that fresh vegetables prevented it. They had no knowledge of vitamins, but, Turnbull wrote, there was in articles of diet, particularly vegetable matter, 'a certain principle . . . absolutely necessary to give tone and vigour to the solids, to preserve the fluids in their proper state of cohesion, and thus to render the body capable of performing its functions in a proper and healthy manner'.

Nelson had a flair for summing up situations in a few words – 'ships and seamen rot in harbour' is a good example – and in a letter he referred to medicine: 'The great thing in all military service is health; and you will agree with me that it is easiest for an officer to keep men healthy, than for a physician to cure them.' While cruising with his ships he gave the men plenty of onions ('which I find the best thing that can be given to seamen'), fresh mutton and plenty of fresh water.

Turnbull, in his volume, listed the diseases of the various stations and began with the English Channel, 'the most important station to which a fleet can be appointed'. He divided the diseases into those prevalent in winter and in summer. Those of the winter 'consist of fevers and inflammatory complaints', while those most common in summer 'assume chiefly nervous and putrid form'. The changeable weather and the difficulty at sea of changing out of wet clothes were so extreme, that 'disease becomes a natural and frequent effect'.

The most prevalent winter fever, he wrote, was typhus; then came 'intermittent fevers or agues', which were also common in spring and autumn. Next to fevers came 'various kinds of inflammations', of which the most common was rheumatism. Turnbull reported that acute rheumatism 'generally attacks the younger part of the crew, or all those whose ages do not exceed thirty-five years'. It had been noticed that the right side was affected more frequently than the left and that rheumatism began 'from the sudden application of cold, when the subject is heated, or from changes of weather'. In its chronic state rheumatism produced 'a kind of crackling noise' when a joint was moved. 'A long train of rainy and stormy weather in the Channel renders the body particularly liable to this form of the disease.'

Next to rheumatism, catarrhal infections were the most frequent of the winter illnesses. Dysentery was particularly liable to appear 'after a long series of stormy or rainy weather, and when the ship has been for a considerable time at sea'. It was commoner in the tropics and 'often appears at the same time with scurvy'.

Smallpox 'very often appears at sea' and was frequently fatal. Epidemics occasionally swept England and deaths in one in 1770 were estimated at 45,000. But Jenner had discovered vaccination in

1798, although inoculation against smallpox was known years earlier. Within two years all the men in the ships of the fleets were being vaccinated, on a voluntary basis. Turnbull noted that seamen brought up in the merchant service, going to sea when young, went on long voyages without getting smallpox, but (if not vaccinated) were likely to catch it when brought on board one of the Royal Navy's ships. Surgeons 'found it difficult to combat the scruples of the seamen, arising from religious prejudices against vaccination', although by 1806 'inoculation has been regularly performed'.

Turnbull considered that consumption, which was common, 'is frequently the consequence' of smallpox and dysentery, though it was 'also very apt to arise from external injuries, as falls, bruises or strains, affecting the trunk of the body'.

Scurvy was less likely to affect the Channel Fleet than ships 'where voyages are longer'. Citric acid was the remedy but 'when thrown in too great quantities' it was apt to bring on pains like rheumatism. Venereal disease, like scurvy, 'forms the basis of marine practice from its frequent occurrence, and the various forms it assumes'.

The summer diseases, he wrote, were much the same as winter 'except that the purely imflammatory diseases are less frequent' and fevers and fluxes were most prevalent. At the top of the list were 'fevers, continued and remittent', followed by scurvy, 'venereal diseases and affections [*sic*] connected with it', consumption, rheumatism and then 'dysenteries or fluxes'. The remainder included smallpox, 'intermittents or agues', lumbago, paeripneumony, and pleurisy.

The West Indies station, he pointed out, was next in importance to the Channel and 'avowedly the most unhealthy'. Describing how anyone entering the tropics should prepare his body ('in lowering the diet or in living temperately and keeping his bowels regular'), he wrote that, if this was not sufficient, he recommended bleeding, the loss of ten or twelve ounces of blood being 'a most useful precaution'.

Great care should be taken 'to guard against the cold and unwholesome damps at night'. In fact Turnbull was not expressing himself clearly because in the tropics at sea level 75°F is a low night temperature. Yet, without realising that the mosquito was the worst cause of contagion, he, like so many others, pointed to the direction without recognising the messenger. 'As contagion either from human effluvia, or marshy exhalation, is the most active source of disease in this quarter', every ship should be anchored as far as

possible out of the reach of their influence. The distance to produce
this good effect did not have to be great but 'so far as not to *smell* the
land *air*'. Just beyond the reach of the mosquitoes, in fact, although
Turnbull did not connect the two facts.

The rest of his advice was good: if disease then appeared in a ship,
'a spring [rope] should be put on the anchor cable so that she could
be hauled round broadside on to the wind to secure better ventilation'. Hard drinking should be avoided – it 'augments the ten-
dency to a putrid state of the fuids' and made contagion more active.
Sleeping on deck was bad because 'by suddenly checking the
copious perspiration from the skin' it had the same effect as heavy
drink.

The first step towards keeping a ship's company healthy, he
wrote, was to 'diminish the quantity of salted food administered to
them'. He was a great believer that flannel worn next to the skin 'is
one of the chief preservations of health', and all seamen in the West
Indies should be issued with two thin flannel shirts. They should be
made 'long and full' and be put on after the men had been in the rain
or before going on any night duty. The reason for wool's favour was
that it absorbed the perspiration 'in consequence of the strong
attraction that subsists between wool and the aqueous vapour, and
[it] is quickly transmitted through it', while cotton on the other hand
confined the perspiration 'and renders the fervid heat of southern
climates unhealthy and insupportable'.

Turnbull and many others had noted the fatal effects of land
diseases on ships 'riding safely sheltered in harbours and in secure
creeks'. They had proved 'the destruction of whole fleets' while 'the
cruisers [at sea] have enjoyed perfect health'. Warning that men
should never sleep on shore (he was of course considering the 'night
vapours', not the mosquitoes), he emphasised that, in terms of
general health, 'the great point is to lower the full habit of the
European, chiefly by an abridgement of animal foods and an absti-
nence from strong liquors'.

Captain Frederic Chamier, writing in 1833 of his experiences as a
midshipman twenty years earlier, describes how his frigate in West
Africa had been put on shore in Sierra Leone to stop a leak, and
noted: 'When the dew of the evening began to fall, we carefully kept
our crew on board; a man, subject to the rays of the moon and the
night damp air, after the burning heat of the day, was almost sure of
a fever. The moon, both here and in the West Indies, is more

powerful than the sun: meat hung in the rays of the former becomes tainted sooner than if exposed to the latter.'

Turnbull noted that of the actual diseases fever was the most common, bringing with it a delirium which took away 'sensation and reason' and often led to coma. This was usually followed by spots, 'which always portend considerable danger'. This ship fever or typhus differed little from the one experienced in the Channel, but 'bilious remitting fever' tended to attack men when their ships were in harbour rather than at sea, and often proved fatal. It was most common between June and September, the hurricane season.

The most dangerous was malignant yellow fever, which attacked suddenly and without warning – 'the first symptoms are sudden giddiness and loss of sight, to such a degree as to make the person fall down almost insensible'. Then came an agonising headache, violent pain in the muscles, high fever and usually a vile death, in the last stages of which 'the foam issues from the mouth; the eyes roll dreadfully; and the extremities are convulsed, being thrown out and pulled back in violent and quick alternate succession'.

Turnbull listed six types of white people in the order in which they were most prone to yellow fever. First came sailors, 'especially the robust and young' and particularly those new to the tropics 'and those most given to the drinking of new rum'. Second were soldiers, especially new recruits just arrived from Europe; then white males, particularly young men lately arrived. The fourth type was 'all other white males', particularly those most intemperate or debilitated by recent sickness. White women came fifth, 'more especially those connected with the shipping; and those [people] lately from Europe'.

The treatment for these fevers, particularly yellow fever, varied slightly but had not changed much over the previous century and a half. Next to yellow fever, dysentery was one of the most prevalent diseases and one which, Turnbull commented, if not always fatal was certainly the most disagreeable. It was followed in his list by 'dry belly-ache', the symptoms of which he compared to lead poisoning or 'the Devonshire cholic', and which usually ended in palsy. Young people often recovered; older victims usually could not throw off the palsy.

Tetanus was common but he admitted that lockjaw was difficult to treat – opium, warm bath, laudanum, vapour bath, cold water pumped over the patient, 'mercurial frictions rubbed in in consider-able quantities'. Turnbull noted that 'each of these modes of treat-ment has succeeded at times, and each of them has also failed in its turn'.

'Fish poison', the next on Turnbull's list, 'constitutes an alarming disease' and while he gave the symptoms with considerable accuracy he did not recognise it as the ciguaterra found by Columbus (and still as troublesome today in a band of latitude twenty degrees either side of the Equator, with neither cause nor cure yet known). 'Where the poison does not prove fatal, the patient is long in recovering.' He noted that some people could eat a poisoned fish (there is no way of telling which are poisoned and which are not) without any effect, while others have become very ill, and its random nature is the same today. Treatment included brandy, white or blue vitriol, ginger tea, laudanum, cayenne pepper made into pills, and quinine.

Venereal disease was milder in the tropics than in a northern climate and, he warned, more liable to be concealed by the patient (who had to pay 15s for a cure) and missed by the doctor. Yaws and scurvy rounded off the list.

He gave a table of 506 patients treated in the course of three voyages to the West Indies, which showed that 290 suffered from fevers, 141 from 'dysenteries or fluxes', while most of the rest were 'scorbutic patients'.

Turnbull's view of the West Indies as a surgeon was necessarily detached, but, for the men serving in the ships, disease was an invisible and pitiless killer which struck without distinction. Captain John Markham, commanding the *Hannibal*, was ordered to sea in April 1795 with other ships of a squadron under Rear-Admiral Colpoys. A few days later he took part in the capture of two French frigates, which put £483 8s 6d of prize money in his pocket. A few weeks later he was ordered to sail for Hispaniola, where the British Government, prodded by Henry Dundas, continued its absurd quest for easy propaganda victories among the Caribbean islands. The French held the island with 15,000 acclimatised militia and 6,000 picked troops sent out from France. Against this force of 21,000 defending the island, the British Government sent 870 soldiers from Jamaica.

They landed in September and could hold only where they landed. A few more troops were sent from Jamaica to reinforce them under the command of Colonel David Markham, John's favourite brother. Markham and this tiny combined force fought on for eight months, until three more regiments arrived, in May 1796.

By the time the *Hannibal* arrived the British troops had taken terrible punishment: 300 out of 450 men in one battalion had been killed by the enemy but by September an even worse killer arrived. Within eight weeks 40 officers and 600 men had died of fever and David Markham was dead, too, though killed by a cannon ball as his men captured a redoubt. He was twenty-eight.

The *Hannibal* arrived three months later and, instead of a happy reunion, John Markham wrote to his father, 'God knows what a heavy blow it is to me who came to this spot in the hope of embracing him.'

Sickness continued attacking the troops: at Cape Nicholas Mole, where the *Hannibal* was at anchor, the 81st Regiment lost 120 men in twelve weeks; at Port au Prince only 230 men were fit enough to do duty, and sentries were so far apart that they could not hail each other.

Yellow fever then hit the ships: the *Raisonable* frigate buried thirty-six men in the few hours spent sailing the 200 miles from Port Royal, Jamaica to Port-au-Prince. Then scurvy broke out in the *Hannibal*, which had been far from ready for the West Indies when she received her orders in Plymouth. 'How the Admiralty can account to the nation and their own conscience for sending us on a foreign cruise when they had my representation of the state of the ship's company, I am at a loss to comprehend,' Markham wrote. 'I keep my people out of the sun as much as possible, and use all the preventives accessible to me.'

He added with understandable bitterness and commendable wisdom: 'A time will come when the nation will be apprised of the wretched policy of our government in meddling with this island. Since my arrival six of my people are dead and every man in the ship has scurvy in a degree. . . . We have little fresh provision, and I have kept the men in the state they are at considerable expense to myself.' The survivors of Colonel David Markham's regiment, the 20th, were sent back to England the following year – only six officers and seventy men.

When John Markham wrote that six had died of the scurvy but most men in the *Hannibal* were affected, these were in fact the happy days: within two months Markham was invalided home, and a month later one of his officers was writing: 'Since you left us, Buller and Sargent and young Harrison, with thirty men, have fallen victims within fourteen days. Young Walker, Brandon, Martin and Jones (your late clerk) died at the hospital a few days after you left. One hundred and seventy have been buried already, and many more must go, I fear. We are reduced to 300 men and boys, many of them in a very feeble state.'

Four months later Lieutenant Moss wrote again to his former captain telling of his own recovery from a second attack. 'Buller and Brisky actually bled to death. The former expired in my arms. I now remain the only officer in the ship that you know.'

The *Hannibal*'s losses, mostly in the early part of 1796, were tiny compared with the Navy and Army losses as a whole in the West Indies. In May 1796, for example, the 31st Foot mustered 776 men, but seven months later only fifteen reported for duty. The 57th Regiment lost fifteen officers and 605 men in Grenada in the nine months to February 1797, while the 27th Regiment lost twenty officers and 516 men in the same period.

In the first three years of the war, the combined Navy and Army losses in the West Indies were estimated at about 35,000 a year by the military historian J. W. Fortescue.

These figures have not been chosen selectively: they were not exceptional. For the Army alone, there were 15,881 white troops serving in the West Indies in the year ending April 1796, and 6,480 of them (40 per cent) died from sickness. Reinforcements were slow to arrive and in the following year the average strength of the white troops was 11,500, of whom 3,760 died, 32 per cent.

James Gardner, serving in the *Brunswick* in 1801, went out to the West Indies. Almost at once yellow fever hit the ship and she soon had 287 on the sick list 'and buried a great many'. He records that 'a short time before we arrived, the *Topaze*, 36, on a cruise, buried all hands except fifty-five; the captain (Church) and all the officers died, and the ship was brought in by the gunner.'

William Parker, later to become an admiral of the fleet, wrote to his father from *La Magicienne* frigate on 9 October 1797 from Cape Nicholas Mole that on a six-week cruise with two 74s, two 44s and *La Magicienne*, 'we had intolerable bad weather, owing to incessant rain and heavy squalls, for the space of a fortnight. Reckoning, on an average, the rain never ceased for two hours at a time, and always came in the gusts of wind, though soon over. . . . To finish this pleasant weather, we had a hard gale of wind for two days. This was most unfortunate weather for the poor *Carnatic*, the damps serving to increase their fevers; and I am sorry to say she lost upwards of 90 men during the cruise.'

At the beginning of the Santo Domingo campaign, in 1794, forty-six masters of transport ships and 11,000 men died of yellow fever. Yet long after the war ended in 1815 the deaths continued: Captain Frederic Chamier wrote that in 1826 (eleven years after the end of the war) there had been 3,000 soldiers in Jamaica, but by the end of the year one in three had died. The next year saw 1,100 dying. In the Navy, every seventh man serving in the West Indies died in 1826: the following year every sixth man perished.

Nor were heavy losses restricted to yellow fever and the West Indies: the *Prompte* frigate was one of the escorts of a convoy sailing into Spithead from the West Indies in July 1797 and, wrote William Richardson, 'Many of our men were bad with the scurvy, and if you only made a dent with your finger on the flesh it would remain a considerable time before it filled up again. From a small pimple that broke out on a man's thigh (and which the doctor could not stop) it increased until all the flesh on the thigh was consumed.'

John Markham's *Hannibal* eventually lost 200 men to yellow fever in six months. The ship with the heaviest British casualties at Trafalgar was the *Victory*, with 57 killed, and the total British deaths were only 449. At Copenhagen, the *Monarch* lost the most men (57 killed – the same as in the *Victory* at Trafalgar) and the total British losses were 994, so that the *Hannibal*'s deaths in three months' West Indies service were four times the highest casualties in any British ship during either of the two bloodiest sea battles of the whole war.

As a young lieutenant, Frederic Chamier had just been transferred to the *Lively* frigate in Port Royal, Jamaica, when yellow fever began to spread through the ship. The first lieutenant was one of the first victims, so Chamier became the senior officer, but with the ship alongside the wharf the seamen were taken off to the hospital as they fell sick.

To begin with Chamier kept fit with regular exercise – 'my constant practice was to rise a little before daylight, and to walk in the cool of the morning'. However, 'one morning, in getting out of bed, I was seized with a shivering fit. Well I knew what was to follow.'

Some of the *Lively*'s men were at the capstan house in irons for drunkenness, and Chamier hurried over to order their release. He gave them a stern lecture on 'the dreadful effects of drunkenness in such a climate', but before he had finished he became giddy, collapsed in the arms of a midshipman, and was carried by four marines to a room in the capstan house and put to bed. Thirteen days later: 'I was by now sinking fast; all hope of recovery gone; my former captain had taken leave of me with tears in his eyes; the expectant midshipman for a death vacancy already rubbed his hands, in earnest hope my grave would be his stepping stone.'

The *Lively*'s officers came to see him, 'deploring my loss and lamenting my fate'. Thirty days later Chamier had recovered but the *Lively*'s captain and her officers – all the people that had visited him – were dead, struck down with yellow fever. 'The fever broke out on board the ship the day after she left Port Royal, and a week after her arrival [in Carthagena] she had not men enough to keep the decks clean. She lost three surgeons, her captain, one lieutenant, three midshipmen and forty men; and vessels were obliged to be sent from Port Royal to bring her in safety to Jamaica.'

Such Caribbean losses should be compared with a fleet at sea in the healthier Mediterranean. Nelson wrote in May 1804: 'The health of this fleet cannot be exceeded, and I really believe that my shattered carcass is in the worst plight of the whole fleet.' He had already been at sea a year and another year was to pass before he set foot on land again, yet in those two years, when his force averaged eleven ships and 6,500 men, only 110 men died and 141 were sent to hospitals. The physician at the hospital in Malta, Dr Leonard Gillespie, commented that the figures gave 'the most convincing and satisfactory proofs' of the advantages of improvements adopted for keeping the men fit. The Mediterranean was, of course, mercifully free of yellow fever, though not malaria, so that a fleet of eleven ships of the line could lose 110 men in two years while the *Hannibal* in the West Indies lost 200 men in a few months.

It was a hard job keeping a large fleet fit: between February and September 1804 the agent victualler bought 21,300 oranges and 81,685 pounds of onions for the Mediterranean ships. The Admiralty was buying lemon juice from Sicily – an order in January 1805 was for 20,000 gallons for the Mediterranean Fleet and another 50,000 gallons to be sent to England for the Channel Fleet.

Any long passage would bring on scurvy, but Nelson with his fleet was, apart from a dash to the West Indies and back, able to visit ports sufficiently frequently to keep his ships provided with fresh meat and vegetables. In contrast, the captain of a ship on Atlantic convoy duty, for instance, became desperate as days went by and men died.

Captain Thomas Pasley (who later commanded the *Bellerophon* after she was launched in the Medway) commanded the 50-gun *Jupiter* in the previous war and was operating with some other ships in the South Atlantic off the Brazilian coast. On 11 December he was writing in his private diary that the wind had vanished but he was anxious to reach Trinidada, an island several hundred miles out in the Atlantic, 'as my people tumble down very fast. That dreadful disorder, the scurvy, makes rapid marches among the ship's company.' He was desperate to get 'refreshments of bullocks and vegetables for my people without which they cannot hold out'. Two days later a favourable wind helped but 'one died this morning, the captain of the forecastle and the best man in the *Jupiter*; I have my fears that many will follow in spite of our every endeavour. They have daily one pint of wine, one pint of beer, and as much of the essence of malt made into wort as they choose to drink.' By 15 December he was writing: 'Today buried another man – my God, where will it end?' He should have found the south-east trade winds; instead a north wind headed him, and his diary entries, meant for his own eyes only, reveal his plight. 'Poor wretches – what will become of our scorbutics? Humanity is shocked by this situation without even hopes but from a favourable wind,' he wrote on 18 December. By Christmas Day the wind had come fair and he reflected on the smiling faces of the previous Christmas and compared them with the present – 'all hearts are sunk and heads held down, surrounded by the dead and dying. Last night my surgeon died, today a Marine – no day hardly do we now pass without reading that awful [funeral] ceremony once.'

The *Jupiter* arrived at Trinidada on 27 December to find that there were no fresh provisions, only three British ships of war, all with many cases of scurvy, and a victualler. Pasley had to transfer water and powder, and take on victuals – not the fresh meat and vegetables he needed – and after embarking another forty sick men from one of the ships he sailed again on 29 December, noting: 'This day two more men died; very serious indeed this dreadful disorder begins to be – 120 down on board.'

Pasley had fitted up some trays of earth in which he grew plants and by 3 January he was desperate enough to wonder whether having sick men lying on it would help their recovery. 'Today my garden (which it has been my practice to raise daily salad in) I have given up and buried as many men in it as possible, greatly to their satisfaction. They are happy and seem to have faith in it. So have I, not for an absolute cure on board but as putting an undoubted check on the scurvy's progress – God grant it!' Next day he recorded: 'Yesterday the garden did wonders; the men who were carried and lifted in and out of it, incapable of moving a limb, walked of themselves today. . . . An hour is the time, and from six in the morning till six at night I can receive thirty-six men – it may save lives.'

Three men died before the *Jupiter* arrived at Fernando Noronha on 7 January, but the surf was too high to get the sick on shore. An attempt on the 11th saw fifteen of them nearly drowned when a boat capsized. 'Never surely was a ship in a more distressed situation: 196 men down in this dreadful disorder, an addition of five or six every day.'

Finally he had them all on shore in their hammocks with the main-deck awning stretched out as a tent. Two weeks later he wrote: 'Early this morning sixty of my men came on board, to my utter astonishment almost all recovered.' Next day, 29 January, he recorded: 'This morning early got off twenty-two more men from the sick tent, wonderfully recovered,' and when the last came off next day, only four needed assistance.

By February the *Jupiter* was on her way to England, with the *Mercury* frigate in company, and mustered 350 men. The Azores were sighted on 26 February and the ship arrived in the English Channel on 8 March, with only a few men ill.

Yellow fever was, mercifully, a disease of the tropics and even then usually found only along the coasts. There were some epidemics outside the tropics, but they were rare and brief, though bad while they lasted. One occurred in New York in 1794 and the French *Dauphin* took it to Cadiz in 1800. Nearly 4,000 died of it in Philadelphia a few years earlier.

Lime or lemon juice was of course the most famous weapon against scurvy; the British use of lime-juice in their ships led to the ships being called 'limejuicers' by American seamen, the men in them becoming 'Limeys', the phrase still in use (though the British term for Americans, Jonathans, did not survive the war).

Dr James Lind published his cure for scurvy in 1753, following long experiments at sea on how lemon juice could be preserved.

The Navy did not adopt it until 1795, and, although this seems tardy, merchant ships – which suffered equally from scurvy – had to wait until the Merchant Shipping Act of 1854.

That limes should get the major credit is ironic: in 1918 it was discovered that as an antiscorbutic fresh limes had only a quarter of the value of fresh lemons. Preserving either juice reduced its value as an antiscorbutic, but this was of little consequence because improved eating habits meant that scurvy all but vanished, being generally restricted in the latter part of the twentieth century to alcoholic whites living in the tropics and following a poor diet.

The Navy's fight against scurvy was mostly an inordinately long one, lasting three hundred years, against lethargy and prejudice. The value of fruit in warding off scurvy was well known in Elizabethan times – Sir Richard Hawkins wrote in 1593: '. . . that which I have seen most fruitful for this sickness is sour oranges and lemons.' Although they were used in the next century, by the 1750s the lessons had been forgotten and when Anson made his voyage round the world 1,051 died out of 1,955, most of them the victims of scurvy.

Yet in 1617 Dr John Woodall, appointed surgeon-general of the Honourable East India Company, published *The Surgeon's Mate*, in which he said of lime juice 'how excellent it hath been approved'. He recommended that limes should be used on shore, but does not mention their use at sea. The first English sailor's word book, *An Accidence for Young Seamen*, by Captain John Smith, published in 1626, says that lemon juice should be used.

Although it was known that antiscorbutics such as lemons cured or prevented scurvy, and bark (quinine) could be used for various fevers (an Admiralty order of 1808 laid down that men going off on wooding and watering expeditions in the tropics should be given bark), treatment was all based on experience of what proved effective, with the surgeons knowing nothing of germs, antiseptics or the circulation of the blood. On the Walcheren Expedition, with the Army and Navy operating across the flat land and marshes of the Netherlands, the disease that caused vast casualties was called 'polder fever' and reckoned by the more advanced doctors to be caused by 'exhalations from the soil', although it was in fact malaria carried by mosquitoes.

Surgery was rudimentary: amputation of limbs was, of course, done without any antiseptic precautions or anaesthetics, other than strong drink, and the man who survived the actual sawing and cutting was likely to die from shock. If he survived that he faced septicaemia. Bleeding was recommended in cases of haemorrhage – because it relieved the local bleeding at the actual site of the wound.

Hernia, very common among seamen, was curiously enough little understood by surgeons. Turnbull, in his volume of 1806, referring to the treatment of hernia said that it was important to relax the system, which could be done by 'injections of tobacco smoke, which will take off the tension, as well as prove a laxative'. As a last resort, he recommended 'filling the intestines with tepid water, by means of a particular instrument or pump which . . . seldom fails'.

Seamen were issued with free trusses, and it was estimated that one man in seven had a hernia. 'A well-constructed truss, accurately fitted', Turnbull wrote, 'will enable a seaman to execute whatever is to be done in the body of the ship, equally well, in the same way as we see daily ruptured persons on land follow the laborious employment of porters, paviours, draymen &c.'

Despite typhus, yellow fever, scurvy, hernia, fractures and fluxes, drunkenness was a problem that continued year in and year out, not only without cure but with very few people realising that alcoholism was as much a disease as tuberculosis or cancer. Like tropical fevers it was classless; a ship's lieutenant was as likely to drink heavily as the most sodden bosun's mate, and it was just as likely to kill him.

Many of the reasons why men of all ranks drank heavily are obvious: the cold and the wet of service in northern climates made a tot of rum a welcome and warming drink. Sheer misery or boredom meant that seamen hoarding their tots (against regulations) and officers who could have as much drink as they could afford found a few hours' oblivion. Yet anyone who has made long voyages under sail knows of another reason why some men drink hard liquor: a monotonous diet produces a powerful craving for a sharp, violent taste which is eased by rum. This craving was a major reason why men chewed tobacco: the bitterness almost scorched the tongue and made up for the insipid salt meat and crumbling bread. It could be chewed for hours; tucked away safely while a man slept, it was good for a second day's chewing, conveniently numbing the taste.

The seamen chewed tobacco; the officers spiced their food. A good curry for the wardroom did for the officers' jaded tastes what a plug of cut tobacco did for the seamen. And it was all swilled down with alcohol.

With the exception of the introduction of vaccination, advances in the treatment of the sick at sea continued to depend on lethargy being overcome by prejudice which was in turn eventually brushed aside by knowledge. Admiral Lord St Vincent, one of the Navy's strictest disciplinarians, went to great lengths to make sure his ships, officers and men were efficient – which also meant fit – but occasionally this misfired. Captain John Markham was commanding the *Centaur* in St Vincent's fleet, and when he had some cases of fever on board St Vincent sent over Dr Weir, the flagship's surgeon, to report. Weir said that the filthy condition of the men's woollen clothing was the cause of the fever – whereupon St Vincent ordered it to be thrown over the sides, the lower-deck gun ports to be kept open day and night, fires to be lit on the lower deck all day (braziers were used), and the ship's company to eat on the upper deck. He also ordered that much of the bread for the fleet was to be stored in the *Centaur*'s wardroom.

St Vincent was usually right where discipline was concerned but he was often so arbitrary that he went too far – the bread in the wardroom, for instance, was almost childish. The *Centaur*'s men 'made a respectful representation' that each be allowed to keep a woollen jacket for night wear. Captain Markham wrote to St Vincent describing this request, and sent the letter with an officer who reported that the weight of bread in the wardroom had pressed down the main-deck beams so much that the tiller (the forward end of which ran in a guide fitted on the under side) could not be moved more than a turn of the wheel each way, thus making ship-handling difficult and dangerous.

St Vincent could not admit that he might have been wrong – his greatest fault – and the lieutenant was sent back with the message that the bread was not to be taken out of the wardroom; instead it should be spread more about and the officers' cabins, which surrounded the wardroom, 'might be floored with it'. As the lieutenant was leaving St Vincent's flagship a midshipman came running up with another message from the Admiral: the first lieutenant's cabin in the *Centaur* was to be stowed 'quite full of bread'.

St Vincent's letter to Markham said that 'the filthy state' of the woollen clothing 'was the principal cause' of the fever on board the

Centaur, and he was paying no attention to Markham's letter, 'which I highly disapprove'.

Markham replied that he was sorry if conveying 'the humble representation of seamen' to the admiral was regarded as improper, and anyway he would have failed in his duty 'if I had neglected to remonstrate when I was convinced that their apparel was insufficient for the night dews'.

Ironically enough, St Vincent had originally set a great store by men wearing flannel next to the skin: he had quarrelled with Dr Trotter, the enlightened physician of the Channel Fleet, on this very question. Trotter's attitude, written in his volume *Medicina Nautica*, was 'clothe them as warm as you please, but in the name of cleanliness give them linen or cotton next to the skin'. Now St Vincent had changed his views and had adopted Trotter's view, and Captain Markham seems to have been one of the first to fall foul of the Admiral's new policy.

Cleanliness was certainly one of St Vincent's aims. Soap was not supplied in the Royal Navy until he ordered it for his fleet in 1796, and he and Trotter were responsible for proper sick bays being installed. Better ventilation by using windsails – canvas cylinders open at the top and hoisted through hatches like chimneys working in reverse – and fumigation helped keep the ships drier down below and kill some of the vermin. Braziers helped dry the decks in cold climates.

The major improvement in health at sea, though, depended upon discoveries in the field of medicine. Considering the structure of a ship of war, the sailor's life was only slightly more unhealthy than that of his brother living in a town or city. The water he drank might be smelly but it was unlikely to be polluted by sewage, and anyway his ration of small beer was intended to take the place of water. If the seaman was ill he could report sick and see the surgeon, but it was unlikely that his brother in a city could afford to see a doctor. The farm labourer worked long hours and had as strenuous a life as a seaman, and his risk of hernia was about the same.

CHAPTER TEN

The Eighth Man

The purser in one of the King's ships was a man for whom there were fourteen ounces to a pound, and the spectre haunting his life was the fear of 'being brought in debt'. The purser was the Navy's shopkeeper and storekeeper who divided the world into the one-eighth allowed to him – and from which his profit or loss came – and the seven-eighths he issued to the men.

The purser was the man standing between the tons of provisions in the Victualling Board's warehouses and its arrival in ounce measures on the mess tables in various of the King's ships. He was allowed a commission of an eighth of the value of everything issued by weight or measure, except tobacco (where he received 10 per cent) and clothing (called 'slops') where he received £5 for every £100-worth he sold. His business was conducted with a profit margin of 12½ per cent (one-eighth) on the bulk of his stock, and 10 and 5 on the rest. His enemies were the rats, mice, weevils and cockroaches which combined with sharp contractors, time, heat and leaking casks to diminish his provisions after they had been issued to him. This was 'wastage', and was why he was allowed an eighth of the value.

To become a purser, a man first needed some capital: the Navy Board required him to put up a bond, to make sure he kept on the path of business righteousness. This ranged from £1,200 in a first-rate to £400 in a sixth-rate or smaller.

The man himself needed a very good business sense and a knowledge of the regulations: the line between legitimate economy on his own part, the required economy on the Navy's behalf, and fraud was finely drawn and very twisty. If he did not know the value and price of everything, and his commission on it, then he would quickly become bankrupt. If he kept his accounts carefully and gave no man credit unless there was no choice, he could expect a comfortable old age.

His pay was poor: he received the same as the gunner, carpenter and boatswain, from £4 a month in a first-rate down to £2 in a sixth or smaller. The attraction of the job came in the commission, and in the bonus paid at the end of each year (providing his accounts balanced), ranging from £25 in a first-rate to £7 in a sixth or smaller.

But the purser's main profit came from a tradition of issuing fourteen ounces of every kind of allowance when the Navy's regulation specified a pound. For every pound issued, the purser made a profit of the value of two ounces. It was all completely illegal and it was practised in every ship in the Navy.

The purser had a long and complex list of instructions covering every aspect of his official life, ranging from the general ('He is to be careful to inspect the good order, stowage and preservation of provisions, and that the oldest to be expended first') to the particular ('He may at appointed times, and in some public place, sell tobacco to the seamen, not exceeding two pounds per month to a man, at the rate settled by the Navy Board'). Nowhere did it say that where the Navy had laid down the 'Daily Allowance for one man', every pound he issued should weigh only fourteen ounces. The Admiralty and the Navy Board knew about it – it had been going on for scores of years – and did nothing. The alternative would have been to increase the purser's pay.

When the Fleet mutinied at Spithead in 1797 the very first of their demands was: 'That our provisions be raised to the weight of sixteen ounces to the pound, and of a better quality; and that our measures may be the same as used in the commercial trade of this country.'

A seaman's weekly ration was strong on quantity and weak on quality. He was allowed a pound of bread every day and a gallon of beer. The bread was hard biscuit which had probably gone soft and dusty from age, assisted by weevils; the drink was small beer, little more than water in which hops had floated but which would keep much longer than water. It was far from being the kind of ale which would leave a toper thumping the bar and terrorising the potman; in fact a serious drinker would dismiss it as fit only for exercising a blacksmith's bladder.

A pound of bread and a gallon of beer was a regular daily ration; the rest of the items were issued on different days of the week. He received each week 4 lb of salt beef (2 lb on Tuesday and 2 lb on

Saturday), 2 lb of salt pork (one on Sunday, the other on Thursday), 2 pints of pease (in half-pints on Monday, Wednesday, Thursday and Friday), 3 pints of oatmeal, 6 ounces of butter and 12 ounces of cheese, issued a third at a time on Monday, Wednesday and Friday.

That was the 'daily allowance' but there were modifications. Once a week the man was issued with flour, suet and currants or raisins instead of his piece of beef, so that he could have a duff 'as a change of diet, and preventive against scurvy'.

The total quantities involved were considerable. A frigate with a complement of 300 men, provisioning for three months (a short period), would be carrying (in 'pursers' weights and measures') 25,200 lb of bread, 25,200 gallons of beer, 3,600 4 lb pieces of beef, and the same number of 2 lb pieces of pork, 3,600 quarts of pease and 5,400 of oatmeal, 1,800 lb of butter (in pounds of 12 oz), 3,600 lb of cheese (in pounds of 9 oz), and 6,300 quarts of rum or 12,600 quarts of wine.

It will be seen that in the table of 'Proportion for three months', in pursers' weights, butter weighs not 14 oz to the pound but 12, and cheese is 9 oz to the pound. The reasons for this are given later but, in case it seems the dice are being loaded deliberately against the purser, it is worth quoting from *A Treatise on the Office Of Purser*, written 'by an old-established Officer in that Line in His Majesty's Navy' and published in 1788. This volume gave 202 pages of advice to pursers on how to avoid being 'cast in debt', and made mild criticisms of the Victualling Board.

In his instructions, a purser had to provide the ship with coal, wood, candles and lanterns, and this brought a warning in the treatise. When a ship was abroad she was sometimes careened (heeled over) to repair seams in the hull planking, or the deck seams were re-payed. In either case the pitch kettle had to be heated. Pitch kettles were like enormous cooking pots (those at the dockyard in English Harbour, Antigua, are 4 ft 6 in. in diameter), and often some of the ship's supply of firewood was needed to heat them. This was paid for by the Navy Board, the purser was told, 'on his producing proper certificates for the quantity expended'. But, the 'old-established officer' grumbled, the fires burned below decks in cold or damp weather, using braziers or the new Brodie's stove, were 'a constant extra expense to the purser', despite the benefit to the health of the ship's company.

After many pages on keeping books and handling money, the

author then deals chapter by chapter with the various types of provisions, starting with 'bread, the staff of life'. He then refers to it as biscuit, which was a far more accurate name because it was baked into hard rectangles. He wrote:

> It is issued to the seamen at the rate of fourteen ounces to the pound, an eighth being reserved, and allowed to the purser for waste, which is frequently found, in long voyages and warm climates, not to be adequate to its loss of weight, occasioned by dust and vermin, particularly weevils, cockroaches, and maggots. Rats and mice, though very destructive do not half the mischief as those insects.
>
> I have frequently seen biscuit entirely perforated by the weevil, and, when knocked on a table, the whole has fallen to powder; and I may venture to assert that a quantity of biscuit which, in its original state, weighed twenty pounds, did not then weigh ten.

All bread, supplied in 224 lb puncheons and 112 lb bags, should be weighed when taken into the ship, 'particularly what is received from a contractor abroad'. The book makes it quite clear that, along with vermin and insects, the purser's worst enemy was 'a contractor abroad', who could halve the weight of a bag of provisions merely by muttering 'a contract price'.

A purser did have a legitimate complaint about returning bread. A ship could be commissioned and provisioned for a foreign voyage and then, with the Admiralty changing its mind, paid off, when all the provisions were returned to the Victualling Office. The 'old-established officer' cites a case where the bread, stowed in bags, was on board a ship for only ten weeks before being returned to the Victualling Office and sifted and reweighed. In that time 41,440 lb had powdered sufficiently to produce 2,420 lb of dust, for which the purser was charged. The purser's complaint in a case like this was that he could charge his eighth only when the bread was issued; while it was stowed in the ship's breadroom it was as though still in the King's store – except that the purser, not the Crown, had to stand any loss.

It is in the section on bread that the 'old-established officer' also admitted that serving fourteen ounces instead of sixteen had no legal basis.

Although all the provisions that are issued by weight or measure (fresh and salt meat excepted) have an eighth deducted to make up for waste, by serving out in retail what was received in the gross, yet there is to my knowledge no absolute article in the Naval instructions that gives any authority to the pursers so to do – Custom and necessity of the practice being the only ground on which it is founded; for it is absolutely specified that the weight of the provisions allowed are avoirdupois, and all the liquors wine measure.

Every man serving in one of the King's ships, from the captain to the cook's boy, was allowed a gallon of beer a day, wine measure. That was laid down in the Instructions. The 'old-established officer' felt it necessary to use italics when he added that 'the purser, *by the custom of the service*, is allowed . . . one eighth for waste, leakage and shrinkage'.

Because various provisions were sometimes not available, or were unsuitable owing to the particular climate in which a ship was serving, there was a scale laid down when one thing was issued instead of another. The gallon of beer is an example: it was laid down that if a ship was 'In the Streights' (i.e. had passed through the Strait of Gibraltar and was in the Mediterranean), one pint of wine would be issued instead of the gallon of beer. On the coast of America spruce beer was issued 'if it can be got', otherwise half a pint of spirits. In the West Indies the men received half a pint of rum or a pint of wine.

A seaman therefore received a pint of wine or half a pint of rum a day. From the time of Admiral Vernon rum was mixed with water and called grog (from Vernon's nickname, Old Grogram, the material of which his cloak was made). The amount of water used was left to the discretion of the captain 'and depends on the climate the ship is in, and the quantity of water that is on board'. Usually three half-pints of water were mixed with one of rum, to give the man a total of a quart. This was served twice a day at set times, usually between eleven and twelve in the forenoon and four and five in the afternoon.

In a large ship a considerable quantity of rum was involved, and it was a strict rule that it could be drawn from the cask only on the open deck, because of the risk of fire – the fate of the *Glasgow*, whose rum caught fire while being issued down in the hold at Jamaica, was still fresh in many men's minds. The rum and the water was measured in the presence of a master's mate, who was also present when it was issued to the men.

However, there was a warning for pursers: 'when casks of spirit are emptied, let them always be rinsed with salt water, to prevent the pernicious custom of the quartermaster making bulls'. Given the chance, the quartermasters put fresh water in a newly emptied rum cask. Within a couple of days it had turned into strong grog. 'I have known casks so used, on opening the bung with a candle near it, take fire and go off like the report of a cannon.'

Seamen preferred grog to anything else and were far from fond of wine, which was usually red. The contemptuous phrase for wine was 'black strap', while serving in the Mediterranean was 'being black strapped'. Like much naval slang the origin is lost but, with the current east-going into the Mediterranean, any ship becalmed in the Strait is swept past the Gibraltar anchorage and would be lucky if her boats could tow her into Black Strap Bay, on the east side of the Rock, so that she could anchor and wait for wind.

Once issued to a seaman, a ration of grog was called a tot and, although forbidden by Regulations, he often used it as currency to repay or buy a favour. When he was on shore and free to drink as much as he wished, the seaman had a simple slang to describe how he took his spirits. 'Due north' meant raw spirit and 'due west' meant water alone, while any point of the compass between north and west described the dilution, so that a 'north-wester' meant half water and half spirit. If that proved too weak, the man would demand 'more northing'.

Once again the purser's grumble about liquor was similar to the one about bread: he was allowed an eighth for wastage on all that he issued, but he had to pay for losses when he came to return to the Victualling Office any left over, or when he handed over to a successor on changing ship. All casks were opened and he had to fill them up. 'I have myself known more than a puncheon of rum used to fill up the deficiencies of fourteen returned into store at the end of the voyage.'

This means that out of 1,120 gallons 80 gallons had leaked, so the purser was 'cast into debt' at the rate of eight shillings a gallon, or £32. The debt would have been less had the puncheons contained wine, which was charged at five shillings a gallon.

In hot climates, pursers often found that casks in the bottom of the hold which should have contained wine or spirits were empty – 'the heat has caused the heads to warp and fly out'. When that happened a purser usually tried to get the master of the ship (responsible for stowage) to go to a notary at the next port the ship visited and swear an affidavit describing 'the exact state the casks of liquor were found to be in': this would help the purser persuade the Victualling Office to allow him the loss.

When a contractor supplied the liquor, 'the casks are generally too light and insufficient, and frequently made of green wood'. The wise purser going on a voyage to the West Indies 'reserves a set of King's casks' and 'sends them to the contractor's to be filled when he completes wine and spirits'. In any case, when they are brought on board, the purser should have the bungs taken out, in the presence of the master, to make sure they are full 'and that no trick, by mixing salt water or otherwise' has been played on him.

The days that meat were not issued (Monday, Wednesday and Friday) were called banyan days by the seamen, a reference to an East Indian sect who were forbidden to eat meat. On each of these days the regulations said that every man and boy on board was allowed 2 oz of butter and 4 oz of Suffolk cheese. There were the usual variations on this – on foreign stations double the quantity of butter might be issued in place of cheese, which could not be kept in a hot climate, or sweet oil in place of both.

The important thing is that the regulations said a man should receive 2 oz of butter and 4 oz of Suffolk cheese on each of the three banyan days. This meant, by the normal rules of arithmetic, that for the week the man received 6 oz of butter and 12 oz of cheese.

There was, however, a catch: butter was measured in pounds of twelve ounces, not sixteen ounces, and cheese went on scales where a pound comprised nine ounces.

This meant that on the scale of allowances when a man received 'half a pound of butter' a week it was six ounces of a twelve-ounce pound. The scale also gave a ration of a pound of cheese, but at nine ounces to one pound, so that when a man was supposed to have 12 oz of Suffolk cheese, 3 oz was missing.

The mystery of the Suffolk cheese is explained by the 'old-established officer', who wrote that 'Suffolk cheese was formerly issued in the Navy, but it was found to be of so tough and bad a quality as to be more proper to make buttons for seamen's jackets than to afford them nourishment, their jaws and teeth being tired long before their hunger could be assuaged'.

There were so many complaints about it that in 1758 the Navy Board ordered that 'cheese of a superior quality, either good Cheshire or single Gloucester, should hereafter be served . . . but the strict economy that pervades and attends every thing that relates to the Navy, here interfered, and the quantity was reduced to two-thirds . . . and the seaman is now only allowed two-thirds of a pound of cheese, in lieu of a whole pound; which when issued, and the eighth taken by the purser for waste . . . reduces a pound to nine ounces, which is a seaman's weekly allowance, and what a moderate working ploughman, who does not go through half the fatigue a seaman is exposed to would devour at a breakfast.' That verdict on both the quality and the quantity of Suffolk cheese was written in 1788.

Butter was not one of a purser's favourite items. 'In warm climates the butter is in so liquid a state that it is issued by measure, at the rate of a pint for a pound. Great waste (more than the allowance) must naturally be incurred by this method,' warns the old-established officer.

When any provisions went rotten, they could only be condemned by a board of survey made up of three officers, preferably from another ship, who inspected the item and filled in the appropriate certificate, the wording of which had to be according to instructions. Volumes like *The Seaman's New Vade Mecum*, published privately, were full of such certificates – 'of survey on beef and pork', 'of provisions lost in the hold', for instance, and followed by 'letters', from the purser to the captain, 'requesting a survey on currants'. The sample letter given, requesting a survey on decayed provisions, says: 'There being a quantity of bread, butter, and cheese on board His Majesty's ship ——, under your command, which is rotten, maggotty, rancid, and stinking, and unfit for men to eat: I am to request you will be pleased to apply to the Commander-in-Chief for a survey on the same.'

The disposal of condemned provisions was strictly governed. Butter, for example, when condemned as 'rank and stinking', could be returned to store or, if the captain made a written order, 'delivered and charged to the boatswain, for the use of the rigging, for which the purser gets proper receipts'.

The butter, smeared or soaked into rope, helped waterproof it and stopped it drying out and getting brittle in the sunlight. Cheese was the only item which was immediately thrown over the side when condemned because it, 'in a corrupted state, is a nuisance to the ship's company, and cannot possibly be kept in the close confined space where it is stowed . . . without infecting the air and endangering the health of the ship's crew'.

Salt provisions, mostly beef and pork, were also a source of trouble. Each cask was marked with the number of double (8 lb) or single (4 lb) pieces of beef or 4 lb or 2 lb pieces of pork that it contained. However, that was often the number counted by a contractor, who sealed the cask, which was not opened again until it was required on board a ship. There were regulations laid down for this ritual: a cask had to be opened 'in public on the open deck, under the inspection and in the presence of the master of the ship, or one of his mates, together with the purser's steward'.

Together they watched as the number of pieces were counted out, 'and the deficiency of each cask is inserted in the log book'. Every few days an entry appeared in the master's log of any King's ship at sea of which this one, of HMS *Minotaur* at sea off Civitavecchia on Saturday 28 September 1799, is typical: 'Light winds and clear weather . . . Open'd 2 casks of pork No 7883 content 52 triple pieces 1 lb short of weight, No 4523 content 120 double pieces, 22 lb over weight.' The sloop *Diligence* between 9 August and 16 September 1797 used seven casks of pork and four of beef. Each cask weighed 200 lb, and each piece of pork 10 lb.

The master or master's mate, and the purser's steward, made an affidavit from time to time because 'these deficiencies, particularly in large ships, come to a great quantity in the course of the year; for it is astonishing the number of pieces that are found short, more particularly in the salt provisions that are supplied by a contractor'.

The Victualling Board stepped aside in the matter: the shortage, it said, was a private matter between a purser and the contractor, even though the contractor had sold it to the Victualling Board, who in turn had supplied a ship and charged the purser. It was up to the purser to claim against the contractor who, providing he was still in business, allowed 8d per piece of beef and 6d for pork. But if the original shortage of meat meant that the purser had been 'brought in debt of salt flesh' he was charged for it by the Victualling Board not at the rate the Board paid for salt meat but the price for fresh beef, five or six times as much.

The method of cooking and serving food in the King's ships was governed by custom. The men were divided up into small groups of from four to eight, each of which was called 'a mess' and given a number. The men in a mess all sat at the same table and were responsible for a set of metal tallies stamped with the number of their mess, a 'bread barge', which was a metal or wooden box in which the bread was kept, and the nets or bags in which the meat or duff was boiled.

Each week one of the mess was appointed cook, a job for which an ignorance of cooking was no disadvantage. The most difficult culinary feat he would perform during the week would be mixing the flour, suet and currants or raisins into a duff, putting it into a bag, and tying the top. He then put it in a 'kettle mess' or a net bag with a mess tally fixed to it. He had to make sure it was delivered before 4 a.m. to the ship's cook ready to be boiled – along with dozens of others – in the ship's coppers, so it would be done by 11.30 a.m., and he had to collect it when it was done. Vegetables were also cooked in net bags.

The mess cook had to make sure that the table was kept clean and crumbs swept up. In addition to the bread barge, he also looked after the mess's water breaker, kid (a small wooden tub with 'ears' or handles, used for carrying hot food), a tea kettle, and a vinegar keg. At 11 a.m. he had to be on the after deck to collect the grog for his mess, and while the times differed from ship to ship he had to be present when provisions were issued. Most were issued at 2 p.m., although sugar, bread, flour, butter and pease were usually given out at 8 a.m. and sugar and tea at 3 p.m. Vinegar was issued once a fortnight, and was kept in the mess's keg. When cocoa was issued, it came as a block and mess cooks took it in turn to pound it into a powder, one man doing it for the whole ship. It was served boiled for breakfast.

The mess cook made sure he was at the mess table when candles (usually known as 'pusser's glims') were issued. Candles and lanthorns, or lanterns, were of course the responsibility of the purser, for which he made a monthly charge from every man in the ship. The candles were delivered to the different messes by the steward's assistant before evening quarters, and collected again by 6 a.m. next morning. He and his boy had to clean and trim them before divisions in the forenoon.

The mess cook was the man who made any complaint about the

quality or quantity of provisions, and the most common one was about the size of the pieces of salt meat. The chance which gave a particular mess a small piece was no fault of the purser: if the cask was the correct weight and contained the correct number of pieces, the difference in sizes was due to the butcher's assistant who cut them up at the contractor's slaughterhouse. However, any mess cook with a legitimate complaint was allowed to choose a piece on the next meat day.

There were older methods, one of which, blindfolding (hood-winking), was described by William Spavens. Each mess cook was given permission by the ship's cook and purser's steward to choose a piece of meat for his mess. They 'then hoodwink him, and when the steward calls a mess [number] he touches a piece, and the cook gives it to the man it is for'.

The six or eight men forming a mess (three or four when the ship was undermanned) lived so close to each other that unless they were all friends, quite happily putting up with each other's foibles and idiosyncrasies, the atmosphere could become very tense. The Admiralty recognised this, and a man could change his mess at the beginning of the month, when the purser's assistant (usually called the 'steward') made up a new mess book, listing each man's name and the number of his mess.

From the mess book a watchful captain or first lieutenant could learn a good deal about a ship's company. Remembering that a ship could be in commission for two or three years, with the same officers and men on board, few changes of mess meant a settled ship's company. If men changed frequently – a couple of dozen or so each month – it indicated an unhappy ship, unless it was the same man changing each time, in which case the mess book provided a list of the ship's troublemakers – men who were unpopular with their own shipmates.

A man tended to stay in the same mess for the whole time the ship was in commission, so the number of his mess became almost part of his identity, so much so that 'he lost the number of his mess' was a euphemism for dying or being killed, and 'like to lose the number of his mess' an indication of how ill a man was, or the danger he was in.

'Pricking for a piece' was the usual custom when salt or fresh beef was being served. Fresh beef was normally issued twice a week when the ship was in port, and at the rate of 4 lb for a piece of beef on a beef day and 3 lb for a piece of pork on a pork day.

The purser had to buy (at his own expense) 'a quantity of vegetables' to be boiled in the broth, and in return he did not issue pease on pork day, crediting his own account with the value.

When a ship was in an English port, the beef was slaughtered at one of the King's victualling yards on stated days and the ships sent their own boats, unless (at Spithead and Plymouth) there was a large fleet in, when the meat was sent out in victualling sloops, to which the boats went.

The purser was not allowed his eighth with fresh beef, and it was the custom that, to make up for the officers being allowed to have their allowance in whatever size pieces they chose, the ship's company in return had an extra one pound in seven added to their ration.

Whenever the master and purser's steward saw a particularly large piece of meat, it was trimmed down to the average size and the extra put aside. These trimmings, or 'skewer pieces', were issued to the men raw, to dress as they pleased.

All the regular pieces were then given to the cook to be boiled in a broth. It was then put into a tub, the top of which was covered with a cloth. The mess cooks lined up and in turn took a big skewer, pricking down into the tub without seeing what they were doing, and being issued with the piece of meat they stabbed. This ritual followed Regulations, not tradition: they said that when fresh meat was boiled 'it is to be delivered out in the customary method of pricking for it'.

As most children suffered from their parents favouring a particular medicine which always tasted nasty, so the majority of seamen suffered the Navy's administration of 'sour krout'. This is described as 'cabbage prepared after the German method, with salt and water, that keeps a long time and is a great preventative against the scurvy'.

Sauerkraut, to give it its more recognisable name, had been used in the Dutch Navy and was suggested for the Royal Navy by Dr James Lind. Various arguments were used to promote sauerkraut, one being that it was a favourite dish of the King (George II).

The seamen disliked it because of its smell. The 'old-established officer' wrote: 'Its use is to boil with the salt water, and when washed with water it is as clean, and as sweet as any vegetable whatever, and most salubrious when eaten with vinegar as a salad', but he had to admit that the seamen were prejudiced against it because of the 'strong and putrid smell which attends the first opening of a cask'. Until it had been open for ten or fifteen minutes and exposed to the fresh air it was 'as offensive as a jakes; but after that time the offensive smell subsides'. The problem was to prevent the seamen sniffing during the critical ten or fifteen minutes: the powerful smell of a lavatory before the days of the water-closet spoiled most appetites.

Most important was that the Navy issued it for the best of reasons and, with portable broth, it was one of the most important items in a general improvement in seamen's diet. A comparison between the number of deaths from scurvy and the numbers who died in battle shows that the most modest dietary victory was, in the long term, quite as important as a successful naval battle.

Portable broth was in fact solid in its portable stage and looked like a thick sheet of old-fashioned glue of the type which was heated in a pot before use. It was made by boiling down 'the coarsest part of beef' into cakes and then packed into 25 lb containers. A piece was broken off and put in water, which was then slowly brought to the boil. The result was a nourishing soup to which vegetables were added, and an ounce of the cake made a quart of beverage.

By 1794 the Ratcliffe Soup House, which had the contract for supplying it, was getting £1 5s a hundredweight, and it was supplied to the ships only for the use of the sick by the Commissioner of Sick and Hurt of the port where she fitted out. Judging by the bureaucracy, the Navy Board thought highly of portable soup: the purser would part with it only 'on a written application from the surgeon, attested by the captain'.

The purser had to keep an 'Account of Portable Broth', and on one side of the paper, under the heading 'On board his Majesty's ship —— between the —— and the ——', he had to specify 'When received', 'From whom received', the number of canisters and the number of pounds. On the other side of the paper he had to list the amount expended.

For many years the sailor's working clothes and bed (comprising a hammock and blanket) were supplied by contractors' agents in the various ports. The agents went on board the ships and sold the purser whatever was needed. These 'slop clothes' were charged against the men's pay and the contractors received the money from the Pay Office.

The scope for fraud was enormous, with the contractors juggling prices and quality and paying bribes to the pursers for the privilege of cheating the seamen. Finally, in 1758, the Navy Board took over the supply of clothing and bedding, charging a set price and making the purser the ship's shopkeeper.

He was given a commission of £5 on every £100 of slop clothes he sold, although he had to issue beds without receiving payment. The Regulations protected the seamen from exploitation by an over-zealous or cunning purser – the purser could not supply a man with more than 5s worth of slops a month. The purser's 'slop shop' was usually opened once a month at sea, but only rarely in port, when newly enlisted men and 'such as are in absolute want' could buy. The rest of the ship's company could not buy for the simple reason that they would probably sell the items to the various pedlars and women on board the ship in harbour.

Pursers always grumbled at the way slop clothes came from the Navy Board, which all too often supplied bales of mixed clothes. 'For example,' wrote one purser, 'if a quantity of Dutch caps was wanted, there was a number of worsted stockings in the same bale; a thing perhaps quite useless if going to a warm climate.' The situation was slowly improving, with bales being made up containing only the same items, except in the case of woollens, where an exasperated purser always found kersey breeches packed in with jackets. Such breeches were 'a part of sailor's clothing hardly or ever required, as he always prefers trowsers'.

The purser of a ship was something of an executor to anyone on board who died. By custom, the clothes and effects of any officer or man who died or was killed in action were sold to the highest bidders in an auction held by the mainmast, the buyers having the amounts deducted from their wages.

The purser paid the proceeds to the man's next of kin, charging £5 for every £100 raised. There were certain rules about 'Dead Men's Cloaths', as the procedure was called. If the dead man had left any cash, 'no officer or man is to bid for it'. That went straight to the next of kin or executors, minus the purser's 5 per cent. The men were not allowed to bid higher than the value of any item, nor could a man bid for any clothing 'as are of a quality above his wear or station' – in other words the cook's mate could not strut about in the late first lieutenant's ruffled silk shirt.

There was no uniform for the seamen although some captains on joining a ship made it clear what they would like the men to wear. Often the men sewed their own clothing, and anyone skilled in cutting a shirt or a pair of trousers from a piece of cloth could be sure of several tots in return for a few minutes' use of his skill.

The men preferred wearing trousers in an age when breeches were the rule. Trousers, with wide (though not yet bell) bottoms, were much more suitable than breeches: the men wanted something easy to put on and take off, and did not want to be bothered with stockings, except in cold weather. More important, decks had to be scrubbed, quite apart from seas sweeping over, and rolling trousers up to the knee kept the cloth dry. Likewise a seaman frequently had to kneel or crouch, an uncomfortable activity when wearing breeches.

The *Midshipman's or British Mariner's Vocabulary*, published in 1801, the year of Nelson's victory at Copenhagen, referred to 'trowsers' as 'A sort of loose long breeches mostly worn by persons on shipboard', and Landsman Hay describes how, having deserted in 1811 and been pressed again, 'I therefore purchased a second-hand jacket, trowsers and check shirt . . . and packed up my long coat, breeches, vest, white neckcloth etc, lest I should on some future occasion require their services.'

Sunday afternoon usually led to a captain giving the order to 'make and mend', when the sailors, proud of their 'rig', took out needle, thread and scissors, in the regular fight to avoid having to wear slop clothes.

Jeffery Raigersfield, crossing the Atlantic for the first time as a midshipman in the 44-gun *Mediator*, noted that, 'Whilst the ship was running down the trade winds, the sailors generally had much spare time, and the captain, in order to employ the men, directed that slops of light clothing might be served to the ship's company, which was communicated to them by the boatswain and his mates piping all hands to Monmouth Street.' (In those days Monmouth Street was a centre for buying clothes and probably gave its name to the Monmouth cap, which had been very popular among seamen in the previous century.)

'These slops consisted of duck frocks and trousers which the sailors altered to a kind of uniform, which the captain chose to establish for the ship, and the watch off deck were employed at this every day, from nine to half past eleven, upon the quarterdeck, so that these alterations took up some time.'

Raigersfield noted that 'at this time it was a fashion for your bucks of the Navy to wear their hair in a pigtail behind, close up to their neck, and as some of the midshipmen in the ship were in a certain degree old stagers, of course they, as well as younger ones, were bucks in this respect'. The captain, who was Cuthbert Collingwood, the friend of Nelson and to be his second-in-command at Trafalgar, decided that he would like to see the midshipmen calculate a noon sight ('work a day's work') in front of him on the quarterdeck. Only three or four of a dozen or more came up with the right answer. Collingwood 'observed to them how remiss they were, and suddenly, imputing their remissness to their pigtails, he took his penknife out of his pocket and cut off their pigtails close to their heads above the tie, then presenting them to their owners, desired they would put them into their pockets and keep them until such time as they could work a day's work'.

Collingwood's choice of a style of clothing for seamen that needed so much work was an indication that Raigersfield was writing of a peacetime voyage. But a captain was not above having his boat's crew rigged out in special clothing – one captain of the *Harlequin* frigate had his men dressed as harlequins.

The prices the Navy Board charged for slop clothes were reasonable when they are compared with the cost of living at the turn of the century. A jacket cost 10s, trousers 3s 2d, shoes 5s 10d a pair, waistcoat 4s 3d and shirt 5s 3d.

Belfry and four-hour watch glass

CHAPTER ELEVEN

The Day Begins

A ship, when in commission, led two separate lives, depending upon whether she was in port or at sea. In either case the day began in darkness, but in harbour it usually started with a good deal of confusion and noise as the boatswain's mates made their way among the slung hammocks, rousing out the men with hoarse shouts which invariably included: 'Show a leg, there! Out or down! Show a leg!'

The order 'Show a leg, there!' was given because a woman was as likely to be in a hammock as a man, and 'Out or down' was the threat to cut down a hammock if a man tried to stay in it. A smooth leg meant a hammock and its female occupant was left in peace; a hairy leg meant cutting the lashings at the head – or at least a closer investigation.

Each man had between fourteen and twenty inches in which to sling his hammock, depending on the ship, so in port he brushed his neighbour on each side if he or they took up more than that width. At sea he had plenty of space because, with the ship's company divided into two watches, the men were alternated so that every other hammock was empty with its owner on watch. Space was not the problem, but the lack of fresh air meant that in port, particularly when women shared many of the hammocks, increasing the crowding, the sleepers woke up with a taste in their mouths as though they had been sucking copper coins.

The next order was 'Lash up hammocks', when the hammock and blanket was rolled into a long sausage and lashed at intervals with a regulation number of turns. At the order 'Stow hammocks' they were hoisted up into racks which were fitted along the top of the bulwarks on the upper deck and formed by netting secured to U-shaped supports. Each hammock had to be rolled into a cylinder of a certain diameter, and before being stowed a bosun's mate watched it being passed through a hammock gauge, a metal ring of the correct size. The hammocks, now nestling in the nettings like dozens of greyish-white sausages, were covered with long strips of scrubbed canvas to protect them from rain and spray. Now, cleared out of the lower deck where they spent the night suspended from eyebolts in the deckhead, they would form a barricade against small-arms fire if the ship went into battle.

From the time the hammocks were stowed, the rest of the day's routine depended, with a few exceptions, on an individual captain and the day of the week, although the times depended on daybreak and changed with the season. No man in a ship of an anchored fleet had any doubt when it was daybreak: in every ship a drum began to beat, and all the drummers kept thumping away, the ominous sound echoing across the anchorage, until a man 'could see a grey goose a mile', when the flagship fired a gun. Each ship hoisted her colours – ensign and jack – at sunrise. The only exception to this was when it was blowing very hard, and the ship had lowered her yards and topmasts to reduce the windage. (The word 'lowered' was rarely used afloat; yards were struck; casks of provisions put in the hold were 'struck into the hold'.)

The events that did not vary were, apart from stowing hammocks, the order at 6.15 'watch below clean lower deck', followed by 'Lower boats, wash round ship's side' and 'Coil down ropes', when any dirty marks on the hull were cleaned off, breakfast (half an hour from 7.15 a.m.), divisions at 9.30 (when the men paraded under their officers), 'clear decks and up spirits' at 11.30, when the first half of the grog was issued, dinner which lasted an hour from noon, 'pump water and serve out' at 2 p.m., 'clear decks' at 4.15 p.m., which marked the end of the working day, supper at 5 p.m. and 'Coil up ropes and sweep decks', the last task of the day, the time of which depended on sunset. 'Down hammocks' was usually piped at 8 p.m., followed almost immediately by 'ship's company's fire and lights out'. The officers had another two hours' use of the purser's candles; the last order of the day, at 10 p.m., was 'gunroom lights out'.

The rest of the ship's activities depended on the day of the week and the climate. A ship in a warm climate would have 'Watch spread awnings' piped at 6 a.m., to keep the sun off the decks. In the Mediterranean during the summer, and in the tropics all the year round, the sun was hot enough to make it uncomfortable to stand around on deck, and the heat dried and shrank the planking, making the pitch in the seams soft and often sticky. A man lying down on deck for a sleep was likely to find on wakening that his shirt and trousers were marked with parallel thin, black lines of pitch from the seams, which led to the slang phrase 'taking a caulk', meaning having a nap. Awnings were furled at 4 p.m., by which time the heat had gone out of the sun.

Scrubbing and holystoning the upper deck was a routine that varied according to the captain. Usually the upper deck was scrubbed every morning, often before dawn, and holystoned only on Sundays and Thursdays. The lower decks were scrubbed once a week (usually on Wednesdays) and holystoned on Saturdays, providing the weather was fine to make sure the decks would dry out quickly. Dampness was not only bad for the men's health but affected stores and provisions.

While some men collected scrubbing brushes others rigged head pumps, which were simple pumps rigged over the side. The men then rolled up their trousers and, with the pumps sending streams of water over the deck, began scrubbing. Although scrubbing 'got the worst off' it rarely left the decks as clean as most captains wanted. For pristine decks holystones and bibles had to be used.

A holystone was a block of Portland stone the size of a large pillow, flat on one side and usually rounded on the other. An eyebolt was fitted on the rounded side and two lengths of rope were spliced to it. With the deck wet, sand was sprinkled over it, and men holding the ropes pulled the holystone back and forth, the stone, sand and water scouring the planking. In narrow spaces too small for the holystone, men used smaller stones the size of a family bible, the similarity leading to their name, 'bibles'. Each 'bible' was worked by one man on his knees, the weight of the stone helping scour.

Holystoning was hard on the wood – the effect was similar to giving a plank a light rubbing down with sandpaper – and eventually wore down the soft wood and left knots standing proud so that occasionally the carpenter had to plane them down. The Regulations and Instructions for captains and commanders said quite flatly: 'The decks or gratings are not to be scraped oftener than is necessary; but are to be washed and swabbed once a day, and air let into the hold, as often as may be.'

The brasswork was usually polished at the same time, using brick dust and a rag. This put a polish on the metal because the fine powder wore off a thin film, and the cynical might note that keeping a ship clean and bright was achieved by gradually wearing it away.

The routine before breakfast was concerned with cleaning the ship and its men. On Mondays, for instance, 'wash clothes' was piped immediately after the hammocks were stowed, and an hour was allowed before the order was given for hanging up the clothes to dry on specially rigged lines. 'Down wash clothes' was usually piped at 1 p.m. whether or not they were dry, followed by 'make up clothes lines and sweep decks'.

The first job after breakfast was mending sails, followed by 'square yards'. The expression 'I soon squared *his* yards', meaning that someone else had been put right or told off, probably came from the frequency with which an admiral might make a signal to a ship at anchor because her yards were not square – the outward symbol of a reasonably smart ship. Squaring the yards – there were three or four on each of three masts – could not be done properly from on board because they had to be horizontal as well as exactly at right angles to the ship's centre line, so the master or boatswain went off in a boat to check and give the final orders. The system of marking the lifts, the ropes by which the yards were suspended when no sails were set, was not satisfactory because the rope stretched, but never at a regular rate. The only time a ship's yards were not squared at anchor was when her captain had died, or there was some other reason for displaying mourning. Then the yards were a'cockbill, one canted one way and the next another, so from ahead or astern the yards on the various masts made a series of Xs.

With the yards squared the next order was to flemish ropes (to coil them up neatly), clean arms, which meant that cutlasses, pikes, tomahawks, muskets and pistols were wiped over with a greasy cloth, and then clear the deck – in mustering dress on Sundays and Thursdays, ready for divisions at 10 a.m., and in working dress the other days.

Divisions each day, when the men paraded under their lieutenants, was followed by divine service on Sundays, and for the rest of the week the routine depended on the captain. From 10 a.m. until 11.30 it was a variation on the theme of exercising at the guns or with small arms, furling sails if they had earlier been let fall to air, painting, whitewashing (used extensively below) or blacking (used on guns, shot and rigging). The rigging was usually painted with a mixture of Stockholm tar, coal tar and sea water, all of which were heated up together. The guns were usually blacked with coal tar and a little seawater painted on warm. On a cold day a knowing gunner rolled a hot shot down the bore of the gun to warm up the metal so that the blacking went on more smoothly. The French used a different recipe for blacking their guns: after giving them a coat of black paint they put on a mixture made up of a gallon of vinegar, ten ounces of lamp black and a pound and a half of 'clean-sifted iron-rust'.

One day in every month after divisions the men had to muster with their clothes so that the officers could make sure that the men had enough clothing and that it was clean and mended.

Official birthdays and celebration days were marked by salutes of guns, usually beginning at 1 p.m., after the men had had dinner. Captains of ships had to keep a list of the days to make sure salutes of the correct number of guns were fired. 'Fired 19 guns for anniversary of the Restoration' was a typical log entry, and among the others during the year, laid down in the Instructions, were 'The Anniversary days of the birth [21 guns], accession [21] and coronation [19] of the King, the birth of the Queen [21], Restoration of King Charles the Second [15], and the Gunpowder-treason [17]', which were 'to be solemnised by his Majesty's ships if they are in port, with such a number of guns as the Chief Officer shall think proper, not exceeding 21 each ship'.

This meant that the actual number was decided by the admiral or senior captain in any particular port, and resulted in them using a system of grading where anything connected with the present King and Queen received twenty-one. The discovery of the Gunpowder Plot, celebrated on 5 November, was regarded as worth more guns than Restoration Day.

Admirals, commanders-in-chief, mayors and magistrates usually celebrated royal birthdays. At Plymouth, for example, the Queen's birthday on 18 January and the King's on 4 June were the signal for a parade of soldiers, a royal salute fired at noon by the citadel and forts, a salute at 1 p.m. by all the ships of war in the harbour and dinners given by the commanders-in-chief of the Navy and Army and in the messes of the different regiments. Balls were held in the evening at the London Inn in Plymouth itself and at the Fountain Tavern in the dock.

A ship at sea did not fire the regular salutes, and in port upper-deck guns were, by the Instructions, to be used. This saved powder because they were also the smaller guns.

The various forts and castles in Britain were not saluted, but a British ship of war arriving for the first time in a British port abroad saluted the fort and garrison, as well as the admiral, if he happened to be there. A frigate arriving in Barbados with the new admiral on board saluted the present admiral with fifteen guns on arrival at the anchorage and received thirteen in reply ('was returned 13', as it was noted in the log). The fort then saluted the new admiral with fifteen guns and the frigate returned thirteen.

Sometimes the system of salutes had to be hastily changed – for example during the time the King's son, Prince William Henry (later the Duke of Clarence and William IV), served in the Navy. When he commanded the *Andromeda* and arrived in Jamaica, he saluted the commodore with thirteen guns, and the commodore returned eleven, the correct number for replying to the captain of a newly arrived frigate. The fort then saluted His Royal Highness with twenty-one guns.

If admirals or captains died at sea, the guns fired a salute at the funeral, but lieutenants rated only 'three vollies of small arms'.

Just as no numbers were laid down by the Admiralty for salutes, other than the limit of twenty-one guns, so no method was laid down for the intervals between each round. By custom it was five seconds and a ship's gunner, who was responsible, gave the firing orders, usually muttering to himself the few words which, with practice, took up five seconds:

'Number one gun, fire! *If I wasn't a gunner, I wouldn't be here,* Number two gun, fire! *If I wasn't . . .*'

The most important part of firing a salute was to make sure that no shot remained in a gun. In wartime guns were often left loaded, and in the excitement of arriving in port, when blank charges were rammed home and the gun fired, it was by no means unknown for a captain subsequently having to explain to his admiral why a shot hit a house on shore, or landed near the flagship.

If there were no salutes to be fired, then the first tasks after dinner during the week were varied and for the first fifteen minutes usually included taking down any hammocks, cots, boat sails and awnings that might have been scrubbed after breakfast and hung up to dry. On Saturdays there was usually an hour when the men aired their bedding, mended clothing and washed and shaved themselves for

Sunday's divisions. This ritual included a hair-plaiting session because many of the men still wore their hair in the thick, short pigtail, called a queue, and a man could not tie his own – looking glasses were rare in the gunroom and non-existent on the lower deck.

The order 'Pump water and serve out' was given every day, usually at two o'clock. A sloop with a crew of 135 usually carried about forty tons of fresh water and expected it to last three months, using it at the rate of half a ton a day. The *Surprise* frigate on 24 September 1799, between Jamaica and Venezuela, had $51^2/_3$ tons of water on board and a month later her log recorded the following amounts of water remaining – 21 October, 30 $^1/_3$ tons; 22nd, 29 $^2/_3$ tons; 23rd, 29 tons.

In the tropics, where heat and exertion increased thirst considerably, a butt was often put on deck holding a certain amount of water, and with a mug beside it. Men could drink as frequently as they wished for as long as the water lasted, but only one mug at a time. A marine sentry stood on duty at the butt to make sure this rule was obeyed. Called the scuttle (or scuttled) butt because it had been scuttled – a square piece had been sawn out of it to admit the mug – it became something of a meeting place for the men, when the latest gossip and rumour, known as 'scuttlebutt', could be exchanged. In some ships the butt was not scuttled; instead the barrel of an old musket pushed into the bung hole served instead of a mug: a man could drink as much as he could suck up the tube.

The afternoon's work continued until 5 p.m. when the ship's company had supper, the last meal of the day. The mealtimes in a ship in port reflected habits on shore. Wealthier and more leisured people had dinner – what would be called luncheon today – beginning about 2 p.m., and it was the main meal of a normal day, although supper, usually a lighter meal, could be made more elaborate. So, although the ship's company had dinner at noon, the captain and the officers usually ate a couple of hours later.

The women on board had spent the day gossiping and drinking, occasionally mending their men's clothing and all too often quarrelling and creating so much noise that the master-at-arms and his corporals had to go below to try and restore order. Some of the women were married to the men but the majority were in effect hired for the time the ship was in port. The Admiralty knew well enough that men who had been at sea needed women when they came into port, but they could only rarely be allowed on shore because of the chances of desertion. But, if Jack could not go on shore to meet Polly, then Polly had to be allowed on board to meet Jack – which meant, in practice, having prostitutes on board. Their Lordships could not allow that, openly at least, and in most ships the men had to claim the women as their wives – the true origin of 'having a wife in every port'. It depended entirely on the captain, but the entries in the *Astrea* frigate's log on 19 and 20 October (the same day because the nautical day began at noon, and one entry was before 12 and the other after) were typical: 'All women sent on shore . . . embarked two pilots and sailed.'

Richard Keats, commanding the *Superb* in 1803, took a brisk and practical approach. Among the eighty-eight paragraphs in his 'Captain's Orders' were: '10th. In port, women will be permitted to come on board, but this indulgence is to be granted (as indeed are all other) in proportion to the merits of the men who require them, and upon their being accountable for the conduct of the women with them.

'11th. The commanding officer in port will therefore permit such men to have women on board as he may choose; and he will direct the master at arms to keep a list agreeable to the following form; which he will carry to the commanding officer every morning for his inspection.

Women's names	With Whom	Married or single	When received on board	Conduct'

Keats was one of the more enlightened officers about shore leave, and used it as an incentive, with orders stating: 'As permission to go on shore will be occasionally granted by the captain or commanding officer, it is to be understood that those indulgences are to be proportioned to the general character, sobriety and punctuality of the men who may apply.'

Although in ports like Portsmouth and Plymouth some of the women were married to men in a ship, the whole system of supplying the ships with women was well organised and entirely in the hands of bumboat men. They brought out pedlars trying to sell anything from vegetables to 'gold' shoe buckles and watches, who paid a fixed sum for every ship they visited, and women, who usually paid the boatmen only if they managed to get on board a ship. If they were not chosen, they did not pay. The boatman, knowing that he received women's shillings only if seamen chose them, but faced rowing or sailing back to the quay with all those rejected, was very fussy, as became a pander: the quay sounded like a slave market as he chose the women he would take and tried to avoid the shrill and outraged abuse of those he rejected.

Once alongside a ship, a bumboat was closely watched by the master-at-arms and the ship's corporals: the boatmen and pedlars knew that the men usually had plenty of money, while the seamen knew that the bumboat carried not just women and catchpenny items but bottles and bladders of rum and brandy. A certain amount of tension was added to the proceedings because the master-at-arms and the corporals had the task of preventing any liquor being smuggled on board.

The women were the usual carriers of liquor, and a bladder of rum, brandy or gin was a useful container to sling beneath a voluminous skirt. The master-at-arms was rarely the victor when a bumboat came alongside with women: short of stripping every woman before she was allowed on board, there was no way of preventing her smuggling at least a pint or so of neat rum for her man, who was tired of grog. For him the bladder of raw spirits was the forbidden fruit, not the woman.

Robert Hay tells how in the *Salvador del Mundo* in Plymouth a seaman's wife came on board to see her husband, newly pressed. The ship's corporal helping her up the ladder 'took it into his head that the calves of her legs, at which he had been taking an unmannerly peep, were rather more bulky than chaste statuary required. ' "I am afraid, my good woman," said he, "that your legs are somewhat dropsical; will you allow me the honour of performing a cure?" ' With that he took out a knife and made a small slit in her stocking. 'The point of the knife gently pierced the skin, not of the leg, but of the bladder that was snugly secured there. . . . Colour and smell bore ample testimony that the blood of the sugar cane had been shed.'

Most captains, particularly those whose ships had just come in after a long time at sea, tried for a few days to turn their backs on what happened on the lower deck and, often more important, closed their ears. All too often something like exercise at the guns, or mending sails, was punctuated by the screams of women fighting and 'exchanging mutual Billingsgate'. Scratched faces and torn hair often identified the offenders, who were usually sent on shore by the nearest bumboat.

The cockpit, a particular part of the lower deck, owes its name to the fact that in larger ships the women were confined down there during the day, and their behaviour made it seem like the cockpit on land in which fighting cocks fought to the death.

Once the day's work was done, the seamen were free to enjoy the company of the women, and contemporary artists and cartoonists liked to show the women sitting around among the mess tables and forms, carousing with the men, at least one of whom would be scratching a tune out of an old fiddle.

The 37th Instruction for captains and commanders said flatly: 'He is not to allow of any women being carried to sea' without orders from a senior officer or the Admiralty. As far as their Lordships were concerned, the only women ever to go to sea in one of the King's ships with their blessing would be the wives of men travelling as passengers.

In fact some captains ignored the Instruction, and in the case of transport ships permission was usually given. The 54-gun *Tromp*, an old store ship on passage to the West Indies on 2 August 1800, was in sight of Madeira when, according to William Richardson, 'the captain's wife was delivered of a fine boy'. But there were several other women to help her – Richardson had earlier recorded how he had gone on shore at Portsmouth to say goodbye to his wife but 'found she had fixed her mind to go with me, as it was reported the voyage would be short . . . I gave my consent, especially as the captain's, the master's and boatswain's were going with them; the serjeant of marines and six other men's wives had leave to go; a person would have thought they were all insane, wishing to go to such a sickly country.'

The ship called at Martinique to unload cargo and soon yellow fever struck. 'Every day for some time we were sending people to the hospital and few returned. The captain and purser with their wives left the ship to live on shore. . . . The first lieutenant, Mr Pine, and the clerk, his brother . . . both died; next the master and his wife (large in the family way) both died; then the Marine officer; and the wardroom was cleared of all its officers except the sick second lieutenant, Mr Frankland.

'Next died Mr Campbell, the boatswain, leaving a wife and daughter on board; next went Mr Hogan, the surgeon-assistant . . . next followed nearly all our fine young midshipmen.' After that the deaths included the master-at-arms, armourer, gunner's mate, captain's steward, cook and tailor, then the captain's wife's maid. Richardson's wife caught the fever but recovered.

Three years earlier a frigate based on Jamaica had a woman on board who certainly did not have permission but whose presence was ignored by the captain. The ship was the *Hermione* and the woman was married to the boatswain, William Martin. The *Hermione* was an unhappy ship because of her harsh captain, Hugh Pigot, and soon the ship's company mutinied, murdered all the officers except the master and a midshipman, and sailed the ship to the Main, handing her over to the Spanish in what is now Venezuela.

An hour after the officers were killed, one of the mutineers murdered Martin by throwing him over the side, and then went below. A seaman giving evidence at a subsequent court martial of that mutineer said that he 'remained in the cabin with the boatswain's wife, and I saw him no more that night'. It is unlikely that Mrs Martin made much resistance: she did not add her screams to the cries of her husband as he was thrown over, and she stayed with the mutineer until the ship was handed over to the Spanish, when she did not join the loyal men who became prisoners but went on board a ship going to North America.

Admiral George Vernon Jackson records how he was a midshipman in the 28-gun *Lapwing* in 1801 when she ran aground on the Sovereign Shoal, near Beachy Head. 'Whilst occupied in getting the ship off the Shoal it was amusing to see how some women – forty or fifty in number – who were on board exerted themselves at the ropes. The rules of the service were not always so stringently enforced as they are now [1865], and Jack often smuggled his sweetheart on board for a short cruise.' Captain Edward Rotherham, commanding the *Lapwing* (and four years later, by an ironic coincidence, to command the 100-gun *Royal Sovereign* at Trafalgar), must have been a very easygoing captain because the frigate had been in attendance on the Prince of Wales, who was staying at Brighton.

Even having women on board in port could lead to difficulties. Robert Hay, describing how the *Amethyst* dragged her anchors in Plymouth during a gale and was driven ashore, noted that 'fortunately the women had all been sent ashore on the preceding day so that we had not their screams to add to the general confusion which now prevailed'.

The 18-gun *Orestes* was in Guernsey when a fire broke out in the master's cabin above the magazine, candles setting the curtains ablaze. James Gardner was serving in her and records that while it lasted the fire 'occasioned the utmost terrors among the ship's company. . . . It was ludicrous to see the captain with a speaking trumpet exerting himself to keep order, and the carpenter's wife catching him round the legs, and while he was calling for Water she was screaming out Fire.' The captain was Commander Manley Dixon, the carpenter's wife Mrs Thomas Scriven.

Gardner also records how the *Blonde* frigate, forced to anchor off the Dutch coast in a gale, had to cut her masts away to reduce the windage, and even then parted an anchor cable. At that moment the cook, who was on the focsle 'in the greatest tribulation', said that ' "Betty" (meaning his wife, who was on board) "will go to a better mansion, but I'm doubtful about myself." '

Logship or log

CHAPTER TWELVE

Garbling the Cargo

The women, like all people living on land, had almost to learn another language if they were to understand a seaman's talk, which was rich in slang and colourful phrases. Many ships with long names were dubbed with more pronounceable nicknames – the *Polyphemus* was usually known as the 'Polly Infamous', while the *Bellerophon* was the 'Billy Ruff'n', and the *Royal William* was the briefer 'Billy'.

Many nautical expressions and descriptions passed into the language – 'the bitter end', for example, which was the inboard end of an anchor cable. When it came on to blow, if the anchor dragged the only chance of setting it again was to pay out more cable, but there was only so much: eventually one came to the bitter end.

A ship was 'taken aback' when the wind was the wrong side of the sails and yards, pressing them back against the mast and trying to force the ship astern, instead of ahead. For a ship it was a dangerous situation which, in a strong wind, could smash the yards or even send the masts crashing. A dowager finding her daughter in a compromising situation with the newly arrived young curate would, similarly, be taken aback.

'Brace up' (trimming the yards so that the sails drew better), 'cut and run' (cutting the anchor cable and sailing off in a hurry), 'put about' (to tack, altering course by at least 130° and thus making a considerable change in direction), 'scuppered' (in battle, when the dead and wounded at the guns were hurriedly put in the scuppers out of the way), 'square up' (when the bosun made sure the yards were square after the ship anchored), 'by and large' ('by the wind' means going to windward; 'large' is off the wind, or running), are expressions which the sailor's brother on shore understood and adapted to his own use, so that they and dozens more are part of the language today.

Many others which were common in Nelson's time are less popular today: 'at loggerheads' (a loggerhead was a solid iron ball with a long handle which was heated in the galley fire and then used to keep warm the pitch used to pay deck seams, and was sometimes used as a weapon by quarrelling men), 'try out his metal' ('metal' was another word for guns: the surest way of testing the enemy's strength was to get within range of his guns) 'cut a fine feather' (said of a ship which was sailing well, her bow wave looking like a white feather).

A seaman travelling in a coach was likely to ask a fellow traveller, 'Caulk or yarn?', meaning 'Do you want to sleep or shall we talk?' In describing an easterly gale (which tends to be long-lasting in northern Europe), he might say it was 'going on forever, like the blacksmith's bellows'. His ship was, no doubt, 'snug as a duck in a ditch, never straining as much as a rope-yarn aloft and as tight as a bottle below'. After the gale the sea could be 'as smooth as Poll Patterson's tongue'.

In a reference to sail trimming on board his ship – the sheet being the rope holding the lower corner – he would boast: 'Give her a foot o' the sheet and she'd go along like a witch.' Praising his captain, and referring to the fact that a man to be flogged was tied to a wooden grating which was taken from on top of a hatch and lashed up vertically, he would remark that it 'went against his grain to seize a grating up'. He would inspect the piece of tobacco he had been chewing for hours and remark sadly, 'This is the fourth watch that this chew of baccy has been overhauled by my toothless gums, and now it's as dry as a haddock.'

Just as 'north' meant neat rum and 'west' meant water, with anywhere in between indicating the dilution of the drink, so 'southerly' meant empty, and a seaman was likely to tell the mess cook, 'Lock up the bread barge, or we'll soon have a southerly wind in it.' A rope (especially if it had to be coiled up neatly) could be 'as long as today and tomorrow', while an impatient man would be told that 'what you lose on one tack you gain on t'other'.

Dutch ships tended to be very beamy, with rounded, apple-cheeked bows, so that a plump woman was 'Dutch built'. When anyone was buried at sea, the body lashed in a hammock was slid over the side from a plank lashed temporarily at the point where one end of the foresheet (the 'standing part') was secured to the ship's side, so that another expression for dying, in addition to 'losing the number of your mess', was 'to go over the standing part of the foresheet'.

A depraved character could be 'a gallows man'. Another person could be 'so thin he could get under the lee of a rope yarn', while 'his coat fits him like a purser's shirt on a handspike'. The purser's assistant was usually 'Jack in the bread room', or 'Jack in the dust'; the cook's mate was nicknamed 'Jack nasty-face'. A liar was usually 'Tom Pepper', a man with a hot tongue, while putting out the lantern or blowing out a candle was 'topping the glim', a phrase also used for executions. A man who was dangerously ill was 'dragging his anchors for t'other world'.

'Hold on too long' is another nautical phrase in common use on land, and refers to shortening sail too late: 'holding on too long to his topsails', for instance. 'No great shakes', meaning of no great value, comes from the casks. When they were empty they were taken to pieces ('shaken') so that they could be stowed in as small a space as possible, and the parts were called shakes (the general word for the staves and the hoops). A 'well set up' young man was a common phrase but first referred to a ship's rigging. The process of tightening or slackening the rigging to get the masts straight is called 'setting it up'.

The Irish came in for a lot of teasing from the English, with a hole in the sail being a 'Paddy's reef', an 'Irish pendant' a loose rope's end (and sometimes one that was frayed and needed a whipping), and an 'Irish hurricane' was a calm. The Dutch, too, came in for their share – a ship sailing along with sails badly trimmed was 'jogging along, Dutch fashion'.

'Press into service' followed on the press gang, while 'a clean sweep' was something the sea did when it swept right over the deck. 'Giving someone a wide berth' came from anchoring far enough away from another ship so that they did not hit each other when they swung with wind or tide.

'A roving commission' was one granted to a captain which allowed him to cruise at will, while the meanings of 'clear the deck', 'get one's bearings', 'all in the same boat', 'stick your oar in' and 'even keel' are obvious.

Some phrases with less obvious meanings include 'hand over hand' (the method of hauling on a rope), and 'eat my hat' (a sailor kept a quid of chewing tobacco in his hat; if he ran out of tobacco he would take out the lining – which was soaked in tobacco juice – and chew that).

'Off and on' described a ship beating along a coast, while 'in the doldrums' referred to a ship becalmed in the area between weather systems, the Doldrums or Horse Latitudes, where the wind was light. 'Touch and go' referred to a ship grounding and getting off, her keel touching the bottom. 'On an even keel' meant that provisions had been stowed so that the weights did not make the ship heel one way or the other, nor be down by the bow or stern.

'Tide over' was used when a ship took advantage of a tide (strictly speaking the tidal stream) to help reach a position in time. 'Buoyed up' came from using a buoy to lift up the bight of an anchor cable to prevent it chafing on a rough bottom. 'Garbling' was nefariously mixing rubbish with cargo, making it an excellent word to describe distorted or incomplete messages. A 'first-rate' ship was one with more than 98 guns, while second- and third-rate were progressively smaller, down to sixth-rate. 'Another shot in the locker', 'stemming a tide' and 'sweeping into a room' (sweeps were oars, used in small ships in a calm) were nautical phrases which fitted into the landman's language.

A book published during the war, *The Post Captain*, gave an hilarious description of life in a frigate and on shore, particularly the amorous adventures of her captain and lieutenants. The book is remarkable for its wealth of nautical phrases and details which help it live up to its subtitle, 'a view of naval society and manners'.

The purser's reporting that he was recovering from his seasickness led to a rejoinder from a lieutenant, 'and now you will be occupied in making *dead men chew tobacco*.' Pursers could do this when a man died by marking him down as having previously bought more tobacco, so that the cost could be deducted from the wages owing, giving a double profit since the purser still had the tobacco.

The surgeon asserted that he had been at sea before. 'Yes,' said the lieutenant, 'you have been at Chelsea, at Battersea; and, I dare say, in the Marshalsea.' The last named was not an area of London but the debtors' jail.

Much of *The Post Captain* would have gone over the head of the ordinary reader, and the following passage is an example. The steward takes a bundle of papers to the captain.

'The gentlemen, sir,' said he, 'have sent you their day's work.'

'Very well,' replied the captain; 'put them in the quarter gallery.'

In layman's language, each of the midshipmen had taken a noon sight, written the workings on a sheet of paper, and sent it in to be inspected by the captain, who had told the steward to put the bundle in the lavatory – the quarter gallery.

However, not all the humour was to be found in novels or on the lower deck. The tiny allowance of paint allowed to each ship led Captain Sir John Phillimore to ask the Navy Board whether he should use it to paint the starboard side or the larboard. Captain Pakenham in the *Invincible* at the Glorious First of June found his French opponent had stopped firing but had not hauled down his colours. Pakenham shouted across to ask if he had struck and received the reply 'Non, non!', to which he bellowed: 'Then damn ye, why don't you go on firing?' At the end of the battle Pakenham was passing the badly damaged *Defence*, commanded by Captain Gambier, a deeply religious man. 'Hello Jimmy,' called Pakenham; 'you're pretty well mauled; but "whom the Lord loveth He chasteneth"!'

The toilet facilities in a ship of war were crude. The focsle ended at the beakhead bulkhead, right up in the bow, and doors led into the 'head'. On one side was a row of seats (the actual arrangement varied from ship to ship) for the seamen, while on the other side were 'roundhouses', like small sentry-boxes, for warrant officers and men in the sick bay. 'Going to the head' was the phrase for 'going to the lavatory', with the difference that the head was exposed to the weather and, in rough weather, to the spray as well. In northern winters the surgeon found that many of the less hardy seamen suffered from costive complaints.

A tub on each side of the bowsprit in the head held urine, which was used for washing clothes, the ammonia helping to bleach them. There was no fresh water for washing clothes so that salt water had to be used, even for rinsing, and the material never completely dried, becoming damp on a humid day as the salt absorbed the moisture.

Washing, whether of men or clothes, was always difficult. Society's attitude to cleanliness was then quite different. A bath was something in which a crank might indulge, but most people were convinced that it could only rob the body of essential oils. Bad teeth meant that most people had bad breath, and hair was rarely washed, particularly by women favouring elaborate styles.

After considering the routine on board a ship in harbour and glimpsing the women on board, let us now look at the activities on shore of the men who were given leave. This is largely the story of Portsmouth and Plymouth.

Plymouth was one of the seamen's favourite ports. If they received leave, there were plenty of inns, bars and brothels. The main inn was the King's Arms, in Briton-side. The London mail left at 6 p.m. and anyone wanting a place had to book early. The fare on a post-chaise, travelling inside, was 10d a mile, including turnpike charges and tips, and the journey to London usually took five days. Russell's wagons, pulled by eight horses and, although moving at a walking pace, called 'flying wagons', were much cheaper but took three weeks. Travellers took their own bedding and a stout pair of boots or shoes, because they were expected to walk up hills. The more prudent made their wills before leaving.

The best food in Plymouth was reckoned to be served at the Commercial Inn, in Old Town Street. Navy captains and ship-brokers favoured the London Inn, in Foxhole Street: it was spacious and had a public sale-room for prize goods, as well as being used for balls, exhibitions and concerts. The masters of merchant ships preferred the Prince George Inn, in the same street, as well as the Navy Tavern in Southside Street.

The post office was in Lower Broad Street, at the home of Mrs Rivers, the postmistress. The mail from London arrived at 8.30 a.m. Mrs Rivers closed at 5 p.m. but (on payment of 2d) received letters until 6 p.m., which gave her time to have the bag ready for the mail coach after it left the King's Arms.

Plymouth had its own theatre. There was 'nothing to recommend it in its outward appearance', a contemporary guide book admitted, but it 'is neatly fitted up in the interior and sufficiently spacious for the inhabitants, who are not very constant in their attendance; it derives indeed its support chiefly from the navy and army'.

Seamen paid a shilling each for a place in the gallery, where they felt themselves free to cheer, boo or join in, while officers paid three shillings for a box and midshipmen and masters' mates sat in the pit for two shillings.

The guide, called *The Picture of Plymouth*, kept the more down-to-earth sailors' haunts from its canvas, and said: 'The amusements in the town are not numerous; there is a good ballroom in the Fountain Tavern, where assemblies are held in the winter, and are well attended; but strangers, unless they go with a party, are not likely to be much pleased, as there is no master of ceremonies, nor any steward to pay attention to them.'

One thing that the seamen did not like about Plymouth was that it had a number of toll-gates and the flying bridge. The seaman wanting to go through the Stonehouse Bridge gate had to pay 2d, which entitled him to return the same day. (A coach with two horses paid 3s, a wagon drawn by three or four horses 4s, a drove of oxen 10s a score.) The Sunday charges are almost bewildering – the Stonehouse Turnpike Road charged double on Sundays but the Stonehouse Bridge gate was free. Double was charged on the New Road gates, but normally on weekdays payment at one gate exempted a traveller at the other.

The flying bridge (a ferry comprising a pontoon on chains) guaranteed that 'no person [was] to be kept waiting on the side where the bridge may happen to be above five minutes', but the seaman on leave might find that his fellow passengers varied in type: the scale of charges included 1d for a passenger or sheep, 2d for a pig, 3d for a horse, ass or mule, 8d for a gig and one horse and 1s 2d for a four-wheel carriage with two horses. A wagon or carriage with more than four horses paid the highest fare, 3s 6d.

Officers joining ships or seamen returning from leave and unable to get a ship's boat had to use one of the boatmen working from the western pier. They were expensive: one with two oars charged 1s to the Catwater, 3s to the Sound, 5s to Cawsand Bay or the Hamoaze.

Plymouth was a city of nearly 60,000 people and by the middle of the war the 'vast influx of inhabitants' had forced up prices and new arrivals were 'obliged to pay most exorbitant rents for their rooms' – there were, in 1812, cases of single rooms letting for £10 a year, though 'more moderate' landlords were content with four guineas.

Plymouth Dock itself was a fortified town so that it could not increase in size. How much was going on is shown by the number of 'principal officers' employed. The dockyard dealt with every aspect of the Navy, from building ships to making rope and supplying bread, so the staff included the master shipwright, timber master, foreman of the yard, afloat and new work, master mastman, boat-builder, joiner, smith, bricklayer, painter, sailmaker, rigger, ropemaker, house-carpenter and boatswain of the yard.

The Victualling Office was separate, near the citadel and beside the Catwater Harbour. Immediately inside the gate was the cooper's department, where the barrels used for beer were repaired. Beyond were two bakehouses, each with four ovens. The eight ovens were fired up from great bundles of faggots eight times a day and, by the middle of the war, produced daily enough bread (the hard, rectangular biscuit) for 16,000 men.

Inside the dockyard were the buildings used by the master craftsmen. The basin, nearly 200 feet long and 66 feet wide, could hold a 74-gun ship, and several more could be fitted out at the jetties on either side. Nearby was the rigging house, a building 480 feet long and three stories high, constructed of limestone. Inside, the rigging for the ships was made up. The sail loft was over the rigging house, and sails were cut and sewn for all sizes of ships.

The blacksmith's shop reminded most people of the hell described in Sunday sermons. It had forty-eight forges in a building 210 feet square, and the smiths forged iron bars to make anchors, the largest weighing four tons and worth £550 each. Cranes lifted the bars in and out of the fires, and the heat and noise was almost overpowering. A contemporary witness wrote: 'Those who are unaccustomed to places of this kind, feel strong sensation of horror on first entering: the clanking of the chains used to blow the bellows, the dingy countenance of the workmen, the immense fires and, above all, the yellow glare thrown on everything by the flames shining through the dismal column of smoke that continually fills the building, form together a very terrific picture.'

The heat was so exhausting that, in addition to their normal pay, the smiths received a daily ration of small beer when they were making the lodging and hanging knees, straps for the chainplates, rudder gudgeons and pintles and the dozens of other pieces of ironwork needed to build a ship. But when they switched to making a run of anchors, the hardest work of all, they were issued with strong beer. In 1802, most of which covered the brief period of peace following the Treaty of Amiens, they used 1,127 tons of coal in the forty-eight forges. The anchors resulting from their work were stored at the anchor wharf nearby, where they were painted with blacking and stored upright 'to prevent rusting'.

To the north were the mast house and the pond. The mainmast of a first-rate ship was four inches short of 120 feet, and 10 feet in circumference, made up of many pieces of wood which were formed to fit into each other and, after being rounded, were held together by iron hoops, made at the nearby forge and pressed on while red hot so that as they shrank in cooling they made a tighter fit.

The pond was used for storing masts and yards. It was nearly 400 feet long and sea water flowed into it through big sluices. Except in times of acute timber shortage, dozens of masts and scores of yards floated in the pond, the water preventing them from drying out and warping in the sun and causing long 'shakes', or splits.

The ropehouse was in fact two stone buildings running parallel. Twine was made on the upper floors and the yarns prepared, when they were taken to the ground floor and layed up (twisted together) into cables. The largest cables made in the ropehouse were 23½ inches in circumference and 720 feet long and weighed almost seven tons. A first-rate ship carried five of them, with a sixth weighing a ton, and a seventh half a ton – more than thirty-six tons of cable, which began upstairs in the ropehouse with bundles of twine.

Nearby there were three dry docks, one of which could hold two ships at a time. The rise and fall of tide meant that pumping could be kept to a minimum. The ship was brought in at high water and the gates shut. Sluices built into the gates were opened and as the tide fell water flowed out of the dock until low water. The sluices were then shut and the remaining water pumped out, the pumps being powered by horses.

The Navy's powder magazine was higher up the river, several stone buildings 'erected with every precaution to prevent fire by fire or lightning'. One of the problems the Navy Board faced was how to dry gunpowder which had been damaged by water. Until recently all such powder had to be sent round to Kent, at the other end of the Channel, where there were kilns to dry it. Now kilns had been built even farther up the river to deal with the damaged powder brought to Plymouth and the people of the city were assured that 'every precaution is taken to prevent an explosion'.

Robert Hay arrived in Plymouth on board the *Culloden* in July 1809, exactly five years to the day after sailing from Spithead to India. He said: 'The practice of giving seamen, on their return from a specified number of years of foreign service, one third of their wages and a fortnight's liberty to visit their friends, had lately come into use, and all those of us whose service entitled us to this gracious treat obtained liberty.'

With a friend, Robert Wright, he left for his home in Scotland, but only three miles outside Plymouth, at 'one of the stations where soldiers are stationed to intercept deserters, we were very strictly examined, but Wright and I having our passports were permitted to pass on'. A shipmate with them who had lost his passport was, despite the arguments of all three of them, taken back to Plymouth as a deserter.

After a meal at Tavistock, Hay and Wright walked on to the village of Sourton. 'We had sufficient time on hand to have advanced somewhat farther, but having for many years had no practice in walk ashore, we found ourselves greatly fatigued.' Reaching Barnstaple, Hay discovered that a ship had sailed for Scotland the previous day but there would be no more for several weeks, so he and Wright had no choice but to spend their leave exploring England. They spent three days in London, bed and board costing them 10s 6d. 'The architectural appearance of this great city fell far short of the ideas I had formed.' But he admitted that 'this was more than compensated by the opulence and magnificence that everywhere met the eye'.

He added that 'when our time was nearly expired we again mounted the coach box. . . . The sum I received when I quitted the ship was £14 and although I considered that I had been pretty economical I found that the end of the fourteenth day would bring me to my last shilling. Few of my shipmates however could boast of such economy, many of them having gone through double the sum in half the time.'

The passport he referred to was in fact a document which identified him as a sailor on leave, giving the dates, which could be shown to patrols and press gangs. It said that he should report to a particular ship by 15 August.

There were clubs for officers in some ports, and in London, but they were often sad places. Captain Glascock, in his *Naval Sketch Book*, devotes a chapter to a 'Naval Club House', noting that it was usually empty on a fine day but 'the more dreary the day, the more thronged the assemblage of the dismal within', Going upstairs he saw two elderly post captains 'who, from their sickly aspect, were evidently much nearer their grave than their Flag, poring over the last number of the Navy List, and betraying a peculiar satisfaction in their looks as the elder struck his pen through the names of their seniors who had died since its publication.

' "Well!" said the veteran, as he concluded the agreeable task of blotting so many brother officers out from the list of the living, "thank God! There are five more within these three months have resigned their flags in our favour!" '

A ship of war had two roles to play and for each one her men needed to be organised in a different way. One role, and the most usual, was simply sailing from one place to another, or patrolling, with the normal sail handling; the other was taking her into action. The routine of sailing the ship was the same in peace or war.

As soon as all the men were on board the first lieutenant and captain drew up a general quarter, watch and station bill. This was a list showing the task of every man in the ship at quarters (the 'action stations' of the Royal Navy today, although the US Navy still retains the fine old phrase), on watch, and at his station for various evolutions, from weighing anchor to reefing sails.

The first group of men chosen were usually stationed on the focsle. Called focslemen they would work at the anchor when weighing or anchoring, at the foresail (the lowest and largest on the foremast), jibs and bowsprit when sail handling and at the six forewardmost guns in action (when they would all be armed with cutlasses, and all but one would have pistols, the exception having a musket and tomahawk). The focslemen were usually prime seamen getting on in years.

The next group were the topmen. They were divided into three sections, one for each mast. They were usually young, agile and well trained. When the ship was weighing and anchoring they manhandled the heavy cable and worked at the capstan. When 'reefing, furling or loosing sail' they worked high over the decks on the yards of the topsails, topgallants and royals. Their work was the most dangerous – they were the men who had to reef or furl thousands of square feet of flogging canvas in bad weather, when one slip meant being thrown or falling to an almost inevitable death. In action they were spread out among the guns' crews and most of them were armed with pistols or boarding pikes, which were weapons like spears, 7½ feet long, used to repel boarders or spit the enemy when boarding his ship.

The third group were the waisters, so called because for sail handling they were stationed in the waist of the ship, the section amidships between the focsle and quarterdeck. They handled the fore and main sheets. Because their tasks (which usually included pumping the bilges and looking after the livestock) required application rather than brains, the waisters were often the landmen and doltish seamen. In action they formed guns' crews.

The afterguard formed the fourth group and, as their name implies, they worked the aftermost part of the ship, handling the braces, the ropes that braced round the yards to which the sails (controlled by the sheets leading aft and the tacks leading forward) were attached.

In the social scale that formed among the seamen, the topmen were the aristocrats, with the focslemen one step lower. The afterguard came third and the waisters were fourth, the butt of the others. But all four joined in jeering at the fifth group, the idlers.

Like the waisters, their tasks bore little relation to their description and they were called idlers only because they did not stand a watch: they were the ship's dayworkers. They included the cook, carpenter and his mates, officers' servants and purser's assistant.

Each of the first four groups was divided into two watches, known as starboard and larboard, and every man had a number, the even numbers belonging to the larboard watch and the odd to starboard. (At the time of Trafalgar the left-hand side of the ship, and anything to the left, was called 'larboard'; 'port' was used instead of 'larboard' for helm orders but it did not supersede the word 'larboard' in general use until 1844, when it was officially changed by an Admiralty order of 22 November which said that because of representations 'that the word port is frequently although not universally substituted on board Her Majesty's ships for the word larboard, and the want of a uniform practise in this respect may lead to important and serious mistakes, and the distinction between "starboard" and "port" is so much more marked than that between starboard and larboard', the Board ordered that 'larboard' was no longer to be used to signify left in HM ships.)

Because he had a number, a man could always consult the 'quarters, watch and station bill' to check on his various tasks. The bill varied from ship to ship because there was no standard method laid down by the Admiralty – each captain had his own system, one which had perhaps been copied years before from another captain, and certainly modified in the light of experience and sometimes because a bill for a frigate with an official complement of 250 men needed drastic revision when the ship mustered a hundred men short. Such revision was not only a question of giving men extra duties – it had to be physically possible for one man to get to the various places in the sequence of events likely to happen.

The bill therefore listed every task to be done in the ship when under way, in battle or in an emergency, and we can choose quite arbitrarily number 75 in a bill designed for a large frigate. He was in the starboard watch, and was one of the crew of the ship's barge. In battle he was captain of number ten gun, starboard side; was in the second division of boarders (should 'Away boarders' be piped as another ship was attacked); and would be armed with a cutlass and pistol. For reefing, furling and loosing sails he had to be at the maintopsail yard. When the ship was weighing anchor he would help pay down the cable – which meant he had to be quick if the ship immediately set her topsail.

When the ship had her sails set and was manoeuvring he had various tasks, of which working at the maintopsail brace and the foretopsail brace were the most important. His duties when making sail, whether shaking out reefs or setting studding-sails, were given in detail next to shortening sail. Finally his jobs in sending down sails for mending or hoisting or lowering yards were listed.

The ship's boys, normally working as servants to officers, had their duties listed for all these manoeuvres, and by tradition in battle they were the 'powder monkeys', carrying the flannel cartridges of gunpowder from the magazine to the guns, using a lidded, wooden cartridge case into which the cylindrical flannel bag fitted. When the ship was weighing anchor, the bill gave their duties as 'assist and holding on and carrying forward nippers', which led to boys being called 'nippers', a word later used much more widely.

It was impossible to put a thick anchor cable round the capstan, although the power of the revolving capstan was used. Instead of the anchor cable another thick and endless rope, the messenger, went round the capstan and round a big block forward or occasionally a second capstan aft. As seamen pressed against the radiating bars and turned the capstan, the messenger rope moved round it, like a thread round a spool.

The anchor cable was led past the moving messenger and men quickly seized cable and the moving messenger together with short lengths of line called nippers. The moment a seaman tied a nipper he stepped forward ready to tie another, leaving a ship's boy to walk aft with messenger and cable, holding an end of the nipper until he reached the hatch down which the cable was led, when he quickly unlashed the nipper and ran forward with it so that it could be used again.

The marines formed a separate group but had various duties like the seamen, but these were modified. In battle half of them were usually stationed on the upper deck with muskets, to act as sharp-shooters, and the others were at the great guns. When weighing anchor they (and seamen of the afterguard and mizentopmen) worked the capstan.

The bill also gave the duties of the carpenter and his mates (most of them below decks with their tools and shot plugs ready to fill shot-holes), bosun and his mates (mostly on duty at various positions to keep order), quartermasters (the senior at the con and two at the wheel) and the gunner and his mates (in the magazine issuing cartridges).

A seaman thus had two numbers to remember – the one in the quarter, watch and station bill, and his mess number. He had two hammocks (one a spare). If he was an ordinary seaman his pay was 25s 6d a month, and, if he 'went over the standing part of the foresheet' on his next voyage, the odds were heavily on sickness being the cause, not wounds. Whether his service was pleasant, tolerable or hateful depended on the man himself as much as his captain, and from the written accounts that have survived about life on the lower deck in the days of Nelson it is clear that the majority of men found it tolerable, and certainly preferable to serving in the Army, garrisoning for years some disease-ridden Caribbean island, storming over the hills and plains of Spain, or crossing the malarial swamps of Holland, with duty as harsh as at sea but usually with only sodden mud or hard earth to sleep on and food not only as bad as that served in a ship but, on active service, uncertain in its arrival. Seamen were never more than a few score feet from the galley, but a field kitchen had a knack of getting lost, along with the battalion cook and provisions.

CHAPTER THIRTEEN

All at Sea

The time the ship's day began at sea depended on the longitude, the time of the year, and the captain, but usually it started at 4 a.m. with the off-watch men being called, the men at the wheel and the lookouts being changed, and the log being hove to get the ship's speed.

The wheel in most ships was in fact a double wheel, two wheels on the same axle and each more than 4 feet in diameter. In normal weather there were two men at the wheel, one each side, with the man to windward doing most of the work. A quartermaster ensured they steered the proper course and watched the sails to make sure they were drawing properly.

The compasses were kept in the binnacle, which was a long locker rather like a small sideboard fitted athwartships in front of the wheel. In the middle was a place for a lantern which, at night, lit up a compass on each side. The men at the wheel could see each compass through a glass window.

There were often drawers in the top of the binnacle in which the slate, a telescope (usually known as a 'bring 'em near') and a nightglass were kept. The nightglass had to be used with care because it gave an inverted image, so not only was a distant ship shown upside down but it appeared to be on the opposite tack from the one it was actually sailing.

A frigate in wartime had at least six look-outs on deck at night – on either bow, one each abreast the mainmast, and one on each quarter – and the officer of the watch usually hailed them every fifteen minutes to make sure they were awake and not 'taking a caulk'.

The officer of the watch wrote on the slate the courses steered during his watch, the wind strength and direction, and the speed if the log was hove. At 4 a.m., or soon after, he ordered the idlers to be called, and the cook and his assistant began preparing the galley fire. This was never lit until daylight because in wartime every one of the King's ships at sea met the dawn at quarters, ready in case daylight revealed an enemy ship in sight. The galley fire had to be out because of the danger of fire from a random shot and the risk of explosions if there was gunpowder on deck.

The carpenter and bosun were also called, along with their mates. The carpenter's first task was to sound the wells, to see if there was any water in the bilges. Because the planking of most ships 'worked', it was usually a question of seeing how much there was, and reporting it to the officer of the watch so that it could be pumped out. The bosun and his mates would check the rigging as soon as there was enough light, and the gunner and his mates the guns.

But first, at least fifteen minutes before the first sign of dawn, the ship went to quarters and two look-outs were sent aloft. As soon as it was light enough to report 'horizon clear' the captain, standing on the quarterdeck, would send the ship's company about its normal day's business.

While the carpenter, bosun and gunner supervised their mates and the cook and his mate struggled to get the galley fire to light – a daily battle with green wood and conflicting draughts coming down the galley chimney from the foresail and headsails and no paper to start the wood burning – the day's work began with the order for the duty watch to scrub the upper deck while the off-duty watch, called for quarters, went back to their hammocks for two hours more sleep. Scrubbing the upper deck removed the sand which had been sprinkled on the wetted planking as the men went to quarters, and as soon as it was done any other scrubbing was disposed of – clothes, windsails, boat sails, hammocks (one a fortnight), tables, stools, forms and gratings, depending on the day of the week.

Sails were frequently adjusted while the decks were being scrubbed; halyards would be slackened a few inches or taken up, so that a different part of the ropes bore on the sheaves of the blocks. Sheets had the same treatment, the whole thing being part of the daily war against chafe, which did its best to wear out the rope of the running rigging and flax of the sails.

In merchant ships, where appearances mattered little, patches could be sewn on the sails at the places where they could chafe, and the foot of the sails was cut in a high curve (the roach) to avoid chafe against the mast. The King's ships had a much flatter roach – a big curve reduced the area of the sails, and the lack of hundreds of square feet could be critical when chasing or fleeing from an enemy. Chafe on the roach had to be accepted, and few captains and even fewer admirals would allow extra chafing patches: they took the view that the flax was going to chafe anyway, whether patch or sail, and when the sail chafed it was just as easy to sew in a new patch as to sew on a chafing patch.

At any time between 6 and 6.45 a.m., depending on latitude, longitude, season and captain, the off-watch men were called and went through the ritual of lashing and stowing hammocks. Then came 'watch below clean the lower deck' while the duty watch had the order 'flemish ropes' and, in a warm climate, 'spread awning'. The awning covered the quarterdeck and was tightly stretched and laced to the rigging to prevent it flapping. It shaded the two men at the wheel in a frigate and those others on watch who had to stand out in the sun – the quartermaster, officer of the watch and a midshipman, two seamen to handle the signal flags if they were in company with other ships, the captain and often the master.

At eight o'clock the hands were piped to breakfast, trooping below to their messes, sitting on forms on either side of the tables. It was not an inspiring meal. The mess cook might have taken some of each man's weekly ration of three pints of oatmeal and made it into a gruel. There would be more than enough bread in the bread barge, and the meagre butter and cheese could be used to help it down. Inevitably some of the men had managed to horde their tot of grog from the previous evening, and now drank it to pull the world into focus. Some messes had coffee to drink. It was not recognisable as coffee, being made of bread toasted over the galley fire until it was hard as a board, then hammered into crumbs and boiled with water. The mixture, providing the cook would boil the water, warmed the men on a cold day, although it did little else.

Half an hour was allowed for breakfast, and then for the next half an hour the routine was the same as when the ship was in harbour – clean in working dress, followed by 'stow bags and sweep decks'. Each mess cook stowed the bread barge, mess kid, knives and spoons. Forks were little used, the point of knife serving well enough if – an unlikely event – the food was too hot for the fingers.

Occasionally the mess cook changed what passed for a napkin. The mess table was usually hung from the deckhead (the name for what would be the ceiling in a house, though the ceiling in a ship was something quite different) by two ropes at the inboard end, the outboard end fitting to the ship's side. A piece of rope about eight inches long was unravelled and the yarns at the top end were lashed round each of the ropes supporting the table, like a thick grass skirt, and providing something upon which the men could wipe their greasy hands. These greasy yarns eventually made good candle wicks and, dipped in hot wax, gave the men more light to reinforce the 'pusser's dips', which were scrawny affairs, the minimum of poor wax clinging to the thinnest of wicks and, in the tropics, given to bending over in the heat like wilted sticks of asparagus.

Divisions at 9.30 a.m. made a distinct break in the day. The men paraded with their lieutenants and midshipmen and the marines with their officers. The number of marines for each class of ship was laid down, although it was usually a maximum, with little more than two-thirds actually serving. A 32-gun frigate had a first and second lieutenant, two sergeants, two corporals, one drummer and forty privates; a 74-gun ship had a captain in addition to the two lieutenants, four sergeants and four corporals, two drummers and 110 men. (The Marines became 'Royal' Marines in 1802.)

If any men were to be punished, it was administered now, with the whole ship's company watching. There was a ritual attached to flogging, and one which was carefully followed (see Chapter 15). The seamen's reaction to a flogging provided a competent captain with another insight into the morale of his men. They never disapproved of a well deserved flogging, and in cases where the captain had any doubt about the culprit he usually knew if he had the right man by the time the flogging was over, the sucking of teeth, shuffling of feet and general restlessness telling him when he had made a mistake.

By 10 a.m. the idlers were at work and the duty watch might be exercising at the guns (the cannons were referred to as the great guns, in contrast to muskets and pistols, which were small arms) or sending down a sail for repairs, hoisting up a spare from the sail room and bending it on. The sail area of a 32-gun frigate totalled more than 15,000 square feet, with the main course – the lowest and largest sail on the mainmast – measuring 3,000 square feet.

At 11.30 came the most welcome order of the day, 'clear decks and up spirits', followed at noon by dinner. An hour later the duty watch exercised or worked and water was pumped out and served at 2 p.m., the scuttlebutt filled and bread issued at the same time on

Mondays, Wednesdays and Fridays. At 4 p.m. 'up spirits' was piped, for the second part of the day's grog, and soon after 4 p.m. the day, which had started twelve hours earlier, began to end with 'clear decks and furl awnings'.

Half an hour before sunset the ship went to quarters, and the captain or first lieutenant inspected the men and the guns. The master-at-arms usually went round first, looking for any men who might be tipsy, having previously hoarded their grog and used it to augment the four o'clock issue.

At dusk the look-outs at the masthead were called down and six more men were placed round the ship, each to watch a particular arc of the horizon. The day finished with the same routine as used in harbour – down hammocks, ship's company's fire and lights out, and then 'gunroom lights out'.

Sunday and Thursday at sea were special days, when the men had to shave, put on clean shirts and change their trousers. They were given plenty of time to prepare: most captains set aside Saturday afternoons at sea for mending clothes and preparing for Sunday's divisions by washing and shaving, the marines 'paying particular attention to arms and accoutrements'.

The Sunday inspection was followed by divine service. After breakfast, when the decks were swept, the men spent their time relaxing or getting ready. Queues (or pigtails) were tied and retied, the clean shirts were put on. Mess cooks made sure that the mess tables were clean and the bread barge, breaker, kid, tea kettle and vinegar keg were stowed properly, and the kettle messes well scrubbed, along with the net bags and tallies.

The various mates made a preliminary inspection and then reported to their warrant officers, who then went to the first lieutenant. If he was a wise man he took a precautionary cruise through the ship before reporting to the captain that all was ready for the inspection.

The captain now told the first lieutenant to beat to divisions, an order passed to the marine drummer through the officer of the watch. As soon as the drum started beating men came up from the lower deck and lined up in single file along the gangways on either side, and across the quarterdeck, each division with its officer in front. The marines by tradition paraded across the after part of the quarterdeck, smart with pipeclayed cross-belts, polished boots and gleaming muskets, their officers standing in front.

All officers wore full uniform with swords and finally the captain came up the companionway to begin an inspection which usually showed him every part of the ship and every man on board. Some captains insisted that the first lieutenant came with them, armed with notebook and pencil to note down defects; others relied on a midshipman.

With the inspection completed, the men were dismissed and the order given to 'rig Church'. This was done on the quarterdeck, when a pulpit was made from a flag put over a box or the binnacle. Chairs were brought up from the wardroom and put at the after end of the quarterdeck for the officers, while the seamen brought up the forms and stools from their own quarters, and ranged them in rows across the forward side of the quarterdeck and facing the 'pulpit'. The chances were that, unless she was a flagship, there was no chaplain on board.

The part of the service which the seamen liked best was the singing. Occasionally one of the men could play a fiddle and would be ordered to strike up the tune, and all the men joined in the singing. Many good captains regarded the men's singing as the best barometer available – happy and contented men sang hymns with gusto; sulky or bullied men put little life into it.

The officers and men in ships carrying chaplains usually liked a brief, blunt sermon, but all too often the chaplain, who had spent the whole week in close proximity to a large number of men of various social classes who were no strangers to blasphemy and the sins of the flesh, tended to preach long sermons. Captains, less endowed with patience than most people, tried to curb the loquacity, and at least one of them regularly gave the chaplain ten minutes, and after that ordered all hands to reef or furl the foretopsail.

In all ships that did not carry a chaplain the captain took the service, though he rarely preached a sermon. Occasionally a captain used up the time to read the Articles of War to the ship's company instead of holding a service. The thirty-six Articles (nearly four thousand words which combined old usage with brevity to warn everyone, from admirals to boys, what would happen to them if they were guilty of anything from treason to wasting stores, by way of provoking gestures and sodomy) could always be extended by including all the subsequent clauses – another four thousand words, each paragraph beginning 'And be it further enacted', or, as a change, 'And it is hereby further enacted . . .' (twelve times in all), or 'Provided also . . .', or 'Provided nevertheless . . .', with an occasional 'Provided always, and it is hereby enacted and declared' (a total of ten times), to wake up anyone dozing in the back row. The men were usually saved from listening to these twenty-two examples of the literary inventiveness of their bureaucratic masters by the fact that the noise of the wind, the creaking of the ship and the rending of rope through blocks meant that the Articles had to be read in a loud voice, and even the most leather-throated captain usually made do without the additions. They were in any case milk-and-water stuff, going on at length about court-martial procedure and (by comparison with the thirty-six Articles) mundane offences like perjury. Nor were seamen shivering with cold because of the downdraught from the mainsail, or sweltering under a tropical sun, likely to greet the last paragraph with anything but relief – 'Provided nevertheless, and be it enacted, that the repeal of the said before recited statutes, or any part thereof, or anything herein contained, shall not extend, or be deemed to extend, to discharge or avoid, or prevent any prosecution or suit commenced . . .', and so on for another ninety-six bewildering words which could have meant nothing to educated officers, let alone the seamen, many of whom were illiterate.

The other religious service held in a ship, unfortunately all too frequently, was a funeral, and it was and still is one of the most moving of all ceremonies. When a seaman died, his messmates by tradition usually prepared his body for burial, and with the master-at-arms present helped the sailmaker sew it into the man's hammock, two roundshot being placed at the feet to make sure it sank. The body was then taken up on deck and put on the after hatch with a Union Flag draped over it.

On the following day a grating was rigged on the lee side, over the standing part of the foresheet. The grating was secured by a rope which, at a given signal, would cant the grating up at a steep angle. With the grating level the body was placed on it, covered in the flag, and the ship's bell was usually tolled a few times so that anyone who wanted to could attend the service. This was conducted by a chaplain, if one was carried, otherwise by the captain. As soon as he had read the service a signal was given, and while a seaman held the flag the grating was tilted up so that the body slid over the side – over the standing part of the foresheet – but the flag and grating could be used again.

Any of the King's ships at sea was run 'by the watch': with the chance of an enemy sail coming over the horizon any moment of the day or night, minutes counted in carrying out most orders concerning sail handling and preparing for action.

Starting with the topmen on deck, they would be up the ratlines and out on the main royal yards in one minute, with thirty seconds allowed for casting off the gaskets, the canvas strips holding the sail in a great roll against the yard. Most ships could set all sail in from four to six minutes.

Replacing damaged yards and topmasts, or sending them down on deck because of bad weather, was a frequent evolution but a difficult one because of the rolling of the ship and the size and weight of the spars, and ships achieved some remarkable times. A few decades after the end of the war, as the Navy reluctantly concentrated on steam, sail handling was still fast. The *Comus*, crossing the Pacific in 1895 and, according to one of her officers, 'not very good at drill', could, with royal yards across, send her topgallant masts down in two and a half minutes and could shift topgallant masts (starting and finishing with her royal yards across) in under five minutes, and shifting topsails could be done in less than ten minutes. (The *Comus* spread about as much canvas as a 74-gun ship but had many fewer men.)

The sloop *Wild Swan*, of 1,400 tons, boasted that she could carry out any drill in the signal book in under half an hour. However, ships specialising in sail drill – of importance when in a squadron under the eye of an admiral – suffered many casualties from men falling. In the 1890s one Mediterranean fleet ship killed a man a month. Often, experienced hands became careless, and an important reason for fatal accidents was the men's own keenness: they would make illicit preparations. For example, anticipating the order to shift topsails, they would let go or slacken the sheets, clewlines and robands on the furled sail. Then, if the admiral instead made the signal 'Make all plain sail', they had to be secured again, or just let fall, which led to men falling off the yard. The blame could be shared: between the admirals and captains who demanded fast times to the pride of the seamen who wanted their own ship to beat the rest of the squadron.

A midshipman in the 131-gun *Marlborough*, who later became Admiral Swinton-Holland, recorded the following times: up topgallant masts and yards and loose sails – 2 minutes; unbend sails (sails not loosed) – 1 minute 45 seconds; bend and make all plain sail – 10 minutes 20 seconds; up topgallant masts and make sail to studding-sails both sides – 7 minutes 41 seconds.

In preparing for battle a frigate could clear for action in five minutes while a ship of the line took a quarter of an hour. A frigate had an advantage because, with no guns on the lower deck, she could leave the hammocks slung, while a ship of the line had to stow them because they would otherwise get in the way of the guns.

The time needed to fire broadsides varied, being affected by the amount the ship was rolling (because of the need to run the heavy guns out each time before firing), but Collingwood recorded three broadsides in ninety seconds, and at Trafalgar the *Victory*'s 32-pounders fired three rounds in two minutes. An 18-pounder carronade fitted in a boat needed eight men to load and fire it, firing eight rounds in about six minutes.

Ships' speeds also varied considerably. If she had just come out of the dockyard with a clean bottom and stowed with just the right provisions to make her float at the draught giving her best performance – and if she had a captain who was a good seaman and prepared to 'crack on', risking sails and spars for speed – a ship might break records. Long after the war the *Sutlej* frigate, designed by Sir William Symonds, averaged 14 knots for eight days in the trades, sailing full and by with her foretopmast studding-sails set.

In wartime, though, the majority of ships were making passages with dirty bottoms (despite popular accounts, copper sheathing did not always keep hulls clean), using sails whose flax and stitching was weakened by strong sunlight and damp, and with masts getting brittle from too much exposure to tropical sun or soft from rot.

A typical situation was one in which the 28-gun *Hind* found herself in 1796 while escorting a convoy to Quebec. One of her lieutenants was James Gardner, who describes how they were chased by two French ships of the line. It was blowing hard and 'We immediately let two reefs out of the topsails, set topgallant sails and hauled the main tack on board, with a jib a third in and spanker. It was neck or nothing,' Gardner wrote, adding that 'for my part I expected we should be upset [i.e. capsized] and it was with uncommon alacrity in making and shortening sails between the squalls that we escaped upsetting or being taken'.

He gave credit to the French seamanship: the ship of the line chasing the *Hind* parted a maintopsail sheet but replaced it in ten minutes, then split a jib, which was unbent and another set in twenty minutes.

The *Hind* was racing along – heaving the log showed that she was making ten knots, with the sea nearly abeam. But the Frenchman was gaining on them 'and we should have been captured for a certainty if the Frenchman had possessed more patience. And so it happened: for a little before six, when he was within gunshot, the greedy fellow let another reef out of his topsails, and just as he had them hoisted, away went his foreyard, jib-boom, foretopmast, and maintopgallant mast.' The chase had lasted twelve hours, in which time the *Hind* had sailed nearly 120 miles. The frigate then shortened sail and wore round to rejoin the scattered convoy.

There were many tricks for increasing speed. Many captains believed in wetting the sails, the idea being to close the slightest space in the weave through which the wind might escape, while others swore it made the sails hang too heavily. With a strong wind on the beam it was common to have the men up to windward, each clutching a couple of roundshot, acting as movable ballast. As a last resort the ship was lightened by emptying the fresh water from the casks into the bilges and pumping it over the side, followed by throwing over the guns.

One lieutenant records a sequence of orders from the captain as: 'Get the [fire] engine to work on the sails – hand butts of water to the stays – pipe the hammocks down and each man place shot in them – slack the stays, knock out the wedges and give the masts play. Start off the [fresh] water, Mr ——, and pump the ship.'

In the *Thetis* frigate the four foremost guns were brought aft, abreast the mainmast, to trim the ship, and the lee guns hauled in towards the centre-line and secured against the coamings of the hatchways to get the ship sailing on an even keel.

All sails used in the Royal Navy up to the abolition of sail, incidentally, were made of flax. Numbers 1, 2, 3 and 4 canvas were made of flax, with very severe penalties for any departure from the quality used. Only two kinds of flax were allowed, both coming from the Baltic, although Italian hemp was sometimes permitted. All the canvas had a coloured 'King's yarn' woven into it to show that it was government property and to prevent peculation and smuggling. (Rope was also laid up with a King's yarn, and both were popularly known as the 'Rogue's yarn'.)

Several types of smaller ships had oars, or sweeps, as well as sails.

They were rarely used to propel the ship in a calm but 'out sweeps' was a frequent order when tacking or wearing, because some vessels were difficult to handle. The sweeps were used to force the bow round. 'Strong gales and heavy squalls with rain, at 11.40 wore by signal, lost six sweeps out of the main chains' was an entry in the *Bittern* sloop's log for Friday 30 October 1807.

Log reel and half-minute glass

CHAPTER FOURTEEN

Guns and Signals

While a ship was under way, the log board – a slate similar to the type once used by schoolchildren – was kept up to date, usually by the master's mate of the watch. 'The mates generally marked the board and it was certified by the officers of the watch,' one master recorded.

The master took a sun sight at noon (weather permitting) and, using the details from the log board, giving the courses steered, wind direction and strength, sail carried and speed, filled in his own log. Two log books were kept in a ship of war, one by the master and one by the captain. They tended to be almost identical, the captain calling his a journal and generally using the details in the master's log.

Log entries were for the most part laconic and mundane but to a trained eye they told a detailed story. Entries from a ship of the line escorting a convoy, for example, said: 'Moderate breezes and pleas-ant weather . . . Ditto weather, parted company one of the convoy . . . 62 sail in company . . . fired two shots at some of the convoy ahead . . . Saw and gave chase to two strange sail to the north-west, made the signal for the convoy to come under our stern . . . The chase was his Majesty's ship —— . . . . Employed working up junk . . . Ditto weather, handed mainsail . . . Spoke a Venetian brig, from Venice bound to Amsterdam.'

In this particular ship, the *Ramillies*, the various instructions – including the order of sailing of the convoy, giving the positions in which the various merchant ships were supposed to sail – were kept in 'the bittacle [binnacle] drawer', with the telescope. The fifth lieutenant who one night went up to the maintopgallant yard with a night glass to watch for enemy ships was asked at a subsequent court martial if he was used to looking through it, and if he was 'acquainted with the principles of its construction'. He said he was, and that in it 'objects appear inverted'.

Close distances were usually described as a pistol shot, a musket shot or a gun shot, which were easier to visualise than yards but corresponded to no official length. 'We ranged up within a pistol shot' or 'pass within a gun shot to avoid the outlying rock' were phrases frequently used. Generally, a pistol shot meant about 25 yards, a musket shot 200 yards (a cable) and a gun shot 1,000 yards (five cables), and represented not the extreme but the effective range of the various weapons.

In bad weather, after sail was reduced, it was often necessary to get the upper masts down, and some of the yards, to reduce the weight aloft. The masts were basically in three sections: the lower mast, with the topmast fitted on to it, and the topgallant mast fitted on top of that. The lowest and largest sails were the courses. When a reef was put in the topsails and topgallants, the royals (highest of the squaresails) and the flying jib were brought in. Taking the second reef in the topsails was usually followed by sending the royal yards into the tops, while the third reef meant taking in the topgallant sails and jib. Tucking a fourth reef in the topsails, by which time the courses would probably be furled, was done when the wind was strong with a high sea running, and this meant housing the topgallant mast and sending the studding-sail booms down on deck. As a last resort, at anchor, the enormous lower yards on which the courses were bent were lowered right down until they rested on the bulwarks; then the topmasts were lowered, so that only the hull, bowsprit and jibboom, and the lower masts, were exposed to the strength of the wind.

The word 'topgallant', incidentally, is derived from 'top garland', or above the garland fitted at the topmast head. The garland was a grommet, or ring of rope, beaten down on the stops of the topmast rigging, or sometimes a collar of rope, to prevent the rigging chafing against the wood of the mast.

The weapons used in the King's ships were divided into two classes: 'small arms' and 'great guns'. In battle the muskets were usually left to the marines, all of whom were normally armed with muskets and cutlasses. The seamen were divided into men who had cutlasses and pistols, cutlasses and tomahawks, and boarders who would use pikes.

The cutlass was a simple straight sword with a 28-inch blade, and an iron grip and guard, a cheap and solid weapon worn in a leather belt that went diagonally across the shoulder. It was a slashing and jabbing weapon; the seaman wielding it had none of the subtlety of a fencer.

The tomahawk bore some resemblance to the Red Indian weapon. Officially it was a boarding axe, a name rarely if ever used outside the Navy Office, and looked rather like a mountaineer's axe. It had a wedge-shaped head with a slightly curved blade, and a sharp spike on the back of the blade. It was a dual purpose weapon – if men boarding an enemy ship had to climb up a steep side with no handholds, they drove in tomahawks, using the spikes, to make ladders. It would appear to be an ineffective weapon in an age of pistols and muskets, but 'T' for tomahawk appeared against men's names on the quarter bills long after the war ended because, once fired, guns were useless in a mêlée.

A full pike was like a spear, an ash stave with an iron, three-sided sharp point at one end. An original pike in the author's collection is 7 feet 7 inches long. The point is designed for stabbing, without the victim remaining impaled. The rule for using a pike (designed to keep the enemy at a distance) was 'jab and go on'. For narrow spaces there were half-pikes, usually 4 feet long. The full pikes were usually stowed in vertical racks on the main deck round the masts, where they could be snatched up in a hurry. The stave was usually varnished ash and the point and the butt plate carefully covered with blacking.

The pistol had a flat hook on one side so that it could be clipped to a belt, and had a 12-inch or 9-inch barrel. It was a solid weapon, able to take hard knocks and double up as a club when it had been fired. The long-barrelled model weighed a little under $3\frac{1}{2}$ lb and the calibre of both was 0·56 inches. The muskets, like the pistols, came in long and short models, the barrel of one being 3 feet 1 inch and the other 2 feet 2 inches. Both could take a bayonet and the long-barrelled version had a maximum range of about 500 yards, although anyone firing at much over 150 yards with aimed shots was a skilled marksman using selected shot, or an optimist. Fifty yards was a more practical range.

The great guns varied in size according to the type of ship and took their description from the weight of the roundshot they fired – 32-, 24-, 18-, 12-, 9- and 6-pounders. Smaller guns were carried for use in a ship's boats.

With most of these guns the length of the barrel varied – the 24-pounder, for instance, came in six different lengths. The 32-pounders (the long-barrel version weighing 2¾ tons) fired a shot a little over six inches in diameter and with a full charge had a 'first graze' range at a 2° elevation of 800 yards and an extreme range of 2,000 yards or less at 10° elevation.

There were three types of 24-pounders in general use, ranging in length from 9½ feet to 6 feet, and in weight from 1½ to 2½ tons. The shot was slightly over 5½ inches in diameter and the extreme range just under 3,000 yards. The shot for an 18-pounder was a fraction over 5 inches in diameter and the range was similar to the 24-pounder.

According to trials when 'the ship was perfectly upright and steady [and] the shot were taken as they came to hand without nice reference to their diameter', an 18-pounder with a 6 lb charge of powder had a range of 1,966 yards, which increased to 2,817 yards at 12°. The 12-pounder was the regular armament of frigates, a gun weighing between 29 and 34 hundredweight, depending on the length of the barrel. It fired a shot nearly 4½ inches in diameter with an extreme range of about 1,800 yards, the same as the 9-pounders also carried by frigates.

Roundshot had a surprising power of penetration. At thirty yards – a very common range in battle – an 18-pounder shot would penetrate four oak planks 32½ inches thick, driving up a shower of splinters and hurling them up to thirty yards. A brass 1-pounder gun, firing a shot slightly over 2 inches in diameter, and fired into a solid block of elm, penetrated twenty inches with a half-pound charge of powder.

Describing ranges and penetrations is difficult in a short space because of the different types of guns firing the same weight of shot, and because of the different charges used. The quantity of gunpowder was increased or reduced for a 32-pounder. For example, 'distant with one shot' meant a charge weighing 10 lb 11 oz while 'full with one shot' meant 8 lb. 'Reduced with two shot' required only 6 lb (otherwise the gun might burst), while the same charge was used for 'exercise and saluting' and practice. 'Scaling and blank' – which meant firing a charge to remove rust scale, or to attract attention – was 2 lb 12 oz.

At 300 yards range a 32-pounder's grapeshot did great damage, penetrating 5 inches of fir planking and 4 of oak. In trials against an old 74-gun ship, a double-shotted 32-pounder put one shot through the first side and lodged it in the other, while the other shot dropped before reaching the other side. Muskets at forty yards' range would penetrate a one-inch oak plank every time; four out of six bullets would pass through two inches of oak, but none could get through three inches.

The drill books – written privately because the Admiralty laid down no routine – usually allowed for up to twelve men for the larger guns (a rule of thumb was one man for every 5 hundredweight) and in at least one volume numbers seven to twelve 'are to man the tackles for running out and training, and perform the contingent duties of firemen'. Number thirteen was the powderman, usually one of the ship's boys. 'A stationary powderman to be stationed at each gun, and opposite. An extra powderman is to be allotted to every two guns, and opposite to fetch powder from the magazine, to supply the stationary powderman.'

The guns were actually fired by flintlocks, a complete change in gunnery having been ordered by the Admiralty on 21 October 1755, exactly fifty years to the day before the Battle of Trafalgar. This date had been in doubt until the author recently found a copy of the Admiralty's letter to all admirals, which said: 'Having considered the experiment lately made in our presence at Woolwich by firing a cannon with locks, and the placing the priming into a tin tube', locks were to be fitted to all quarterdeck guns. Locks, replacing the match-lock (in effect a slow-burning fuse wound round a thin metal rod) 'will answer much better at sea than the present method of firing only with a match and ought to be introduced on board'. Flint-locks, the letter added, would be introduced gradually to the other guns.

Equally important was the Board's decision at the same time to stop using paper for the cartridges. These cylindrical paper bags were strong enough but when the gun fired the bottom of each bag (at the breech end) did not always burn and stayed in the gun 'till it is filled up before the touchhole'. Cartridges in future would be made of flannel. The letter was signed by Anson, who was First Lord, and two other Board members, Wellbore Ellis and Thomas Villiers.

The guns, powder and shot accounted for a high proportion of a fighting ship's weight: even in the smallest frigate with 28 guns, the guns and carronades came to more than 31 tons, the powder to 5 tons, shot to 30 tons, and the gunner's stores – which included everything from spare rope breechings to flintlocks – came to another 7½ tons, making a total of nearly 75 out of the 370 tons of water, provisions, masts, spars, sails, rigging, anchors and boats on board.

When any of the King's ships was at sea in wartime it was always on the look-out for other vessels, and once one was sighted there was a sequence of questions to be asked and answered, ranging from 'friend or foe' to 'where from'.

The 'where from' was very important and every captain laid down strict instructions about what was to be done when meeting another ship at sea – or in a foreign port. No officer or petty officer, Captain Keats laid down, was to go alongside any other ship 'before he had informed himself from whence the vessel is and on no account to board her if from Gibraltar, Cadiz, Malaga, Alicant [*sic*], Cathagena [Spain], or any places where the contagious fever is or has been'.

The reason was quarantine: any ship from those places (and anyone 'having held communication' with them) had to be quarantined, a process involving at least fifteen days at anchor in isolated splendour at the quarantine anchorage at the Motherbank for Portsmouth, at Falmouth for Plymouth, or Stangate Creek for London – providing the ship has a clean bill of health. On meeting other ships at sea, ships liable to quarantine were supposed to fly 'a large yellow flag of six breadths of bunting' from the maintopmasthead if free of disease but a similar yellow flag with a black circular mark or ball 'equal to two breadths of bunting' in the middle if there was illness on board.

The first thing that happened on sighting a strange vessel, providing she was not obviously a merchant ship or an enemy, was to make the challenge or give the correct reply if challenged first. Signalling by flags was mainly done by numbers: the Admiralty laid down a code which comprised twelve flags, from 1 to 9, nought, and two substitutes. Each ship was issued with a signal book which was, with the challenges, the most secret document on board. Taking the 1799 edition, *Signal Book for the Ships of War*, as an example, this gave under 'List of the Navy' the number which identified each of the King's ships. It began alphabetically, but sinkings and new buildings meant many changes. The first number was 2, the 98-gun *Atlas*, with the *Agamemnon* 15, *Bellerophon* 89, Nelson's former frigate the *Boreas* 105, *Elephant* (Nelson's flagship at Copenhagen) 234, a blank next to 327 because this had been the number of the *Hermione* frigate, whose crew had mutinied and run away with her two years before the book came out, *San Salvador* 568 and *Salvador del Mundo* 569, two of the ships captured at the Battle of Cape St Vincent, and *Victory*, 703.

In the author's copy some ships' names have been crossed out – including the *Eclair*, of 3 guns, the smallest vessel listed – while some were added in blank spaces, the *Santa Dorotea*, 608, captured by the *Lion* in the Mediterranean the previous year, and the *Santa Teresa*, 632, taken by the *Argo* a few months later.

The signal book was not used for making the challenge: instead 'The Private Signals' were used, and these were issued by individual commanders-in-chief. They were changed as soon as it was known that the enemy might have captured them. Commodore Samuel Hood, for instance, wrote to the Admiralty from Barbados on 16 December 1804: 'I beg leave to enclose a copy of the Private Signals which I have thought fit to issue to the ships under my command, in consequence of having received information that the Private Signals fell into the hands of the enemy at the capture of His Majesty's late sloop *Lilly*.' (The 16-gun *Lilly*, commanded by Lieutenant William Compton and with a crew of eighty, was captured off the Georgia coast on 14 July by a French 16-gun privateer, the captured *Marlboro' Packet*. Compton was killed in bitter fighting.)

In the letter to his commanding officers when issuing the Private Signals, Hood warned that the signals were to be kept 'with sufficient weight affixed to them to insure their being sunk if it should be found necessary to throw them overboard', and he added that, 'As a consequence of the most dangerous nature to His Majesty's Fleet' resulting from the enemy getting hold of them, any officer who let that happen 'will certainly be made to answer for his disobedience at a court martial'.

The Private Signals were made up in a table, with the day of the month in the first column and the challenge and reply in the next. These changed every ten days, so that on the 1st, 11th, 21st and 31st of the month the challenge (called 'the first signal') was a white flag with a blue cross (number 2) at the maintopmasthead and a blue flag with a yellow cross (number 7) at the foretopmasthead. The reply was number 9 and the substitute pendant and 0. The second set of signals were for use on the 2nd, 12th, 22nd, while the third were for the 3rd, 13th and 23rd, and so on.

The new day began at midnight, for the day signals, though of course until 1805 the nautical day began officially at noon. The night signals, set out in the same way, were arranged by the nautical day, so there could be no mistake in the date. The 5th of the month, for example, began at noon on the 4th and ended the following noon.

Night Private Signals were comparatively clumsy: in Hood's list the challenge used every third day was two lights, one over the other, and the other ship answered with three lights of equal height. The challenging ship then lit a flare and showed two lights of equal height, and was answered with three lights, one over the other. The hail was 'Russia' and the answer 'Sweden' (the hails and replies for the other periods were also geographical – Bengal, China; Denmark, Switzerland).

The much more complex Admiralty signal book, although issued to more than 700 ships, was considered sufficiently important that in the front of each copy was a printed page giving an order to each commanding officer, and the author's 1799 edition was signed personally by three members of the Board – Rear-Admirals James Gambier, William Young and Robert Man – and the Board Secretary, William Marsden.

It gave the numerical signals, and then a list of single-flag signals – flag number 1, for example, meant 'an enemy in sight'; number 2 'prepare for battle', and 5 'engage the enemy'.

After that the book listed two- and three-number signals, more than 260 of them (though more than thirty numbers were left blank so that commanders-in-chief could add their own instructions), covering all the orders the Admiralty thought an admiral was likely to want to signal to his fleet or squadron. It was not a satisfactory system and, before and during battle, put an admiral in something of a straitjacket until Sir Home Popham's telegraphic code was adopted.

The Admiralty signal book's first two signals give an indication of the problem: number 11 said: 'An enemy is in sight. The bearing will be shown occasionally by the proper compass signal', while number 12 said: 'A particular ship to signify whether she had, within two or three days past, seen the enemy's fleet. To be answered accordingly by the negative or affirmative signal; if answered by the latter, its bearing and distance from the fleet, and the number of ships of the line which composed it, are to be shewn.'

For the actual tactics to be used in a battle, the admiral was restricted, the most important signals being 27, 'Break through the enemy's line in all parts where it is practicable, and engage on the other side', and 30, which said that the van, centre and rear ships were to attack their opposite numbers and 'the flag officers are, if circumstances admit of it, to engage the flag officers of the enemy'. Other signals allowed the admiral to signal that the van, centre or rear of the enemy was to be attacked, or to windward or leeward, but the signals were more suited to a couple of prizefighters than fencers.

The signals for manoeuvring a fleet were quite adequate, ranging from 45, 'invert the line in succession from van to rear', which made the sternmost ship the leader, to 90, 'shorten sail: the ships in the rear first'.

There was the normal routine of a fleet to be dealt with, and for that there were various signals, including 205, 'send a launch load of water immediately on board the ship whose pendants will be shown after this pendant has been answered', to 208, 'the ships' companies are to be put to two-thirds allowance of provisions'.

Specific flags hoisted by a flagship in different positions had different meanings: the Union Flag at the mizentopmasthead and a ship's signal numbers meant that her captain was to come on board, while at the mizen peak it meant that a court martial was being held.

Fog signals were made with horns, drums or muskets – cannons were used only to indicate that a signal was to follow. The order to tack comprised two guns fired at five-second intervals as a preparative signal and two guns at the same interval half a minute later, the reply being 'drums or bells', while the order to sail close-hauled on the starboard tack was two guns followed by three, with 'horns or drums' answering. The progress of a fleet or squadron in fog sounded like some eastern religious procession, the bells taking the place of cymbals and the muskets replacing firecrackers.

The moment it became known that the signal book was 'compromised' – captured by the enemy – all ships were ordered to add a particular number to all signals. For instance, adding 7 to every signal meant that no prying eye could understand it.

Sir Home Popham's 'Telegraphic Signals, or Marine Vocabulary' was originally designed to make it easier for him in the *Romney* off Copenhagen to signal to Admiral Dickson off Elsinore, repeating messages from ship to ship. Until Popham's code, admirals and captains could communicate with each other with no more subtlety than a traveller using a brief phrase book: if the whole question or statement was not in the book, communication stopped. Popham's code was in effect a dictionary and gave a choice of individual words; specific questions could be made up and asked, and equally specific answers given.

Popham's code used the flag numbers in the Admiralty book, adding a flag (divided diagonally, white and red) to show that the signal following was in his code, and another flag showing when numbers were in thousands. The letters of the alphabet were numbered from 1 to 25, I and J being together and K and following letters needing two flags.

For the first edition of his code Popham chose from the dictionary a thousand words which he regarded as the most useful, using the root and leaving the receiver of the signal to decide precisely what was meant (for example, number 66 meant *appear-ed-ing-ance*, 69 *approve-d-ing-al*, and 78 *ask-ed-ing*).

The first edition contained fifty-nine words beginning with A and numbered from 26 (*able*) to 85 (*away*). There were 138 beginning with B, ranging from 91 (*backward-ness*) to 129 (*by*); and it went on through the alphabet, putting I and J together and placing V before U. The next edition doubled the total of words but, cleverly, each new word's number was formed by putting a 1 in front of a number in the first edition. Thus 253 was *England-ish*, and 1253 meant *esteem-imate-ion*, while 269 was *expect-ed-ing-ation* and 1269 was *extinguish-tinct*; 261 was *ever-y-thing-where* and 1261 *except-ed-ing-ion-able*. 370 was *his* while 1370 was *hinder-ed-rance-most*; 863 meant *that*, while 1863 was *then, thence*. Number 471 (*man*) began the letter M, while 1471 was *Madeira*, 958 *will-ing-ly-ness* and 1958 *wilful-ly-ness*. 220 gave *did, do, does, doing, done*, and 1220 *disguise-s-d-ing*.

Home Popham's code was carried on board the *Victory* and all of Nelson's ships at Trafalgar, and was used for the most famous naval signal ever made. Nelson, as his ships went into action, went up to John Pasco, the lieutenant temporarily in charge of signals, who was on the poop. 'Mr Pasco,' he said, in his high-pitched Norfolk drawl, 'I wish to say to the Fleet, *England confides that every man will do his duty*. You must be quick, for I have one more to make, which is for *Close Action*.'

Pasco answered, 'If your Lordship will permit me to substitute *expects* for *confides*, the signal will soon be completed, because the word *expects* is in the vocabulary, and *confides* must be spelled.'

Nelson agreed and the signal was made, involving only thirteen flags:

Telegraph flag

253	England
269	expects
863	that
261	every
471	man
958	will
220	do
370	his
4 21 19 24	DUTY

The *Euryalus* frigate, whose job was to repeat the *Victory*'s signals, recorded that it took four minutes to make the signal.

Earlier Nelson had made a much longer signal using Popham's code to give his precise intentions: 9 *I*, 418 *intend*, 873 *to*, 337 *go*, 1870 *through*, 864 *the*, 247 *end*, 570 *of*, 864 *the*, 249 *enemy's*, 456 *line*, 873 *to*, 642 *prevent*, 865 *them*, 318 *from*, 335 *getting*, 396 *into*, 2126 *Cadiz*.

When Popham brought out a new edition of his code he was able to claim that 'it consists of nearly 6,000 primitive words, exclusive of the inflexion of verbs &c, making in all upwards of 30,000 real words; the sentences have also been extended to about 6,000 with 1,500 syllables, a geographical table, a table of technical terms, a table of stores and provisions, and a spare table for local significations'.

Rope rammer (on left) *and sponge, powder horn and priming wire*

CHAPTER FIFTEEN

Crime and Punishment

Punishment was always carried out in public; indeed, the 'spectacle' aspect was regarded as most important. 'Punishment' usually meant flogging or hanging.

Keelhauling was never ordered by a Royal Navy court martial, though it was resorted to by captains in the Navy and merchant service until some time after the Civil War, and it was still used in the Dutch Navy in 1813. A line was passed from one end of the main yard under the ship and up to the other end, and the victim was secured to one end with a deep sea lead tied to his feet, dropped and hauled under the ship and up the other side. The weight of the lead kept him clear of the hull – otherwise the barnacles would tear him to pieces, apart from the possibility of being stuck against the keel.

'Starting', when a man was hit across the shoulders by a rattan cane wielded by a bosun's mate, was not regarded as punishment in the same way as flogging; more frequently an exasperated officer would order a bosun's mate 'to start that man' because he was slow. Most captains had stopped it by the time the Admiralty forbade it entirely after the court martial of Captain Robert Corbett in 1809, commenting that it was 'extremely disgusting to the feeling of British seamen'.

Two years later Captain Robert Preston of the *Ganymede* was court-martialled on a charge of cruel treatment, made by the ship's company. Found 'partly guilty . . . in practising the summary punishment of starting', he was warned by the court to change his conduct.

The ship's boys, the 'nippers' and officers' servants, were often caught in some mischief and they would be 'put to the hoop'. Each boy would be tied by his left hand to a hoop (often from a cask but occasionally a large grommet of rope) and given a 'knittle' or piece of light cord, which he held in his right hand. When the word was given the boys had to run round in a circle, flogging the one in front with the knittle, an endless progress which usually brought laughter to watching seamen and tears to the boys.

Liars on board a ship were only slightly less unpopular than thieves, and a particularly bad one was usually hoisted up to the mainstay by one of the forebraces with a broom and shovel lashed to his back, and with the ship's company shouting 'A liar! A liar!' at him. When he was lowered to the deck again he spent the next week or so cleaning the seats in the head.

One of the worst crimes in a ship is theft: in a ship of the line with 800 or so men on board, the presence of a thief on board could make everyone's life a misery, poisoning the air with suspicion, particularly because most men could not lock up their valued possessions. For minor offences a thief was made to run the gantlet (probably from the Dutch gantlope: *gant*, all; *loopen*, to run). For this men were given rope yarns which they plaited into knittles, with a half hitch in the end. They then stood in two rows, facing each other and leaving a corridor between them. The thief then had to strip off his shirt and was made to pass along the corridor, the master-at-arms walking slowly backwards in front of him and holding a cutlass at his chest and a ship's corporal following with another cutlass. The men then thrashed him with the knittles as he passed – as he slowly walked, not ran, the gantlet.

Major theft was punished by flogging, and the seriousness with which it was treated on board a Royal Navy ship is shown by the fact that *only* for theft was the cat of nine tails knotted: three knots at three-inch intervals were put in each tail. (For all other offences, including desertion and mutiny, the tails were not altered.)

Swearing as an offence depended on the captain: some were foul-mouthed, others occasionally relieving their feelings by a broadside of oaths. Some captains, though, and particularly those with strong religious feelings, forbade any cursing and punished men severely. One method, the most usual, was making the offender wear the cangue, a wooden collar made of two pieces of plank three inches thick and with a nine- or twelve-pound shot fixed to it. The man had to wear it – performing his usual duties – for a set time. In the *Blandford* frigate, according to William Spavens, the captain made offenders walk the lee side of the quarterdeck 'until he should hear another swear'. This meant that the men in the cangue 'would often stagger with design, and tread on the toes of some of the after guard or maintopmen, who would perhaps say, d—n your eyes, why don't you keep your feet to yourself . . . when the prisoner would cry out, "Sir, such a man swears!", when the collar was taken off him and fixed on the other.'

Spavens noted that 'sometimes an exceeding noisy fellow is gagged with a pump bolt in his mouth'. This was secured by spunyarn behind the neck, and the man was then put in the weather mizen shrouds for an hour, facing to windward.

The important point about punishment in the Royal Navy, despite all the nonsense written in twentieth-century accounts, is that it was intended to be a rough and ready and swift justice aimed at fitting the crime. A petty thief was an object of contempt and it was fitting that his shipmates, whom he robbed, should punish him. Even a dirty man, repulsive to anyone having to work, eat and sleep near him, was given a suitable punishment, being stood in a tub of sea water and scrubbed with stiff brooms by some of the ship's company, or at worst given a ducking, when he was lashed astride a thick batten, weighted with the lead, and ducked over the side a few times from a yardarm.

More serious crimes needed more serious punishment but it must be remembered that the Navy was always short of men, so the sentence of death was rare, particularly when the size of the Navy and the attitudes of the day are understood. The court-martial records show that officers were brought to trial at the slightest hint of a breach of the Articles of War. In 1800, for instance, five lieutenants, two surgeons, one gunner and two boatswains from various ships were tried for offences ranging from throwing a cup of tea at another officer to behaving in a riotous and mutinous manner. In every instance the case was proved and all ten men were punished severely.

Sir Edward Hamilton, who had just received a knighthood for his bravery in cutting out the *Hermione* from a Spanish port on the Main in circumstances which make it one of the bravest acts in the Navy's history, was dismissed the service for seizing up the gunner and four seamen in the *Trent*'s rigging. He was later reinstated, but two admirals had to answer for their conduct in 1805 and the first lieutenant of the *Hazard* was hanged two years later after being found guilty of unnatural practices. One of the more ludicrous trials in 1807 was of the Lieutenant of Marines and the surgeon of *L'Aigle*.

The lieutenant was accused of pulling the surgeon's nose and the surgeon was charged with provoking him to do so. The court found them both guilty, putting the lieutenant at the bottom of the list for 1804 (which meant that he lost three years' seniority) and dismissing the surgeon from *L'Aigle*, which was less of a punishment because having a provocative nose proved no bar to finding another ship.

The captain of the *Ulysses*, the Hon. Warwick Lake, marooned a seaman on a deserted island and was tried by court martial and, on 5 November 1810, found guilty and dismissed the service amid a lot of unfavourable publicity, the Admiralty behaving remarkably well.

Lake's trial, on board the *Gladiator* at Portsmouth, caused something of a sensation as the story was told. Robert Jeffery, from Polperro in Cornwall, was eighteen years old and a blacksmith's apprentice when he signed on in the *Lord Nelson* privateer at Plymouth in 1807. Little more than a week later the *Lord Nelson* put into Falmouth, when the 18-gun brig *Recruit*, commanded by Captain Lake, sent a press gang on board and took up Jeffery Lake was anxious to get men because the *Recruit* was sailing for the West Indies. She was small and made a slow passage, so that in November, well inside the tropics, the crew were put on short allowance of water.

Jeffery, who because of his training with metalwork had been rated an armourer's mate, was then said by Captain Lake to have taken 'a bottle with some rum in it' from the gunner's cabin, and a few days later (as he subsequently confessed) he went to the cask of spruce beer and took two quarts of it. He was seen by one of his shipmates, who reported him. Captain Lake ordered the Sergeant of Marines to 'put him on the black list'.

Up to that point, Captain Lake had dealt with the youth lightly: either offence could have resulted in Jeffery getting a dozen lashes; instead he was merely on a list of people given the unpleasant jobs. But on 13 December 1807, three days after the beer episode, the ship passed Sombrero, an uninhabited island thirty miles north-west of Anguilla and 125 miles north-west of Antigua, astride the channel joining the Atlantic and the Caribbean. Captain Lake saw it, asked the master and lieutenants the name of the island, and they described it to him. It is small and jagged, crevices being cut by the sea washing away the coral rock and giving the appearance of creases in a hat. The only fresh water comes from rain lying in the coral rock; the only plants are prickly pear, a type of cactus. The island's sides are steep and at first sight the island appears inaccessible to all but the limpets stuck to the rocks.

'Captain Lake then ordered Jeffery to be landed upon that island,' wrote the chronicler of the war. 'Accordingly at 6 p.m., the poor fellow was placed in a boat, with the second lieutenant of the brig, Richard Cotton Mould, a midshipman and four seamen, and landed . . . without shoes on his feet, or any other clothes than those on his back, and without even a biscuit for food.'

The author can vouch for the fact that it is impossible to walk twenty yards on Sombrero with bare feet without being crippled by the long, thin, sharp and almost invisible spines of the prickly pear, which if not removed at once (and one incautious step can mean twenty almost transparent spines stuck in the flesh) usually become septic. Yet Jeffery would have to seek water among the rocks, and the sun all the year round is so hot that half an hour's exposure can cause bad burns.

'Observing that his feet were cut by the rocks, Lt Mould gave him a pair of shoes, which he [Mould] had begged one of the men together with a knife, and his own and the midshipman's pocket handkerchiefs for making signals. The lieutenant then advised this victim of tyranny and oppression to keep a sharp lookout for vessels, and pulled back to the *Recruit*.

'Her captain's vengeance being thus gratified, the brig filled and made sail from an island until then little known except as a landfall or point of bearing for navigators but,' wrote the contemporary chronicler, William James, 'subsequently blazed about in every quarter of the globe, and never named without any execration upon the (must we say?) British officer who had acted so inhuman a part.'

Some weeks later the *Recruit* put into Antigua and the brig's officers made sure that the Commander-in-Chief at the Leeward Islands heard what had happened. He immediately sent for Lake, reprimanded him and ordered him to go straight back to Sombrero 'and bring away the man if he should chance to be alive'.

By 11 February, two days short of two months after Jeffery had been marooned, the *Recruit* was anchored in nine fathoms off the western end of the mass of rock and both lieutenants, the master, two midshipmen and several seamen scrambled up and searched among the crags and slots. There was no sign of Jeffery: no piece of cloth, no sign that he had ever been on the island.

The officers returned to the *Recruit* and reported to Captain Lake, who now had to deal with Jeffery's name in the muster book. He could have put 'D' in the appropriate column, for 'discharged' – to another ship, or to hospital; 'D.D.' for 'discharged dead', meaning that he had died or been killed. Or he could put 'R' for 'run' or deserted. True to his type, Lake put down 'R', and the *Recruit* sailed once again.

Lake was relieved of the command of the *Recruit* by Captain Charles Napier, who almost immediately distinguished himself in battle with the 18-gun French *Diligence*, tackled a 74-gun ship a few months after that in a confused action off The Saintes, and by January 1809 was distinguishing himself in the capture of Martinique.

Early next year reports began reaching London from Marble-head, across the Atlantic in Massachusetts, that a former British seaman in the Royal Navy, once marooned on Sombrero, was now working there as a blacksmith. The Admiralty, learning about the episode for the first time, acted very quickly – it promptly ordered Captain Lake to face a court martial, which assembled on board the *Gladiator* at Portsmouth on 5 February 1810, almost exactly two years after he had gone back to Sombrero and found it deserted.

In a trial lasting two days Lake was accused of marooning a seaman, and he admitted it, although he claimed that he 'thought the island was inhabited' – a claim proved untrue when he admitted that he had not recognised the island and had to get the details from his officers. The court heard the story only from Lake – Jeffery was still in Massachusetts – and the man condemned himself: he was found guilty and sentenced to be dismissed from the Navy, a sentence confirmed by the Admiralty.

In the meantime orders were crossing the Atlantic to send Jeffery home; general anger was expressed in Britain by people ranging from admirals' wives to Members of Parliament, some of whom were genuinely outraged and some looking for a cause to champion. Jeffery, now twenty-one years old, was taken up to Halifax, Nova Scotia, where the 10-gun schooner *Thistle* was waiting for him, and her captain, Lieutenant Peter Proctor, had orders to bring him at once to Portsmouth. By the time Jeffery arrived back in England, Lake had been a civilian for nearly six months, pointed out as a man who, but for what seemed a miracle, would have been a cold-blooded murderer.

The Admiralty questioned Jeffery and discovered that as soon as the *Recruit*'s sails dropped over the horizon he began looking for food and water on the bare and jagged rock. There were a few small pools of stagnant rainwater, but no food; he did not know that the spine-covered prickly pear cactus could be opened and eaten. He climbed down the almost sheer sides of the island and found limpets, which he managed to prise off and eat.

Occasionally he saw the sails of ships passing, but none came close: the unusual-shaped Sombrero was used as a landmark for ships from the Atlantic bound south to the Leeward or Windward Islands, or south-west through the Anegada Passage, one of the main entrances to the Caribbean. After seven days of living on limpets and lapping up water from the tiny rock pools, most of it brackish from spray, Jeffery was almost too weak to crawl; the sun had scorched his face and arms, the glare left him dazed. Finally, and almost unbelievably, on the ninth day he saw a schooner passing northwards and quite close. Frantic, he waved the handkerchiefs left him by Lieutenant Mould, and they were seen, the schooner sailing into the lee of the island and anchoring.

She was the *Adams*, of Marblehead, Massachusetts, and Jeffery was soon on board being fed and telling his story to the master, John Dennis, who agreed to take him to Marblehead, to which the *Adams* was bound. Once on American soil, with sympathetic ears to hear of his experiences, Jeffery set up as a blacksmith, but in time his story was printed in the local paper, and copied by others, until eventually it was heard by the British minister, who in turn reported it to London.

On 21 October 1810, exactly five years to the day after the Battle of Trafalgar, Jeffery arrived in London by coach and the next day he reported to the Admiralty, where he found himself telling his story to the Lords Commissioners. They at once ordered the removal of the 'R' put against his name by Lake, which meant that, apart from not being listed as a deserter, he was owed more than three years' accumulated pay (at £1 16s 6d a month). In addition, a group of friends of the former Captain Lake collected a sum of money for him, so he went back to Polperro a comparatively wealthy young man with a regular discharge in his pocket for good measure.

The cat of nine tails was a product of its times. To understand how it formed a part of the history of the Royal Navy it is necessary to view it through the eyes of society at the time it was used, otherwise any judgement is distorted because attitudes towards punishment change every decade. The author spent the whole of his school life in an atmosphere where any master could cane, and half of them did, yet when pupils were given the choice ('six whacks or a hundred lines') almost invariably they chose the 'whacks' rather than spend some of the evening copying out a hundred lines from a dull text-book.

With flogging, the seaman was given no choice, although it must be remembered that while his brother on land could be hanged for stealing a handkerchief from another's pocket a seaman could be hanged only for mutiny, treason or desertion. On land a man could be given long jail sentences for trivial offences – and put in jail for debt if his creditor felt so inclined. For most of the war, it was usual at Newgate jail for twenty prisoners to be kept day and night in a cell measuring twenty feet by fifteen. Many years after the war the Inspectors of Prisons called Newgate 'a monstrous place'.

For an offence bringing a seaman a dozen or so lashes, his brother on land might spend a year in jail or be transported for life. This did not ease the pain of a flogging, but it provides some much-needed perspective on discipline in the Navy, especially when it is remembered that many men avoided a few years in cramped cells by joining the Navy in the first place. That in turn conjures up a picture of jailbirds becoming seamen, which is true – except that often the jailbirds were not toughened criminals but men like sturdy poachers caught once again with a couple of brace of pheasants slung over their shoulders, or bricklayers celebrating on a Saturday night by tossing argumentative plasterers out of the inn and breaking furniture as well as the peace.

An agile young poacher soon made a good topman; a hefty brawler avoiding six months in jail by joining the Navy could become a handy focsleman; the nimble fingers of a pickpocket were better employed in one of the King's ships tucking in a splice than picking oakum at one of the King's jails.

The cat of nine tails used in the Navy was heavier than that used by the Army and the reason may have been that, up to 1806, the Regulations and Instructions laid down that a captain could not 'inflict any punishment beyond twelve lashes upon his bare back'. For any offence deserving more a seaman was supposed to be court-martialled. The regulation was largely ignored; captains noted in their journals that they had awarded more. One captain in

1795 recorded fifteen floggings in his journals in nine months – five of 12 lashes, seven of 24, one of 36, and two of 72 (for desertion). The journals went to the Admiralty, where they were inspected, but nothing was done, and it was in many cases an advantage to the seamen. In the case of the two men given 72 lashes each, the ship was in the West Indies, and bringing them to trial would delay the ship and require at least five captains to form the court. It might take several weeks to assemble the court, and during that time the men would be under arrest. But much more important was the fact that a court would certainly award a much heavier sentence – the 300 lashes for desertion awarded George Melvin, a seaman from the *Antelope*, was typical. As though recognising the advantage of speedy though probably lighter punishment, in 1806 the Admiralty lifted the limit on captains. The new Regulations and Instructions said only that a captain was never to order punishment 'without sufficient cause, nor ever with greater severity than the offence shall really deserve'.

The naval cat of nine tails was made in a traditional way. The handle was usually made of rope in wartime (sometimes, after the war, it was made of wood), about two feet long and an inch in diameter – the size of the average broom handle.

The nine tails were made of line a quarter of an inch in diameter and each, two feet long, was secured to the rope handle, usually by tucking three tails into each of the three strands of the rope and putting on a whipping or turk's head to secure them. Such a cat weighed thirteen or fourteen ounces.

There was a ritual attached to a flogging. A man was seldom flogged on the day that he was accused. He would be brought before the captain, his offence would be described, the details heard, and his guilt determined. If the captain sentenced the man to a flogging it would normally be set for the next day and a bosun's mate would start to make a new cat of nine tails.

The same cat was never used twice. The sight of the bosun's mate cutting up the lengths of rope and line, making the tucks and putting on the whippings, no doubt had its deterrent effect, and he finished the job by covering the handle with red baize and making a red baize bag, into which the cat was put until it was needed.

The tradition of carrying out the flogging the following day was a good one because it gave the captain time to reflect on the punishment. Lashes were usually awarded in dozens, although there is at least one case of eighteen being awarded: the *Niger*, Captain Edward Griffith on 26 December 1797, logged: 'Thomas Wright, seaman, was punished with eighteen lashes for plundering the prisoners' (from the French privateer *Delphine*, captured off Bolt Head on Christmas Day). Some captains awarded fewer than a dozen.

Curiously enough it was not the actual number of lashes that led to the worst mutiny in a single ship in the Royal Navy but the frequency of the floggings. When Captain Wilkinson commanded the *Hermione* he ordered 72 lashes for each of two men. At the same time Captain Pigot commanded the *Success* on the same station.

Wilkinson in nine months ordered fifteen floggings in the *Hermione* while Pigot, during the same nine months, ordered more than seventy in the *Success*. Only five of Wilkinson's fifteen were for a dozen. Pigot awarded only one of four dozen and one of three in his total; the majority were for a dozen lashes. Yet when the captains exchanged ships and Pigot started his more-frequent-but-fewer-lashes in the *Hermione* it was he who was murdered by his crew.

Part of the reason was the irrational nature of Pigot's punishment: if a man decided to get drunk on a Saturday night at sea by hoarding his tot, he expected to get a dozen lashes the following Monday: that was, in effect, the going rate. If a man deserted he knew he risked being hanged and would certainly get at least 300 lashes. But Pigot played havoc with these accepted values: he gave a man 36 lashes for desertion; nine days later another man was given only 24 for the same offence. Ten days later a man received only 12 lashes for desertion – and on the same day a man received 12 for disobedience. Thus he showed his men, on 12 March 1795, that disobedience and desertion were equal in his mind. A fortnight later he awarded one man 24 for mutiny, another 24 for disobedience, and three others 24 each for drunkenness. So the men saw they could mutiny and get only the same punishment as they would if they were found drunk. Then, a month later, a man who only attempted to desert was given the most lashes that Pigot had ever ordered, four dozen.

Pigot's inconsistent punishment meant that the men's sense of values was given a violent shock. Throughout the Navy some men regularly got drunk and were regularly punished; it was as though an agreement existed – being quietly drunk meant a dozen lashes, and many men thought it worth it. Men rarely deserted, though: they had seen men flogged through the fleet, with drums beating; they had seen the smoke of a gun disperse to show a deserter dangling from a noose at the yardarm. Except that suddenly, under the new captain in the *Hermione*, it was all jumbled together – drunkenness, desertion, disobeying a petty officer, behaving mutinously towards an officer – it brought a dozen or so on your back. Except that suddenly someone received four dozen lashes for *attempting* to desert, something for which several men who had lately been caught after initially *succeeding* received only a dozen.

Yet the Pigots and Lakes were rare; in more than twenty years of bitter war when Britain fought France at sea all the time, Spain most of the time, and America some of the time, the Navy threw up only half a dozen or so Pigots, an average of less than one every four years, at a time when there were always more than 500 ships at sea.

There were harsh captains, men who enforced strict discipline, but they were rarely unpopular among the men for the simple reason that with such captains they knew where they stood. A good example was Edward Hamilton, who won a knighthood when he cut out the *Hermione* and was then dismissed the service, as mentioned earlier, for seizing up men in the rigging. In the *Hermione* affair he had received a head wound which may have unbalanced him, because Admiral Jackson, who first served under Hamilton as a midshipman, wrote: 'I should be loth to say what my opinion of Sir Edward Hamilton might have become had I stopped much longer in the *Trent*. As each new day passed, so did I conceive new terrors of this man. A more uncompromising disciplinarian did not exist, or one less scrupulous in exacting the due fulfillment of his orders, whatever they were.'

Jackson wrote that, 'The *Trent*, I must admit, was in excellent order; indeed, as regards discipline and the general efficiency of her company, she was equal, if not superior, to any other frigate afloat; but those qualities had all been prompted at no small sacrifice of humanity. No sailor was allowed to walk from one place to another on deck, and woe betide an unfortunate fellow who halted in his run aloft.'

Yet Jackson's next captain was Robert Fanshawe, in the *Carysfort*, who 'increased his kindness by making me always write my journals in his cabin, where I could be overlooked and instructed'. Fanshawe was, incidentally, less than twenty-one years old at the time and Jackson sixteen. 'In addition to his abilities as a commander,' Jackson added, 'he possessed all the attributes of a gentleman and was deservedly esteemed. As regards the ship herself, we were also specially favoured, as she was believed to be the handsomest frigate yet built by English hands.'

Jackson's next captain, George Bettesworth, commanding the 14-gun *St Lucia*, was only twenty years old and, by the time he was killed in action three years later, had been wounded twenty-four times. He was, Jackson wrote, 'a kind and considerate man', but was replaced by a man whose name 'would soil the paper upon which it was written . . . low objectionable fellow, who would at one moment be cracking unseemly jokes with the least on board, and the next assuming the consequence of an admiral . . . a queer mixture of gun-room officer and a marine store dealer. Whenever he could he cheated the men of their rations right and left and did not hesitate to deprive them openly of their legal quantity when the meat was being weighed out.

'He was accordingly watched like a cat in the larder, and it was amusing to observe the men scrutinising his conduct at the scales. "Please, sir, take your thumb off the meat; you're pressing down the scales." '

Yet a rough and ready justice caught up with him: he had been challenged to a duel by Bettesworth and refused, and later challenged by another officer he had insulted. He again refused, and was regarded as a coward and ignored by all officers he met. Subsequently he learned that he was to be court-martialled for his peculations and shot himself.

Jackson's later captains were generally good – Captain Nairne 'was essentially a kind and considerate man to everyone under him'. Another left a mark on a hungry young midshipman because when inviting the 'young gentlemen' to breakfast he sent them away little heavier than when they sat down. Captain John Shortland in the *Junon* 'bore the character of an austere disciplinarian', but Jackson liked him.

Young Robert Hay's first captain was Cuthbert Collingwood in the *Culloden*. 'How attentive he was to the health and comfort and happiness of his crew! A man who could not be happy under him could have been happy nowhere; a look of displeasure from him was as bad as a dozen at the gangway from another man.'

The ceremony of a flogging began with the order for all hands to muster aft 'to witness punishment'. A heavy grating taken from one of the hatches was put up vertically at the gangway in some ships.

The officers in full uniform stood to one side, the marines lined up aft, and the prisoner was brought on deck with a guard of two marines or the master-at-arms and his corporals. The bosun's mates stood by, one of them holding the red baize bag containing the cat of nine tails.

Finally the captain came up on deck, bringing the slim volume of the Articles of War. Although the actual routine varied from ship to ship, he usually related the man's offence and, while all officers and men removed their hats, read out the particular Article of War that had been broken.

Quite frequently the Article was the thirty-sixth, generally known as the 'Captain's Cloak' because it covered any offence that an inventive seaman might contrive that was not covered in the previous thirty-five. 'All other crimes not capital,' it said, 'committed by any person or persons in the Fleet, which are not mentioned in this Act, or for which no punishment is hereby directed to be indicated, shall be punished according to the laws and customs in such cases used at sea.'

With the offence and article specified, the captain awarded the punishment. The man's shirt was stripped off and a leather apron tied round his waist, protecting the lower part of his back. The next order was 'seize him up', and the man was spreadeagled against the grating, his ankles and wrists being seized to it with pieces of spunyarn. In some ships a man was seized to a capstan bar. The bar protruded horizontally from the barrel of the capstan like the spoke of a huge cartwheel at the height of a man's chest, and his arms could be lashed along it. The bosun's mate then took the cat from the bag and, at the order, laid on a dozen lashes. If the punishment was more than a dozen, a second bosun's mate laid on the next dozen.

Captain Frederic Chamier describes how as a midshipman he saw his first flogging. 'The Captain gave the order "Give him a dozen". There was an awful stillness; I felt the flesh creep upon my bones, and I shivered and shook like a dog in a wet sack. All eyes were directed towards the prisoner, who looked over his shoulder at the preparations of the boatswain's mate to inflict the dozen: the latter drew his fingers through the tails of the cat, ultimately holding the nine ends in his left hand, as the right was raised to inflict the lash. They fell with a whizzing sound as they passed through the air, and left behind the reddened mark of sudden inflammation. . . .

'At the conclusion of the dozen I heard the unwilling order [from the captain], "Another boatswain's mate!" The fresh executioner pulled off his coat.' The prisoner had said nothing during the first dozen, but 'on the first cut of his new and merciless punisher, he writhed his back in acknowledgement of the pain; the second stripe was followed by a sigh; the third by an ejaculation; and the fourth produced an expression of a hope of pardon. At the conclusion of the dozen, this was granted, and the prisoner released.'

Because the cat was a standard weight and each blow was struck with roughly the same strength, 'the effect of a dozen lashes varied only with the type of victim; some men were more sensitive to pain; others had more pride, a sense of honour, which was damaged. Three dozen lashes could kill one man; another would survive 200. Probably the greatest indictment of indiscriminate flogging was that the number of lashes were ordered on the assumption that every man had the same kind of physique and personality, making no allowance for the sensitive man or the type who was by nature tough and brutal and who would be a criminal in any age or environment.'

The foregoing was written after experiments with an actual cat of nine tails weighing thirteen ounces, using pieces of wood lashed to a shipyard trestle. The first piece of wood was $\frac{1}{2}$-inch by 2-inch pitch-pine which was unsupported for only fifteen inches, and a man 5 feet 10 inches tall and weighing 152 lb broke it in half with a blow intended only to try out his stance. A second piece, $\frac{3}{4}$ inch by $\frac{3}{4}$ inch, free of knots, broke into three, and a third piece, 1 inch by 1 inch, broke in half at the second stroke. It was clear from these experiments that a man standing braced but unsupported would have been knocked down; a man lashed to a grating would be severely bruised.

The very few existing descriptions by men who experienced floggings are so different as to be almost contradictory. One man described it as 'Nothing but an O, a few O my Gods, and then you can put on your shirt'. But another man, a soldier flogged with the lighter Army cat, wrote that after the first two or three strokes 'The pain in my lungs was more severe, I thought, than on my back. I felt as if i would burst in the internal parts of my body.'

After two dozen lashes with a naval cat, according to one eye-witness, 'the lacerated back looks inhuman; it resembles roasted meat burnt nearly black before a scorching fire'.

A flogging through the Fleet as a spectacle approached something arranged by a Roman emperor, and could be ordered only by sentence of a court martial. A typical sentence was that on Marine John Briscow, of the *Diadem*, who was sentenced to receive '200 lashes from ship to ship, and to be imprisoned six months in the Marshalsea', while a seaman was later sentenced to 500 lashes and a year in the Marshalsea.

The Admiralty was of course much more concerned with the deterrent effect that such a flogging might have on others than the actual punishment for a particular man. At the time it was administered there would probably be ten ships of the line in the anchorage, quite apart from frigates and smaller vessels, so that 8,000 or more men would be watching from the ships of the line alone. As soon as the court's sentence was confirmed by the Admiralty the admiral gave orders to the captain of the flagship. The man concerned was usually held prisoner in the flagship, whose captain was told: 'You are hereby required and directed to hoist a yellow flag at the fore-topmasthead of his Majesty's ship under your command, and fire a gun at nine o'clock tomorrow morning, as a signal for the boats of the fleet to assemble alongside of his Majesty's ship ——, to attend the said punishment.'

The captains of all the other ships were ordered: 'When the signal for punishment is made tomorrow morning, you are to send a lieutenant with a boat manned and armed from the ship under your command to his Majesty's ship ——, in order to attend the punishment.'

The total number of lashes was divided by the number of ships present, and if they did not make an even number the extra were always given alongside the man's own ship, whose captain was told officially of the man's punishment, the court 'having sentenced him to receive —— lashes on his bare back, with a cat-of-nine tails, alongside such of his Majesty's ships and vessels at this port.'

The order added that 'You are hereby required and directed, when the signal is made for that purpose on board the [flagship] tomorrow morning . . . to cause one of your lieutenants of the ship you command to attend and see the said sentence put in execution, by the said [prisoner] receiving —— lashes alongside such of his Majesty's ships named in the margin.'

It was unlikely that the whole sentence could be carried out in one day, and another order to the captain of the prisoner's ship from the admiral said that 'as I would not have more of the said punishment inflicted upon him at one time than he is able to bear, and as the lieutenant may not be a proper judge of the prisoner's case, you are hereby required and directed to cause the surgeon of [your] ship to attend in the boat with the lieutenant for that purpose, as well as one of his mates, in the long boat, with the prisoner, and you are to give the lieutenant directions to stop the punishment until further orders when the surgeon shall give it as his opinion that he cannot bear any more with safety, and return on board with the prisoner.'

That did not mean that the rest of the sentence would be forgotten: the man would be kept in the care of the surgeon until he was recovered enough to have the remainder, and was technically still the prisoner of the provost marshal, who had also been ordered to attend the punishment. He was told 'to read publicly the copy of the sentence . . . alongside each ship respectively; and when the said prisoner shall have received the whole of the punishment adjudged him, you are to release and deliver him to the Commanding Officer of the ——.'

When the punishment day came, and the yellow flag was hoisted on board the flagship and a gun fired, the boats from all the ships headed for the flagship, looking like a swarm of water beetles. The flagship's boat was ready: a grating was already rigged up, tripod fashion, and as soon as the time approached for the punishment to begin marines climbed down into the boat and with them was a drummer, his drum usually covered with a piece of black cloth to muffle it. The prisoner was brought down, followed by the lieutenant, surgeon and surgeon's mate of his own ship, the provost marshal, and one of the bosun's mates of the flagship, carrying a red baize bag containing the cat.

By now at least a couple of dozen boats would be surrounding the flagship, and at the set time the flagship's captain shouted down to the provost marshal to read out the sentence, and as soon as this was done, ordered the punishment to begin. Once the flagship's share of the lashes had been laid on, the man would be given a blanket to cover himself and the boat would be cast off, to be rowed to the next ship.

The drummer standing in the bow would begin the slow steady beat of the Rogue's March, and the rest of the boats would join up astern in a long column. At the next ship the crew would already be mustered – some admirals insisted they manned the rigging – and as soon as the flagship's boat arrived alongside it was secured and the provost marshal read out the sentence once again. The captain would then order one of his own bosun's mates down into the boat to lay on his ship's share of the lashes, and as soon as this was done the provost marshal ordered the boat to proceed to the third ship on his list.

The steady thumping of a drum carries a considerable distance across water, and the leading boat was always very obvious because of the bright coats of the marines and the tripod of the grating, quite apart from all the boats following astern. The ships were always some distance apart, and the long row between them gave the prisoner a little time to recover. William Spavens records how he saw one such flogging, when the sentence of 600 lashes was carried out at the rate of 200 lashes at a time, once a fortnight. 'We attended there through the process of the first day,' he wrote, 'when one of our Marines on guard in the bow of the boat fell asleep and lost the bayonet off the mizzle [*sic*] of his piece, and narrowly escaped getting a dozen for his offence.'

The men's attitude towards flogging was that it was often necessary and it is significant that in the Great Mutiny flogging was not mentioned once in the mutineers' list of complaints and demands. Even while the fleet at the Nore and Spithead were under the command of the mutineers, they ordered floggings.

Captain Glascock noted that the mutineers 'still felt it necessary to maintain the discipline of the service on board, in the same way they had been accustomed to see it preserved under the old regime; and during the period of the mutiny there were repeated instances of severer corporal punishment on board the two fleets than would have taken place for similar offences under the then existing regulations, severe as it must be acknowledged those regulations comparatively were.'

There seems little reason to argue with Captain Francis Liardet, who wrote: 'The best conducted seamen in the Navy will now candidly tell you that in ships where the cat is not used on proper occasions, that they are the most uncomfortable vessels to sail in, as the willing and hard-working men do the work of the lazy ones.'

Captain Chamier, against too much flogging but seeing no other way of maintaining discipline with the Navy as it was, wrote: 'I have known a man faint before he was seized up; but, although I have seen four hundred lashes applied, and at each dozen a fresh boatswain's mate, yet I never knew a man who died of the punishment in my life. I speak of this merely to mention that naval punishments, although unquestionably severe, and by no means pleasant either to order or to receive, are not of the dreadful, merciless, flagitious order so frequently asserted.'

Linstock and match

CHAPTER SIXTEEN

The Prize Money

While one of the King's ships was at sea the men always had a chance of prize money. Avid readers of the *London Gazette* would see items like:

> *Resource and Mermaid.* The head money for the *Gen. Laveau*, French privateer, taken Dec 4, 1796, paid Nov 29 by Mess. Poulain and Keys, Salter's Hall Court, [Cannon Street], London. Recall same place every Monday and Thursday. . . .
>
> *Anson and La Nymphe.* The bounty money for the *Daphne*, French national corvette, and for the *Hazard* and *Avanture*, French privateer, taken Dec, 1797, paid on board the *Anson*; and that for the *Legere*, taken Feb, 1797, paid on board the *Anson* and *La Nymphe*, Nov 28, 1798. . . .
>
> *Royal George, Atlas, Mars, Saturn, Revolutionaire* and *La Nymphe*. A distribution of the proceeds of the hull and stores of the *Hercule*, taken by the *Mars*, April 21, 1798; paid on board the above ships as they arrive in port. . . .
>
> *La Raison.* A remittance from Antigua, on account of the capture of the *St Anne* (alias *St Dalgo*), Spanish brig, paid at the White Lion, Wych Street, London, Dec 15. . . .

Thirteen ships were to share in 'the proportion of the Navy', £40,000, for 'the reduction of the island Trinidada &c, Feb 17 & 18, 1797', while the *Melpomene*'s crew had money due to them from 'the salvage of the *Eliza*, American ship, and the bounty money for the *Triton*'.

These advertisements were inserted by prize agents, who by law had to publish the date when money would be paid out and also be ready to pay late arrivals – hence the mention of 'recall days' – and who took 5 per cent.

Although the seamen loosely referred to it all as 'prize money', in fact the capture of an enemy ship belonging to the French Navy (referred to as a 'French national ship') could yield head and prize money, which was shared according to a traditional scale.

Head, bounty (not to be confused with the bounty paid for joining the Navy) and gun money were the same thing, a payment for capturing an enemy warship. In the days when it was called 'bounty money' it was a payment of 'ten pounds a gun', to be shared among the captors. This was so little (barely £1 a man when one 74-gun ship captured another) that it was later changed to 'five pounds a head', counting every man in the muster book of the enemy ship, which would have meant a payment of £4 a man for the same ships. In the meantime some prize agents referred to it in their announcements as bounty money, but others used the more popular and official 'head money', and by half-way through the war it was generally known as 'head and gun money'. The Regulations and Instructions of 1808 laid down that it was paid only on men who were alive on board the enemy ship when the action began, and captors needed a copy of the 'sentence of condemnation' and a certificate of the men (excluding passengers) on board.

The prize money yielded by a captured ship depended on whether she was a warship or a merchant ship, because the money came from different sources. If the *Alpha* frigate, for instance, captured the French frigate *Beta* in January 1801 and took her in to, say, Jamaica, she then had to be surveyed and an inventory made of everything on board. In a place like Jamaica where, unlike Plymouth, Portsmouth and Chatham, King's ships were not built, the survey would be carried out by the master shipwright, Mr Henry Fishley, whose wage was £200 a year, with £30 extra for rent, and the master attendant, Alfred Wylie, who received the same pay. For the survey of the ship they would be assisted by the carpenters of two or three of the largest ships present – certainly from the flagship – and once they had checked over the hull and valued it (with allowances for any necessary repairs) they would be joined by the muster-master and storekeeper, Mr John Dick.

They would then list and value everything on board, ranging from sails to anchors, guns to watch glasses, roundshot to copper kettles. The survey report on the hull, masts and spars, and the inventory and valuations, would then be delivered to the Commander-in-Chief, with a suggested price for the ship based on her tonnage.

The Commander-in-Chief would then have to decide whether or not to buy the ship on behalf of the Admiralty (who had eventually to approve the transaction) and the total price. At this time a frigate was worth about £14 a ton, and a 32-gun frigate would total about 750 tons.

Her equipment would comprise hundreds of items and the values would be based on the prices *in Jamaica*. These were the prices charged to merchant ships wanting to buy anything from the naval store, which in turn was usually the price in England plus 60 per cent. Watch glasses (hour and four-hour glasses) would be listed at 2d each; a copper kettle in the galley, used for boiling the bags of meat or puddings, at about £12, which would also be about the price of a maintopgallant sail.

The actual valuations made for a particular captured frigate at this period were £10,038 for the 'hull, masts, yards, booms, rigging and fitted furniture', and £6,057 for the equipment, making a total of £16,095 prize money paid for the ship (providing the Admiralty, in consultation with the Navy Board, approved the prices).

Capturing an enemy merchant ship was a vastly different thing and financially much more dangerous for the captain because he had to produce bills of lading, charter parties and various other documents to get the ship and her cargo 'condemned' by an Admiralty court, a process which put money into the pockets of unscrupulous proctors and lawyers, who hung round courthouses like pimps and crimps lurking on the jetties. Providing ship and cargo were enemy-owned, all was well; but if the master, owners or shippers could prove that the ship was neutral they could – and usually did – sue the Royal Navy captain for damages, which he had to pay out of his own pocket.

Whereas 'head and gun money' was payment divided equally between every man on board the captor, prize money was shared out in a manner which in these more egalitarian days seems both scandalous and startling in its unfairness, although it should be recorded that at the time there was no great outcry.

The total prize money was divided into eighths and then shared out so that the admiral commanding the station or fleet received one-eighth and the captain of the ship two-eighths. The lieutenants, master, surgeon and Marine captain shared an eighth; the principal warrant officers, master's mates, chaplain and admiral's secretary had an eighth; midshipmen, inferior warrant officers, mates of principal warrant officers and Marine sergeants had an eighth, while the rest of the ship's company shared two-eighths. (This scale was changed in 1808, reducing the admiral's and captain's share.)

All of this meant that the admiral received £2,000 from the capture of the *Beta* frigate and the captain £4,000. There was £285 each for the four lieutenants, master, surgeon and Marine captain, while the next group's share could vary, but would be £222 if there were the boatswain, carpenter, gunner, admiral's secretary, and four master's mates (it was unlikely that a frigate carried a chaplain). The next group received well under £100 each, while there was £4,000 left to be shared among the remaining ship's company which, at this stage of the war, was unlikely to number more than 125, so they would receive £32 each.

The best way of assessing the value of such a prize payment is knowing that the capture of an enemy 32-gun frigate in good condition in the year 1801 was equal to more than thirty-five years' pay for the captain, four years for the lieutenants and master, and just under a year and a half for each able and ordinary seaman.

On top of that came the 'head and gun money', and because such an enemy frigate would have about 250 men on board each member of the ship's company would have more than £5.

These figures show that the man who became rich from prize money was the admiral, whose role usually was, on stations like the West Indies, making sure that his frigates were patrolling areas most likely to yield prizes. Sir Hyde Parker as Commander-in-Chief at Jamaica in the four years referred to earlier was reputed to have made £200,000. But, although a few admirals and captains made a great deal of money from prizes, it is important to remember they were the exception.

Prizes brought out the worst in men, whether the prize crew bringing in the ship, the proctor, the agent or, in all too many cases, the judges of the prize court, but the Regulations tried to cut down the pilferage and peculation at the beginning.

'Prizes are not to be broke open, but the hatches are immediately to be spiked up, and her lading and furniture secured from imbezzlement, until condemn'd in the Admiralty Court,' William Mountaine warned in *The Seaman's Vade-Mecum*. He added: 'When a privateer is taken, great care must be had to secure the ship's papers, the Commission especially; for if no legal commission be found, they are to be committed as pirates.'

The share-out of the prize money could be affected by the circumstances of the capture. Obviously, if a second ship helped take the prize she shared, but so did any ship of war that was in sight, even though she did not fire a shot – indeed, might have been almost hull down over the horizon at the time. Being in sight was what mattered, because an enemy ship may have surrendered to one ship because, with another – perhaps several – in sight she knew that flight was impossible, or the appearance of another ship to windward or leeward showed that she could not escape. The second vessel thus contributed to the capture, and deserved a share.

A captain only gave up an eighth of his share to his admiral when he was in fact sailing 'under the command of a flag', in other words was attached to a particular admiral or station. But a captain sailing under Admiralty orders – a frigate taking orders to a distant admiral and then due to return to England, for example – did not have to share: her captain had three-eighths.

Prize money made some admirals both greedy and litigious, and to avoid any misunderstandings the Instructions laid down that an admiral sent out to command a distant station 'shall have no rights to any share or prizes taken by ships employed there before he arrives within the limits of his command' – nor, when he returned home, was he entitled to any share 'after he has got out of the limits of his command'.

The dream of prize agents was to receive the money for a rich prize and then, because of some technicality, avoid having to pay it out for many months, and sometimes many years, so that the sum could be drawing interest. In the case of the *Magicienne*, because her captain, Ricketts, was drowned in 1805, the prize money for several captures made in 1796–8 was not paid out until 1826, so the agents drew more than twenty-eight years' interest.

The gossips and press delighted in exaggerating the amount of prize money, and an open letter by 'A Post Captain' addressed to the First Lord of the Admiralty in 1811 complained that the system did nothing but 'fatten the parasites of the admiralty court, together with the agents'.

He cited a case 'when the *Valiant* captured the French frigate *Commerce* . . . which ship netted £60,000, it was asserted in various newspapers that she had specie on board to the amount of upwards of a million sterling; and recently it has been stated that Admiral Bertie, General Abercrombie and Commodore Rowley . . . will receive £200,000 each.' He pointed out that for them to receive £200,000 each, the prize would have to amount of £7,200,000. He added ironically that the captors would have been only too delighted to receive a total of £200,000 for the capture (instead of £60,000) because, with head money, it would have yielded the three officers £5,550 11s 5d.

Convoys were hated by the men that sailed in them, whether they were in merchant ships or the escorts, but they were necessary and ships sailing alone (called 'runners') usually had to pay much higher insurance premiums and needed a licence from the Admiralty. The captains of merchant ships and the captains of ships of war had completely different objectives and training, so all too often the great convoys sailing to and from England – some of the West Indies convoys comprised up to 150 ships of various sizes – quarrelled their way across the Western Ocean.

The captain of a merchant ship, then as now, was required by his owners to transport a cargo from one place to another as cheaply as possible. Time was usually of little consequence except in peacetime, where occasionally there was need for haste to catch the market. All this entailed sailing with as small a crew as possible, feeding them the lowest quality of food they were likely to accept and paying the lowest possible wages (but still appreciably above the Royal Navy rates in order to attract the men who had only to set foot on board to risk being seized by the press gang).

The need to save money by having a small crew suited the masters well because, to save risking extra wear and tear on canvas on being caught in the darkness by a squall, it was customary to reduce sail at night, jogging along under reduced canvas. This was such a habit that it was done by most merchant ships even when it was almost calm and the weather was obviously set fair.

With the exception of the ships of the Honourable East India Company, known familiarly as 'John Company', most merchant ships were, then, in no hurry. By contrast, from the day he first went to sea, the Royal Navy officer was trained to make the fastest possible passage – most Admiralty orders to captains included the phrase 'You will make the best of your way.' And except in unusual conditions (when half the ship's company was down with scurvy, for instance) there were always enough well trained men to reef or furl any sail on the windiest night.

It was by no means uncommon for a couple of frigates to be the sole escort for a hundred merchant ships. Convoys usually sailed for particular destinations at set times of the year – in the days of sail due attention had to be paid to weather and seasons. West Indies convoys normally left England four times a year to arrive in Barbados in December, February, April and June, the aim being to avoid arriving or leaving during the main hurricane months, August and September. After July the insurance rates doubled; ordinary policies said that ships must sail from West Indies ports by August.

The actual dates the convoys left England were arranged by the Admiralty, dealing with a committee of shipowners and traders, who received the correspondence and met at Lloyd's Coffee House. The majority of the ships were 'established', chartered by merchants to go out in a convoy to collect a specified cargo, usually sugar or molasses from a named planter in the case of the West Indies. Other ships were 'seekers', in effect tramp ships going out with or without cargoes and bargaining with merchants for a homeward freight.

The ships were usually between 200 and 500 tons; in 1808 they averaged 298 tons. But ships as small as twenty registered tons were not unknown. The routes that convoys took were well established, governed as much by the prevailing winds as the whims of captains and the orders of the Admiralty. Convoys to the West Indies usually arrived at Barbados, splitting up so that the Leeward Islands ships went off north and the Jamaica ones sailed on across the Caribbean. The Windward and Leeward Islands convoy usually left the Caribbean for England from Tortola, in the Virgin Islands, while the Jamaica convoy went out the Windward Passage between Cuba and Hispaniola.

Convoys took an average of nine weeks from the Channel to Barbados (about the same time as surface mail in the late 1970s), with ships from London, the Solent, Bristol, Liverpool and Glasgow meeting at Cork by a certain date, where they sailed as a single convoy.

The most vivid descriptions of convoy escort work comes from Captain (later Admiral Sir) Thomas Pasley while commanding the 20-gun *Glasgow* and then the 28-gun *Sybil*. A typical convoy left Jamaica in August, escorted by the *Glasgow* and the sloop *Chameleon*, with another sloop going as far as 32° North (i.e. near Bermuda).

There were forty-seven merchant ships and on the first day Pasley 'found some horrid dull goers, owing to their being uncommonly deep loaded. The freight of suggars [*sic*] being high, a cursed rage for money put prudence out of the question with many of them.' After the second day the convoy was at sea Pasley recorded that he was 'obliged to lie-to near three hours this evening to allow the rear of the fleet to join me, tho' I had during the day carried only two topsails'.

On the fifth day out he was commenting sourly that 'there are such heavy sailers in the fleet that we make but poor way of it – 20 leagues (sixty miles) a day will not run down our thousands these twelve weeks and more'.

A few days later the convoy was joined by the *Royal George* from Montego Bay, 'an old India ship' which had sprung a leak the day before sailing. She 'took part of her suggars [*sic*] out, stop'd it the best way she could and pushed after the convoy, which nothing but 8 days of calms and light winds from the S.W. (never known before in those seas) would have given her the smallest chance of joining. Providence seems to have been interested in the preservation of the people's lives on board her, it being my opinion that ere she gets half way home, if the weather prove the least boisterous, she will go down with them – as all the old India ships hired by government have done.'

The seamen in the escorting warships hated convoy work because they were forever making or reducing sail, or tacking or wearing in the constant task of chasing ships back into position as they began to drop astern or sag off to leeward. A long and tedious passage meant scurvy for certain and probably reduced rations. There was no chance of prize money and almost none of any excitement; the sight of ships all round the horizon and all going slowly in the same direction is boring in any century.

After three weeks, a sorely tried Pasley noted that at daylight nearly fifty ships were out of position. 'How can I pretend to answer for the safety of ships commanded by such a set of mules? Thus is a captain of a man-of-war's character sported away, who happens to have the misfortune to command a convoy. Not one of those vessels ahead (if taken) . . . but their captains would swear that it was in consequence of the *Glasgow*'s having left them.'

Next day the straggling was even worse, but he 'resolved in future not to fret or teize [*sic*: tease] myself with their bad conduct'. A day later he signalled to a ship 'but the dam'd mule her captain' ignored him for hours, and the following day he commented that 'surely I should be justified by God and man for leaving this said rascal'.

Pasley had taken a small tender with him – this he had used in the Caribbean – and two days later she lost her masts and was taken in tow by the *John* of Liverpool, which brought her up to the *Glasgow*, an attention Pasley admitted 'I never should have expected from a Liverpool man'.

The *Glasgow*'s carpenter and his mates were soon busy with spare masts and spars, and Pasley noted for 26 August, 'masted the tender again, though they were about 9 or 10 feet shorter than the former ones, found she could with her reefed sails run round the fleet'.

After a few days free of trouble ('I daily rise with a heart full of grateful adoration to the wise disposer of all things'), September began with a hail from the *Catharine*, 'a mutiny being on board'. That was sorted out and nine days' bad weather followed, and on the 10th he saw a brig in distress. She was the *Catharine* with topmasts and sails lost, so he ordered the *Chameleon* to take her in tow while helping with repairs.

After a few days of hard gales he was surprised and pleased that on 19 September 'our whole number still in company', but very soon the *Mary Agnus* and another Bristol ship made signals of distress. The *Mary Agnus*, of but fifteen tons and suitable only for coastal trading, 'was leaking and sinking for want of men to pump her, two being sick; himself [the master], mate, one man and boy, being all remaining and [needing] both pumps kept going. N.B. – this fellow came out so badly man'd that at Bluefields [Jamaica] he applied to me for men to weigh his anchor; I think him a rascal but could not see him sink – therefore gave him four men.'

Pasley's last entry about this convoy concerned his own ship. He had seen the Dublin, Liverpool and Glasgow ships leave to go north through the St George's Channel, followed by the Bristol ones, and had only a dozen left, for London, Hull and Leith. They anchored in St Mary's Sound, in the Scilly Isles, and then weighed on 20 October for the last leg of the voyage, which had began on 1 August.

'At $\frac{1}{4}$ past 4 our stupid rascal of a pilot run the ship's stern upon the Crow Rock, the ship then going 4 or 5 knots through the water. She tumbled immediately down on her beam ends; but as this Rock was steep-to all round, by backing our sails in ten minutes we were off again. The shock was so great that it broke several bottles in one of my cases of rum; what damage she has received I cannot ascertain. She makes now four times the quantity of water, that is 18 inches every hour. . . . I hope we shall be able without further disaster to bundle the old bitch into one King's Port or other; then farewell, *Glasgow*!'

The Admiralty's instructions concerning convoys acknowledged that the masters of merchant ships were a law unto themselves. If a master misbehaved himself by delaying the convoy or leaving it, or disobeying instructions, the commander of the convoy escort 'is to report him, with a narration of the fact, to the Secretary of the Admiralty'. But the only thing the Secretary could do was write to the owners or complain to the committee at Lloyd's representing all the shipowners sailing their ships to the West Indies. The captains of the King's ships knew it was useless to lodge a complaint and most of them took matters into their own hands. William Richardson reported some incidents at the time the *Prompte* was escorting a convoy across the Atlantic. After a near-collision with a merchant ship and an exchange of insults, 'our captain then told him to heave to, and seeing he would not, we sheered close up alongside of him, beat to quarters, and got the guns ready to sink him; but the mate of the ship, fearing the consequences, ran to the wheel and brought the ship to.

'We then sent a lieutenant in the jolly-boat to bring her captain on board; but he judging their intent, ran to the cookhouse, seized the cook's axe, and swore he would split the first man's head in two who dared to take hold of him.'

The *Prompte*'s captain then sent over the pinnace with a party of marines, and they brought the master back – 'a dark-looking, daring fellow, and not the least humbled'. Finally the *Prompte*'s captain took the man over to the Commodore's ship, where the merchant ship's master was reprimanded 'and cautioned for the future'.

A few days later he described 'a Scotch brig which sailed so badly that she, being always astern, detained the whole fleet very much. One day, she being so far astern, our signal was made to tow her up to the fleet, and when we got a good hawser made fast to her bows, we set steering-sails alow and aloft and dragged her bows under; she lost the use of her helm, and nothing but the tow rope kept [her] end on.

'They were so alarmed on board her that they hailed us to cast her off, and would have done that themselves, but could not get at the tow rope for the rush of water over her fo'c'sle. When we got her ahead of the fleet we cast her off, but she had got such a twisting that she wanted no more towing during the passage.'

James Gardner, serving in the *Gorgon* and escorting a convoy from the Mediterranean to England, said that 'our admiral [Cosby] was a glorious fellow for keeping the convoy in order, and if they did not immediately obey the signal, he would fire at them without further ceremony'.

Some captains brought trouble on themselves for bullying the masters. Richardson's ship was part of a squadron which 'saw a ship to windward steering towards us in a very wild manner'. When it was discovered that she was a homeward-bound merchant ship which had lost her rudder and mizen topmast, Lord William Fitzroy of the *Macedonia* was ordered to tow her to Lisbon.

'But when she arrived near the place the wind headed them, and the two ships got foul of each other, and when they got clear his lordship took all the people out [of her] and set her on fire, and this valuable ship and cargo were totally destroyed. We heard afterwards that his lordship had to pay the underwriters the whole value of the ship and cargo, which served him right. But this was not all, for when the ships were foul of each other he abused his [the *Macedonia*'s] master and put him in irons, for which he was tried by court martial at Lisbon and dismissed the service.'

Match tub

CHAPTER SEVENTEEN

Rough Justice

The system by which a seaman or officer was court-martialled had much in common with an errant man brought before the elders of his tribe, who dispensed justice not from written precedents but on the basis of how it seemed to them.

All that the Admiralty had to say on the subject was represented by sixteen paragraphs in the Regulations, which began by citing the Act of Parliament under which they were held. Before 1808 this said that a court was to assemble in the mornings, and ended: 'Every matter in the court is to be determined by a majority of voices; the youngest officer to vote first, and so proceed up to the president.' After 1808 the morning rule was dropped.

A court martial needed at least five post captains, a copy of the Articles of War, a Bible, and pen, paper and ink for the deputy judge advocate to keep the record. It did not need any legal books describing procedures or precedents, nor were there any useful books on court-martial law and precedent until 1813, when John McArthur, who had been secretary to Admiral Lord Hood, wrote two volumes called *Principle and Practice of Naval and Military Courts Martial*.

Yet even McArthur did not help in some cases. 'Officers of the Navy have a very limited knowledge of the law of evidence,' wrote Frederic Chamier long after the war, 'so little indeed that I recollect a doubt having arisen from the president of the court if he could call the prosecutor as evidence against the prisoner. Even when McArthur was shown him on the subject, he took the opinion of the court.'

Chamier asked that 'a short essay on the law of evidence' should be issued to captains and commanders, and pointed out that much time would be saved by the appointment of shorthand writers in the major ports – 'the consequence would be that the work of ten days might be done in two'.

The reason for this was that everything had to be written down in longhand: the prosecutor's question had to be copied into the rough record, then the prisoner's answer. Chamier noted that if the accused man 'is inclined to equivocate, he has sufficient time to form a guarded answer: he hears the question put to the judge advocate first, it is then written down, and then generally read to the captain asking the question to ascertain that it is correctly given, and then it is at last offered to the evidence [*sic*: the accused] . . . surely this is a waste of time, patience and breath – and which gives the evidence about five minutes between each question to arrange his answer. Now, we all know very well that in cross-examination of a suspicious witness, the rapidity of the questions generally confuses the man who is not on the firm basis of truth; whereas if you allow that man five minutes to collect himself – if he has a good memory, as liars always should have – he will bother the court, rather than the court should bother him.'

One of the worst aspects of courts martial in wartime was the need for at least five captains to form the court: at times this meant that a trial had to wait weeks before enough ships were present; often it meant that ships were then delayed in sailing.

Chamier recorded going into Jamaica to find that 'a certain captain had about a dozen courts-martial in store for us on our arrival in the hot bed of yellow fever'. The whole squadron was delayed more than three months and several ships had bad outbreaks of yellow fever, that in the *Scylla* occurring the day she sailed, killing the captain, one lieutenant, three surgeons, four midshipmen and about forty seamen.

There were certain traditions about trials. For example, all the members put on their hats while the sentence was read, and when an officer was to be tried on a serious charge he surrendered his sword. When he was brought into the cabin to hear the court's verdict, some presidents had the sword lying on the table, the hilt towards the man if he had been cleared, and the point if guilty.

The Admiralty's court-martial indexes give an interesting postscript to the great mutinies at the Nore and Spithead in 1797: the trials for mutiny for the first nine months of 1798 show eighty-nine accused of mutiny – including twenty-five from the *Defiance* and twenty-two from the *Caesar* – with twenty-five hanged. Thirteen others were sentenced to death but reprieved. The most lashes ordered were for four men who received 500 each, one with 400, three 300, five 200 and one 150. One of the eighty-nine was a lieutenant of the *Dordrecht* at the Nore, who was dismissed the service for making mutinous speeches. Four seamen in the *Renommée* in the West Indies were included – they tried to persuade their shipmates to follow the *Hermione* frigate, killing their officers and sailing the ship to an enemy port on the Main. Three were hanged and the fourth imprisoned for thirteen months.

Whenever there was a particularly important trial, it was customary afterwards to have posters printed giving the sentence, and these would be pasted up in various countries. When some of the mutineers from the *Hermione* were tried, the Commander-in-Chief, Sir Hyde Parker, had the printer make such posters, and copies were sent out.

Beginning with 'At a Court Martial' in bold type, it went on to list the four men accused of being 'part of the crew of the French privateer *La Magicienne* . . . and also part of the crew of his Majesty's said ship *Hermione* and were actually on board . . . at the time the Mutiny, Murders and Piracy were committed'. They were also charged with 'being taken in arms against his Majesty'.

The sentence was that they were 'to be hung by their necks until they are dead, at the yard arms of such of his Majesty's ships . . . as shall be directed by the Commander-in-Chief'. However, Sir Hyde had a much grimmer warning for the seamen entering and leaving Port Royal, as the posters announced: 'And as a further example to deter others from committing, or being an accessory to such shocking and atrocious crimes; that when dead, their bodies be hung in chains upon gibbets on such conspicuous points, or headlands, as the commander-in-chief shall direct. And they are hereby sentenced to be so hung until they are dead, and their bodies gibbetted accordingly.'

The captains forming the courts were lucky because until a few years earlier, once the trial had began, the captains had to stay on board and not leave for any reason until the sentence was given. This was not changed until the twelve officers forming the trial of Admiral Keppel wrote to the Admiralty on 11 February 1779, that 'Having now been in confinement six and thirty days since we first assembled' they could not see why they should be made to suffer 'so severe a hardship' which they could not conceive to be necessary.

In most courts martial, the punishment was already set out in the thirty-six Articles of War. Numbers 3, 10, 12, 13, 15, 25, 28 and 29 laid down that anyone found guilty 'shall suffer death'. The court had no option in these eight articles, but 2, 4, 5, 6, 7, 8, 9, 11, 14, 17, 19, 20, 21, 22, 23, 24, 26, 27, 30 and 32 gave the court discretion. Articles 16, 18, 31 and 33 said that a guilty officer should be cashiered. The majority of the Articles of War were in fact aimed at officers, but they also ranged in scope from relieving 'an enemy or rebel' to using 'profane oaths, cursings, execrations'; from robbing a prize, deserting to the enemy, making a mutinous assembly, or committing the 'detestable sin of buggery or sodomy with man or beast' to sleeping on watch.

The main role of the captains forming the court was therefore acting as a jury: listening to the evidence and deciding whether or not a man was guilty. In the few cases where they had to decide on the sentence, they were supposed to act 'according to the nature and degree' of the offence 'or according to the laws and customs in such cases used at sea'. A court martial was a lay court; unless it sat at one of the main ports, where a judge advocate was available, no one forming the court had any legal training because the deputy judge advocate was usually someone like a purser, or a flag officer's secretary.

Despite – or because of – the lack of legal training, courts martial were rarely unjust. By modern standards some of the sentences they passed seem harsh, but not by the standards of the days in which they sat. The captains, being practical men who understood far better than anyone else the problems facing both seamen and officers in the King's ships, paid more attention to the spirit than to the letter of the law.

Some courts martial explained the need for much of the form-filling that took up a great deal of people's time, and also revealed something of conditions. Lieutenant William William Walker, commanding the *Sparkler*, was court-martialled on board the *Gladiator* at Portsmouth on 1 July 1800, on a variety of charges that he put other people's provisions and money in his pocket. He was accused of having entered the name of his own son, aged one year, in the muster book as William Walker, rated him able seaman, and answered for him at musters. Whenever asked about him, Walker said he was on shore duty. Not content with his illicit £1 4s a month, he told one of the seamen on board the *Sparkler* to assume the name of William Walker and sent him to receive the £5 bounty in Portsmouth. By now £5 better off and drawing his son's £1 4s a month, Lieutenant Walker did not put 'R' against the name of any of the *Sparkler*'s men who deserted; instead he answered for them as though they were still on board and drew their pay too. He 'shortened' the issue of provisions on board for the ship's company 'and drew it on shore for the use of his own table'. He sent salt herring on board the *Sparkler* and sold it to the hungry crew 'without a vegetable of any species'. In addition he drew full provisions for fifty men, a dangerous greediness because it was more than the complement of the ship. The charges were proved 'in part' and Lieutenant William William Walker was cashiered, and his place as the accused was taken next day in the *Gladiator* by John Duncan, a seaman charged with being a mutineer in the *Hermione*, an episode which had happened nearly three years earlier.

The Navy Board were particularly careful about pay frauds, and this was one of the reasons why a copy of the muster book had to be sent in every two months. There were only four legal ways of disposing of Navy goods: consume them, survey them (after which they could be condemned), lose them in a shipwreck, or have them destroyed in battle. However, man's ingenuity devised many variations on the fifth way, fraud. There were the comparatively minor examples of captains juggling with the muster books and drawing pay for men who had actually deserted, pursers serving short measure, and masters and other warrant officers certifying as destroyed in battle items which could be sold on shore.

Although it was difficult to defraud the Navy at the lower levels it was not impossible. Rope could have a coloured thread laid up in it, the 'Rogue's Yarn', to make it harder to sell to an unscrupulous master of a merchant ship, but rigging was almost always painted to preserve it, and a lick of Stockholm tar hid the yarn. Likewise, canvas used for the sails of ships of war had a coloured thread woven in – but many merchant ships gave their sails a coat or two of cutch tan, a mixture of linseed oil and red ochre, which preserved the flax, made it waterproof – and blotted out the thread.

The main frauds took place on land and were on a comparatively large scale. Enormous quantities of timber were needed for building and repairing ships, and most of it was bought from private contractors who, honesty apart, could and did create shortages to force up prices. Suppliers of salt meat were generous with their bribes when it came to securing Navy Board contracts, and so were the people seeking contracts for the scores of things needed to keep the King's ships at sea.

The men they dealt with were, for the most part, ill paid clerks whose salaries had probably been set in the first place on the assumption that bribes would make them up to a respectable figure. The Navy Office dealt with most of the contracts, and the officer in charge was the Comptroller, Sir Andrew Snape Hamond, a man who by the middle of the war had accumulated considerable wealth and influence, and was the Member of Parliament for Ipswich. There was a Commissioner at each of the main yards (Chatham, Sheerness, Portsmouth and Plymouth), paid £800 a year, while the Deptford and Woolwich yards, 'under the immediate inspection of the Navy Board', had a clerk of the cheque at £200. Small establishments had a clerk of the cheque who was also storekeeper (Deal at £200 a year, Harwich £100).

Humorous examples of the ease with which men could enrich themselves were given by a cynical officer who, just before the war began, wrote a light-hearted pamphlet, *Advice to Officers of the British Navy*. He gave amusing 'advice' to most people in the fleet, ranging from admiral to carpenter. That for the surgeon (who was paid £5 until within two years of the end of the war) said: 'When any libertine comes with a certain fashionable complaint', treat him with white vitriol and 'he will be apparently cured in a few days'. The disorder will reappear in two or three months 'which you can attribute to his own imprudence'. And, more important, every time it happened it meant 15s in the surgeon's pocket – his allowance for every case of venereal disease, and in fact a fine deducted from the man's wages and paid to the surgeon. This was in addition to the flat rate of £5 a month for every 100 cases being treated.

There was an even better system, although it meant sharing the money. 'Strive to cultivate the friendship of the purser and captain's clerk, who will assist you in charging 15s. for a venereal cure against the wages of all the run men, to whom it will be no loss, as they forfeit their pay, and as for the scandal – a deserter cares very little about it.'

In battle, when a man was brought in with a wound in the arm or leg, the surgeon was advised, do not waste time thinking of how to save the limb 'but off with it at once. This will save you trouble . . .

besides securing him a tolerable pension, if he survives the operation.'

A ship's purser should stay friendly with the captain – tell tales on the wardroom, for example, and 'make presents from time to time of a few dozen of wine – the captain will then give you a certificate specifying a pipe of wine stove in a gale of wind – for which certificates you will be allowed credit at the Navy Office'.

Officers, he noted, never considered the expense to which a purser was put in supplying candles, so whenever one of them had a light in his cabin and stepped out, 'whip in and blow the candle out, on the score of the fear of fire'.

When correcting the slops book with the captain's clerk, 'and fearful that in the entry some articles have been neglected, to balance the loss you put certain little items' against sailors with most pay due. But, he warned, a purser had to be careful – someone put ten pounds of tobacco against a seaman known to loathe it.

Various other items of advice for the purser told him that if going to sea for three months at the end of the autumn, 'do not carry the wardroom stove but pretend you have forgotten it' – this guaranteed a saving of at least half a chaldron of coal, because the purser had to provide fuel.

A chaplain was advised to be agreeable, get drunk, and in port lend his cabin to any officer with a mistress or 'who sends for a sailor's wife'. Midshipmen were told that when on watch on the poop, where the poultry usually lived in cages, they should stick pins in the heads of one or two of the captain's or wardroom's fowls, and when the poulterer finds them and is going to throw them overboard because they must have died of disease, 'beg him to give them to you, under the pretence you want the guts to bait fish-hooks, and you will find they make excellent soup'.

A lieutenant commanding a cutter was given advice some fifteen years before Lieutenant William William Walker of the *Sparkler* took it and found himself cashiered. As the forfeited pay of deserted seamen 'is applied to a great naval charity', he was told, 'you must work your vessel with as few hands as possible, keeping the full complement on your books, till you are at the eve of going into a King's port [where there was a Commissioner who would pay the men], when you may "run" the superfluous number, and so contribute to this humane institution, at the same time that you secure to yourself their provisions'. (The writer saw the danger of keeping their pay: that would be fraud and could involve a charge of false muster.)

Lieutenants serving in ships of the line or frigates were advised, when fresh provisions were getting scarce, to say to another lieutenant at the table that the pig, goose, or whatever it was about to be served, died of sickness; that the liver was diseased, 'and thus spoil some appetites'.

If you were a lieutenant who disliked his captain, or liked the station and the ship was leaving it, 'ingratiate yourself with the surgeon and get a sick ticket and be sent on shore, where you will enjoy full pay and sick quarters money' – and then ingratiate yourself with the agent charged with the care of the sick 'and he will keep you on his list as long as you wish'.

The advice for admirals was concerned mostly with glory, while that for captains combined glory and prize money about equally with staying alive in battle. When commanding a division in battle and with the rigging of your ship damaged and the signal given to renew the action, 'do not hurry to comply and place your ship alongside the enemy in a lubberly way: knot and splice everything coolly. If the enemy waits and again you are damaged, you can say you were cut to pieces twice in a day. If the enemy escapes – well, that is not your affair.'

The admiral was advised that if he was sent with a light squadron to reinforce a commander-in-chief of a station where the enemy was expected, should he come across an enemy East Indiaman then capture it and take it in tow, even if it made him late – the prize was worth perhaps half the enemy's ships of war 'which you could not have taken with so little loss or damage'.

The art of staying alive, if you were a captain, meant being prudent without it showing; bravely rushing into action slowly, in fact. Without describing it in quite those terms, the author of *Advice* had some tips. If you commanded the leading ship while chasing enemy ships of the line and they begin firing their stern guns, then bear away or luff up and fire a broadside. This turn away – necessary so that the broadside guns could be aimed – gave the rest of the squadron time to catch up with you. An even safer way of giving more time for reinforcements to arrive – without, of course, any of your fellow captains thinking you other than a brave fellow, the smoke pouring from your gun ports – was to miss stays as you turned to fire a broadside.

If you commanded one of two frigates attacking two enemy frigates, always go for the smaller: there was more chance of capturing her, and although there was more glory for your consort if he captured the larger, if he failed you could always recapture him as well.

He had a method for dealing with convoys, too: if the master of a merchant ship continually misbehaves and 'gets a sense of superiority', the captain was advised to send for him and give him a few lashes of the cat of nine tails. This, it was pointed out, was provided for in the Articles of War, which subject 'all persons in or belonging to the fleet' to that discipline. (This ingenious move was not, as far as is known, attempted by anyone.)

Then there was advice concerning his own ship: if he had to put an officer under arrest in hot weather, confine him to his cabin and do not allow him to use the wardroom or gunroom. It would be so hot and airless that it would be punishment enough 'even if he finally escapes [punishment] at a court martial'.

When he dined out, a captain was told, he should tell his steward to wash the cabin so that the water dripping on to the officers eating at the table in the cabin below would show them exactly where the deck planking needed caulking or paying.

Ways round the limit of a dozen lashes of the cat were described. One was to give a dozen under one article of war, and then read out another and give a second dozen. If the man about to be flogged demanded a court martial, 'punish the insolence of his appeal' by giving him three dozen lashes instead of the intended dozen, and after that offer him the choice of being released or awaiting his trial in irons.

Finally, if two men make complaints about each other, if one 'is known to be turbulent or an Irishman, flog him without further question and show the ship's company the value of a good character'.

Although all the 'advice' was intended by its author to be ribald, most of the tricks described were practised in the course of the long war by men who had never seen the book but acted out of natural cunning. But this was all petty fraud – putting an undeserved name in a *Gazette* dispatch or a few pounds in a purser's pocket. It was not the stuff of which solid wealth was made. That kind of fraud was the target of Admiral Lord St Vincent's efforts, particularly when he was made First Lord of the Admiralty.

CHAPTER EIGHTEEN

The Artful Dundas

Lord St Vincent had spent months at sea during 1800 with the Channel Fleet, blockading Brest and trying to keep his seamen fit. No fresh provisions had been served in the ships for seventeen weeks and as scurvy broke out St Vincent ordered an ounce of lime juice and half an ounce of sugar, mixed in half a pint of water, to be served daily to each man. When the fleet returned to Torbay on 19 October, there were only sixteen hospital cases out of 23,000 men. A month earlier St Vincent had ordered that all seamen were to be vaccinated who wished it.

When Pitt resigned the premiership and Addington formed a Government in February 1801, St Vincent became the First Lord. He had the choice of two naval members of the six-man Board of Admiralty, and he chose Sir Thomas Troubridge and Captain Markham, who had commanded the *Hannibal* in the West Indies and then the *Centaur*. The three civilian members were Sir Philip Stephens, a former Secretary of the Board, and two Members of Parliament, William Eliot (St Germain's) and William Garthshore (Weymouth).

Their first task was assembling the fleet under the command of Sir Hyde Parker which sailed to Denmark and with which Nelson won the Battle of Copenhagen on Maundy Thursday. But the position in which they found the Navy's administration when they first met on 18 February is best described by Markham's biographer in 1883:

In those days the civil administration of the Navy, including contracts and supply of stores and provisions, as well as the work of the dockyards, was under a separate Board of Commissioners, presided over by the Comptroller of the Navy, called the Navy Board.

These permanent officials, although nominally subordinate to the Admiralty, acted as if they were practically independent, and much of the waste and peculation was due to their negligence, ignorance and incapacity. The comptroller was Sir Andrew S. Hamond, Captain Markham's old commander in the *Roebuck*.

As the representative of the Navy Board, he soon quarrelled with Lord St Vincent, and the proceedings of the junior lords [i.e. of the Admiralty] were equally disliked by this representative of routine and circumlocution.

With a character deteriorated, and judgment warped and dwarfed by years passed in a public office, the jobbing old Comptroller was a very different man from the dashing captain of the *Roebuck*.

Nelson's victory at Copenhagen in April 1801 was followed by Admiral Lord Keith's success on the coast of Egypt, the landing of British troops at Aboukir Bay and the Battle of Alexandria, so that by October all fighting had virtually stopped, and on 26 March 1802 Britain and France signed the Treaty of Amiens, bringing a brief pause to a war which had begun in 1793.

St Vincent had more trust in the word of Napoleon than was wise or justified, but, as ships of war were paid off by the score and anchored in harbours, rivers and creeks all round the coasts, the Admiralty started probing the peculation and inefficiency of the various departments.

'Their Lordships were thwarted at every turn by the Navy Board,' writes Markham's biographer. 'The officials disliked being disturbed; any discovery of cases of peculation and waste would reflect upon them; their supine negligence would be discovered, their ignorance exposed, and they were also influenced by feelings of mortified vanity. They wished everything to go on in the old grooves. What was good enough for Pitt and Dundas ought to satisfy St Vincent.'

Dundas, later Lord Melville, had an influence over Pitt which was almost disastrous; most of the catastrophic expeditions embarked upon by the Army and Navy began in Dundas's head, the ideas brewed and stewed by drink. He was also outstandingly corrupt in an age where corruption formed part of public life, so much so that when he was Viscount Melville it led to his impeachment.

All six members of the Board of Admiralty met on the 20 August

1802 and the minute recorded that their Lordships, 'taking into consideration the extraordinary expenses in the dockyards and ropeyards in proportion to the number of ships employed, and having received reports from various quarters of flagrant abuses and mismanagement existing in the several departments, which there is reason to believe are too well founded', and determined to put an end to it, had decided to visit all the dockyards.

There they would examine 'the conduct and ability of the officers, the sufficiency of the workmen, [and] the condition of the ships and magazines' to decide what reforms were needed, 'especially to prevent unnecessary expenditure of the public money'. And, as if to rub it in, they decided that the Comptroller, Hamond, and three other members of the Navy Board, 'do attend them on their visitation'.

The visitation began with the briskness one associates with St Vincent: three days later St Vincent, Markham, and Garthshore arrived in Plymouth and at 6.30 a.m. on 25 August they were in the dockyard receiving reports from department heads and investigating the system (or rather lack of it) for paying the workmen. The stores department, victualling office and hospital at Cawsand Bay were investigated, then Sir William Rule, the Surveyor of the Navy, was examined and orders given for a general survey of all the oak timber in stock.

Two days later they were in Portsmouth, where they spent a week looking, checking and questioning. By the first week in October they had also investigated the yards at Deptford, Woolwich, Sheerness, and Chatham. By this time there was not a Commissioner of the Navy, clerk of the cheque or storekeeper that was not alarmed: the whole inquiry had been decided on and completed within six weeks, giving no time for books and stocks to be juggled into some semblance of balance.

On 15 October the Admiralty Board met and recorded that they had during their visits to the dockyards observed 'with extreme concern' that the Navy Board 'had neglected to investigate frauds reported to them, but on the contrary had shown a disposition to cover and pass over irregularities'. A letter was to be written to the Navy Board signifying the Admiralty's 'high disapprobation of their conduct, and reprimanding them. By their failure in the execution of their duty,' the minute added, 'the public has been defrauded to a very considerable amount, and delinquencies have been passed unpunished.'

For all that, St Vincent and his fellow Board Members knew that mere words were not going to stop the corruption: men like Sir Andrew Snape Hamond were too wealthy and too firmly entrenched, with all the crooked contractors on their side, to be bothered by stiff letters from the Admiralty. And, more important, they had many allies in Parliament.

The new Admiralty Board was weak in the House of Commons. St Vincent, of course, sat in the House of Lords, but Markham had been recently elected one of the members for Portsmouth, and by now had a year's experience of parliamentary procedure.

Their Lordships decided that the corruption in the Navy – more precisely in the world of the Navy Board – was too vast for them to stop without help: a parliamentary commission was needed to investigate the entire civil branch of the Navy, with powers (which the Board did not have) of examining witnesses on oath and calling for documents.

St Vincent took the whole matter before the Cabinet, who were startled and then scared, noted Markham's biographer, by 'such an attack upon public officers and vested interests'. Only one member, Lord Eldon, supported him. The rest, including such men as Lords Hawkesbury, Hobart, Pelham and Lewisham, said no. St Vincent went back to the Admiralty and told his Board, who backed his view that a commission was absolutely necessary. St Vincent told the Cabinet that unless the measure was adopted he would have to quit the Cabinet – and the Board of Admiralty would resign as well. Addison's collection of mediocrity inspired no trust in the country; only St Vincent gave a weak Government a semblance of strength.

The Cabinet finally agreed and Captain Markham was given the job of introducing the Bill to Parliament, and seeing it through. It was obviously going to be a lonely task because five of the six most important ministers were in the House of Lords and most of the members of the Government were at best lukewarm supporters of the measure.

On 13 December 1802, while captains who had commanded ships of the line settled down to try to live on six shillings a day half pay and lieutenants and masters three shillings, and thousands of pressed seamen were given their freedom, the Board of Admiralty, so often blamed for much that was wrong, started a long and bitter fight to improve the Navy. On that day, Captain Markham rose in the Commons 'to call the attention of the House to the necessity for inquiring into naval abuses, and for leave to bring a bill'. It was a daunting task for a man more accustomed to handling a 74-gun ship because facing him were the two most renowned politicians of the age – Pitt, a close friend of Dundas, and naturally against the Bill, and Fox, who was at best 'critically neutral'.

Markham assured the House that the Admiralty had no intention of attacking its precedessors – he reminded them that two of the six members had served in the previous Board – but 'an interval of peace was the fitting time for the proposed investigation'.

The subsequent debate was noisy. Rear-Admiral George Berkeley, son of the Earl, who had been at the Glorious First of June and reputedly spent £100,000 to get himself elected for Gloucestershire, claimed that the Navy Board itself should carry out the inquiry into the Navy Board. (Lord Eldon had by an irony inserted a clause in the Bill allowing a witness to remain silent rather than incriminate himself.) Berkeley was followed by the Comptroller of the Navy Board himself, because Sir Andrew Snape Hamond was the Member for Ipswich. The man who was more guilty than most told the House 'that he and his colleagues were honourable and liberal men, full of zeal and ardour, who had always done everything in their power to remove abuses'.

In subsequent debates Canning called the proposed commission unconstitutional, Lord Temple likened it to the Star Chamber, Rear-Admiral Berkeley objected to the names of the proposed commissioners, and yet another Member, a friend of Edmund Burke, claimed in a splendid outburst that it was unjust and unconstitutional to make men 'degrade and dishonour themselves by discovering their own malpractices'.

At the third reading Earl Temple remained opposed but Sheridan supported the Bill, saying it should be passed 'with applause and gratitude'. In the Lords it was supported by Lord Nelson, who said that everyone knew that abuses existed, and told his fellow peers: 'From the highest admiral to the poorest cabin-boy, there is not a man that may not be in distress, yet with large sums of wages owing to him. My lords, he cannot obtain payment by any diligence of request and his entreaties will be answered with insults at the proper places of application, if he comes not with particular recommendations for a preference.

'From the highest admiral to the meanest seaman, whatever the sums of prize money due to him, no man can tell when he may securely call any part of it his own. Are these things to be tolerated?'

Yet the Duke of Clarence – who, as Prince William Henry, had been a post captain and a friend of Nelson's, attending his wedding – spoke against the Bill. But by 29 December it was passed.

The commissioners appointed by the Act were headed by Rear-Admiral Sir Charles Pole, who was MP for Newark and proposed by the Government, and they began their investigation of the Navy Board, the Treasurer of the Navy, the Victualling Board, the Sick and Hurt Board, the Transport Board, and the commissioners responsible for the dockyards, hospitals, prisoners of war, the collection of sixpences from merchant seamen for Greenwich Hospital and the Chatham Chest (a pension fund).

It began work at an office in Great George Street in February 1803 – by which time it was clear to most people that war would soon break out again with France, which it did on 16 May. Pitt's subsequent attacks on St Vincent do not belong here, although Henry Dundas, accurately described by Markham's biographer as 'that prince of jobbers and place hunters', was created Viscount Melville and became First Lord when Addison's Government resigned, and was thus in power when some of the Reports of the Commissioners were published.

Each report – there were twelve of them – covered a different aspect of the Navy Board, and a brief survey of them is all that is necessary here to confirm the corruption.

The first report covered peculation in dockyards abroad. At Port Royal, Jamaica, for instance, the government had lost £53,000 in eight years simply by exchanges in the negotiation of bills, caused by fraud and neglect by agents abroad and clerks in the Navy Board. The government had lost another £134,557 because the storekeeper (paid £200 a year and a £50 rent allowance) made a big profit by purchasing stores from contractors abroad instead of sending demands to England. There were many other examples covering other yards in the colonies.

The second report was one that directly affected sick and wounded seamen. It was on the Chatham Chest, a fund begun by Sir John Hawkins and Sir Francis Drake 'for the relief of maimed and worn-out mariners'. The money came from a shilling a month deducted from the wages of every warrant officer in the Navy and provided pensions for seamen and marines. The Commissioners had found a scandalous state of affairs. The money was kept in a chest at Chatham, locked with five keys. Wounded seamen, no matter how far away they were, had to go to Chatham to collect their money. Yet out of 5,205 pensions granted, only 309 were paid to pensioners in person. The rest was scooped up by landsharks who had persuaded the rightful owners to sign powers of attorney – ostensibly to save them the long journey to Chatham each year. Sir Charles Pole cited one sailor who had lost all his limbs and had to travel more than 200 miles each year to collect his miserable pension. (This abuse was promptly stopped: the chest was tranferred to Greenwich and the men were paid at their homes.)

The third report covered the contracts let out by the Navy Board for the supply of blocks (pulleys), capstan bars, handspikes and pumpbrakes. One man had supplied all the Navy's blocks for the past forty years, and despite protests St Vincent gave the contract to Mr Brunel, who had just invented a machine for making them. The Navy Board laughed at the idea that an oval object could be made by machinery, but the machines made by the French refugee father of Isembard Kingdom Brunel continued making them for many years.

Down at the Deptford yards an investigation of the cooperage department showed the Commissioners that £1,020 had been charged for work costing £37 and £2,650 for what cost £227. The report gave scores of similar examples. Five ships needed mast hoops; 192 were received and 720 charged.

Prize agents were covered by the fourth report and, to the surprise of no one from admiral to seaman, it was proved that agents delayed payments for years and frequently defrauded seamen. The lack of a prize list from one ship in a fleet, the report said, could delay payments to all ships for six or seven years – and all the time the agents had the money invested at a good rate of interest. Dozens of examples were given – including that of the *Requin*, when admirals were paid but the agents kept everyone else waiting eight years. Sir Charles Pole cited the case of Sir Charles Danvers, who from thirty-one captures was awarded a total of £163,000. Of this £50,000 was taken by agents and £51,000 went in expenses at prize courts, leaving him with £62,000.

The Sixpenny Office was investigated in the fifth report. Established in 1694, every merchant seaman had to pay 6d from his wages towards Greenwich Hospital, but after 1747 it was increased to a shilling. The masters of ships were responsible for collecting every man's shilling and paying it to the Sixpenny Office, which in theory passed the money to Greenwich Hospital – an establishment which never accepted merchant seamen.

The Sixpenny Office was well organised. It had a Receiver's Office on Great Tower Hill and a staff of eleven. There were three commissioners. The first 'Commissioner and Receiver' was John Rashleigh, who was paid £300 a year – but was an invalid and never went to the office. He had two clerks, John Bryan, who was paid £50, and William Grey, who had £40 a year. The 'Commissioner and Accomptant' was John Clevland, who was paid £200 a year, but he lived at Tapeley, in Devon, and was Recorder of Bideford, as well as Member of Parliament for Barnstaple, serving in six parliaments. He owed his sinecure to the fact that his father, also John Clevland, was a former Secretary to the Board of Admiralty and paid a far from mute or inglorious part in the judicial murder of Admiral the Hon. John Byng. Clevland left the work to his clerk, Charles Eve, who was paid £50 a year.

The 'Commissioner and Comptroller' was John Beverly, AM, who was paid £100 a year, and, because he was an 'Esquire Beadle' at Cambridge, he did not bother to go to Tower Hill either, leaving the work to his clerk – who was John Bryan junior, the young son of the absentee Mr Rashleigh's senior clerk.

These five clerks were looked after during the day by the aptly named Margaret Silver, the housekeeper at £20 a year, while the messenger, William Carey, ran any errands and the solicitor could always be consulted. A sixth clerk belonging to the office, one of the two senior men, actually had a chair and table at the Custom House – John Dalley was paid £50 a year 'to take an account of the daily arrival of the ships'. The other five then checked the names of the ships against the names of those masters who had paid their shillings.

The report recommended that these sinecures should be abolished and the office reorganised, although no one proposed abolishing what was in fact a tax on merchant seamen for the upkeep of Navy seamen. The charge continued until 1834, by which time it was calculated that it yielded an average of £20,000 a year and that since it was started merchant seamen had paid more than £2 million towards the upkeep of Navy pensioners.

The dockyards were covered by the sixth report, and most of its findings could be predicted. The inspectors checking work regularly took bribes: £580,000 in wages were paid out on the authority of a simple certificate from a muster clerk; and for the previous four years £68,000 had been lost because labourers were overpaid.

Yet the most radical improvement resulting from this report did not concern money. At many of the dockyards old ships of the line which would otherwise have been broken up were left on river banks and as they went up and down with the tide they dug themselves beds. The long and spacious decks were then converted into cabins (with dockyard materials) and used as homes by shipwrights, dockyard officers, blacksmiths, coopers – by anyone who needed accommodation. Before long ladies of easy virtue moved in as well, to comfort the seamen serving in ships nearby, and the upper decks of these once-famous old ships sprouted dovecotes, washing lines and laundry houses. 'No species of crime and infamy was unpractised in these rabbit warrens, down to murder.'

The Admiralty now ordered them to be cleared out, and a contemporary pamphlet commented: 'Whoever recollects the nest of harpies which, driven from their impure feasts and orgies in the dockyards, prowled our streets, stunning the ear with their curses and execrations against the virtue which had hunted them from their dark and, as they hoped, impenetrable recesses, will be aware of the necessity which compelled the Admiralty to proceed with the utmost circumspection.'

This report raised the greatest uproar so far in Parliament, the press and the country, yet the officials of most of the other departments knew only too well that their turn had yet to come. The first of them, the Sick and Hurt Board, and all the hospitals, were covered in the seventh report, presented in the late spring of 1805, a few months before the Battle of Trafalgar. This report was perhaps the most shameful so far.

In one ship set aside for sick prisoners of war the officers lived on provisions provided for the patients, although this only supplemented the fare supplied by the surgeon's chief assistant at a cost of £2,000 a year. The report was full of examples of fraud, neglect and corruption in the Navy's hospitals.

The next two reports caused much less stir. The eighth showed that the cooperage department in Plymouth was apparently supplying the neighbourhood with casks, both by way of fraud and theft: sixty-four Navy casks were found in one brewery alone. The ninth referred to stores and revealed no great discrepancies.

The tenth report was the one for which the political world had been waiting. It was on the Office of the Treasurer of the Navy – held from 1783 until 1801 by Henry Dundas who, at the time the report was published, was not only Viscount Melville but had replaced St Vincent as the First Lord of the Admiralty.

When Lord St Vincent became First Lord and the parliamentary inquiry first began, Henry Dundas's town address was given as 'Somerset Place'. This was in fact a suite in the Navy Board's head-quarters which Dundas had occupied rent-free and in considerable luxury for the past nineteen years, and for the whole of that time he had been Treasurer of the Navy, at a salary of £4,000 a year. For the past seven years he had also been Secretary of State for War (at £2,000 a year), President of the India Board (at £2,000), Lord Privy Seal in Scotland (£3,000 a year) and Home Secretary from 1791 to 1794 (at £6,000 a year).

So on New Year's Day 1801, a few weeks before Pitt resigned, the Right Honourable Henry Dundas, Member of Parliament for Edinburgh City, Secretary of State for the War Department, Chancellor of the University of St Andrews, a Lord of Trade and Plantations, First Commissioner for the Affairs of India, Lord Privy Seal in Scotland, Governor of the Bank of Scotland (salary undisclosed), an Elder Brother of Trinity House, Treasurer of the Navy, and holder of various other posts, including that of President of the Society for the Relief of Ruptured Poor, was officially paid a total of £11,000 a year from public funds for political offices. To give an idea of how much this was in those days, he could have used the money to buy himself a new 32-gun frigate each year.

As far as money was concerned, Dundas had a voracious appetite and a canny touch, yet £11,000 a year was not enough. The tenth report on the office of the Treasurer of the Navy, the post which Dundas had held for the past nineteen years, noted that he refused to give full information and on several occasions refused to answer questions, using the clause in the Act which said that a witness need not incriminate himself.

Even with Dundas refusing answers, the report had a miserable story of corruption to tell. Dundas had appointed Alexander Trotter as Paymaster of the Navy (at £800 a year), and allowed him to keep the public money at his private bank, pocketing the interest.

Far more important, £20,000 was missing. Dundas (by now created Viscount Melville and First Lord of the Admiralty) was allowed to address the House of Commons and defend himself on 11 June,

1805, and although he spoke for two hours he refused to account for the £20,000, apart from admitting what most people suspected, that it had not been spent on the Navy. Instead, he said that at the time he had been entrusted with the King's interests in Scotland and he had used the money in a way no consideration would induce him to reveal.

There was little doubt that Dundas had spent the money for his own purposes but there was no way of proving it. He was dismissed as First Lord, his name erased from the list of Privy Councillors, and he was impeached, his trial beginning exactly three months after Nelson was buried at St Paul's. He escaped punishment because the Lord Chancellor, Erskine, arranged one charge which included both admitted and unprovable matters, so peers who would have found him guilty on some items and not guilty on others had no choice but to acquit him. He died in 1811.

The Navy Board, headed by Sir Andrew Snape Hamond, was investigated in the eleventh report, and many examples were given of irregular payments. £100,000 in secret service money, spent in three years, had vanished, and no one could explain who received any of it.

The twelfth report, covering the purchase from Riga of spars and hemp for rope, showed that a Mr Lindegreen received £3,550 as commission for writing one letter to a merchant ordering the hemp, which was found to be damaged when it arrived but was passed by Navy Board officials.

Canister (left) and grape shot

CHAPTER NINETEEN

The Odds

Corruption of civilian officials, many pursers and certain officers, poor food and often much sickness in the ships, cheating prize agents, prowling press gangs and rare leave, the need because of Britain's lonely position for ships of war to be at sea year after year in all weathers – all this should have produced a Navy manned by men who neither wanted to go into battle nor could put up a fight when they did.

Yet the British seaman was firmly convinced that he equalled any three Frenchmen and four Spaniards and by the end of the war the figures from the great sea battles tended to bear out his claim. Only against the Dutch and the Danes (and the Americans during the brief war against them) did he need parity.

Statistics are said to be capable of proving anything, but taking the two greatest battles of the war, Copenhagen in 1801 and Trafalgar in 1805, a straight comparison of the number of ships and men involved, the casualties and the captures and losses, makes the point.

At Copenhagen the British were fighting Danes who were defending their very homes, because their ships were moored within sight and sound of their capital city. The Danes used old ships of the line without masts, powerful forts and floating batteries; the British used ships of the line, frigates and bomb ketches. It is difficult to compare relative strengths but a close study of the battle shows 888 Danish guns of various calibres against 954 British, while the casualties (British figures in brackets), were 476 Danes killed (256), 559 wounded (688), with the total Danish killed and wounded being 1,035 (944). The only possible conclusion, borne out in the full-scale study of the battle, *The Great Gamble*, is that both sides fought equally bravely.

The Battle of Trafalgar, fought four years later but with Nelson again commanding the British ships, is a different story as far as both the enemy and the British are concerned: the British fought as bitterly and achieved an incredible victory.

There were thirty-three French and Spanish ships of the line and twenty-seven British. The British lost no ship but sank, captured or drove ashore twenty-three French and Spanish, leaving only ten to get back to Cadiz badly damaged (two of them had been recaptured).

The French and Spanish casualties (with the British in brackets) were 4,408 French and Spanish officers and men killed (449 British), and 2,545 wounded (1,214). These figures are taken from official French, Spanish and British records.

Lest it should be thought that twenty-seven British ships capturing or destroying twenty-three out of an enemy fleet of thirty-three was a fluke, it should be remembered that at the Battle of the Nile Nelson's fourteen ships attacked nineteen French, capturing nine and destroying two. Yet a year earlier a British fleet of fifteen ships of the line commanded by Sir John Jervis met a Spanish fleet of twenty-five and managed to capture only four of them. Why should there be such a difference? The clue might well be in the fact that the fifth in seniority in the British fleet, a commodore with four admirals above him, was Nelson, who ignored orders and captured two of the four prizes.

Was it leadership, personality, charisma, that made the difference? Sir John Jervis, later Earl St Vincent, had done more than Nelson to improve conditions in the Navy – his long service and period as First Lord of the Admiralty had been well spent, and his battle, from which his title was taken, was still a victory.

Nor was Nelson the only recipe for victory: in the same year as the Battle of Cape St Vincent, Admiral Duncan with sixteen ships of the line fought fifteen Dutch, capturing nine. The fighting was bitter – the British had 244 killed and the Dutch 540, and 796 were wounded, compared with 620 Dutch, making totals of 1,040 British and 1,160 Dutch. The number of guns involved were 1,150 British and 1,084 Dutch, although such comparisons rarely indicate much of consequence. The conditions in the Danish, Dutch, French, and Spanish Navies were comparable with the British when those countries were at war; variations of the press gang were familiar sights.

The point being made, however, is not that the Royal Navy was usually the victor but that it won the victories with ships manned by the men whose lives have just been described.

One conclusion seems obvious, although no doubt others will be drawn. Harsh as conditions were for the seamen in the Royal Navy, they were little better for his brother in the Army. By comparison, little has been written about the terrible conditions in which the Army often existed, and fought, but the number of soldiers killed by disease in the West Indies, for example, referred to earlier, when thousands of men died on garrison duty as a result of the policies of Henry Dundas, make it certain that if a man was given the choice of serving in the Army in the West Indies or Spain, or the Navy, the chances were at least even that he would have chosen the Navy and survived to tell the tale. He had a far better chance of staying alive; at least he would not be pinned down in one island for years on end, as the soldiers were. Ships moved around; rarely was a ship on a particular station for more than two years. By contrast, a regiment sent to the West Indies could stay on one island for ten years, its casualties from sickness replaced by new drafts from England. Soldiers sent to the West Indies from England could be reasonably sure that they would never return – a far less enviable position than that of the sailor, who might not be paid for a couple of years or get leave for three. His chances of living were, however, excellent compared with his brother in the Army.

Nun buoy for anchors or cables

Bibliography

UNPUBLISHED MATERIAL

British
Public Record Office
Admiralty 50/65 Journals of the Proceedings of Vice Admiral Sir Hyde Parker. 31 January–13 May 1801 (for Battle of Copenhagen).
Adm 50/33 Journal of Sir Hyde Parker (for *Hermione* and *Surprise* period).
Adm 1/248 In-letters, Admirals' Dispatches, [Sir Hyde Parker] for *Hermione–Success* period
Adm 36/15900 *Victory* muster roll for Trafalgar
Adm 36/15342 *Elephant* muster roll for Copenhagen
Adm 36/13743 *Monarch* muster roll for Copenhagen
Adm 36/15392 *Ganges* muster roll for Copenhagen
Adm 36/1650 *Pickle* muster roll for Trafalgar
Adm 9254 Commission and Warrant indexes
Adm 9255 Commission and Warrant indexes
Adm 1/248 In-letters, Admirals' Dispatches, Jamaica 1797
Adm 1/4120 In-letters, Secretary of State to Board, 1756
Adm 1/923 In-letters, from C-in-C, Portsmouth, 1756
Adm 2/1331 Out-letters, Secret Orders, Admirals, 1756
Adm 2/516 Out-letters, Public Officers and Admirals, 1756
Adm 2/150 Out-letters (Secret Orders) 1363, 3 September 1805, Orders by Lord Barham for *Agamemnon, Thunderer, Ajax, Euryalis, Defiance, Superb, Royal Sovereign* and *Victory*
Adm 3/126 Board Minute Book, 1 January–31 October 1801
Adm 3/144 Board Minute Book (Rough), 1 January–31 October 1801
Adm 3/64 Board Minutes, 1 January–31 December 1756
Adm 3/256 Tasks of members of the Board of Admiralty as laid down by Lord Barham, May 1805
Adm 1/4186 State Letters (Letters from Secretaries of State to Board of Admiralty)
Adm 2/141 Letter Book, Orders and Instructions, 7 January–15 July 1801
Adm 1/118 Admirals' Dispatches, Channel Fleet
Adm 1/4 Admirals' Dispatches, Baltic Fleet

Adm 2/294 Lords Letters to Navy Board

Adm 1/320 Copy of Test Act in use 1797

Adm 1/4189 Correspondence between Secretary of State and US Minister in London concerning American seamen and Protections

F.O. 5/16 f 369, Original of US Protection issued to 'Daniel Robertson, Mariner'

Adm 1/4352 Secret Letters, Wording of Protection issued by Royal Navy

Adm 36/15392 (*Ganges*), 36/15342 (*Elephant*), 36/13743 (*Monarch*): return of foreigners serving on board, February 1801

Captains' Journals

Adm 51/1102 *Success* (Captain H. Pigot) 4 September 1794–30 September 1795

Adm 51/1104 *Hermione* (Captain Wilkinson) 5 September 1794–9 September 1795

Adm 51/1179 *Hermione* (Captain Wilkinson) 10 September 1795–10 February 1797 (ends as Pigot takes over)

Adm 51/1360 *Blanche* (Captain G E. Hamond, for Copenhagen)

Adm 51/15441 *Nautilus* (Captain Sykes) after Trafalgar

Adm 51/3950 *Ramillies* (Captain Arthur Gardiner) 1756 (including Battle of Minorca)

badm 51/4132 *Buckingham* (Captain Michael Everitt) 1756 (including Battle of Minorca)

Adm 51/1010 *Trident* (Captain Philip Durell) 1756 (including Battle of Minorca)

Adm 51/4301 *Princess Louise* (Captain Thomas Noel) 1756

Adm 51/165 *Captain* (Captain Charles Catford) 1756

Adm 51/1662 *Astrea* (Captain E. Heywood) 1807 until ran aground

Masters' logs (all for the period of Battle of Copenhagen)

Adm 52/3299 (*Polyphemus*), 52/2968 (*Elephant*), 52/3399 (*St George*), 52/2964 (*Edgar*), 52/3231 (*Monarch*), 52/4018 (*Amazon*), 52/2773 (*Blanche*), 52/2702 (*Ardent*), 52/2656 (*Alcemene*), 52/2899 (*Cruizer*), 52/2652 (*Explosion*)

For Battle of Minorca: 52/996 (*Ramillies*)

For *Hermione* Mutiny: 52/2935 (*Diligence*), May–October 1797

Adm 53/3669 Part II, (*Pickle*) log of George Almy, 2nd Master, 20 October 1805–5 November 1805, carrying Trafalgar dispatches

Muster Rolls

Adm 36/12009 *Hermione*, 1792–4

Adm 36/12010 *Hermione*, February 29, 1796–7 July 1796 (for pre-mutiny period)

Adm 36/13193 *Success* for 1797–9
Adm 36/14942–3 *Surprise* for 1799
Adm 36/1650 *Pickle*, at Trafalgar
Adm 36/6463 *Ramillies* for 1755
Adm 36/4664 *Ramillies* for 1756 (the Battle of Minorca)
Adm 36/15900 *Victory* (for Trafalgar)

Courts Martial
For *Hermione* Mutiny (minutes of the trials of thirty-nine men held on various dates): Adm 1/5344, 1/5346, 1/5347, 1/5348, 1/5350, 1/5353, 1/5357, 1/5360, 1/5375
For Loss of *Astrea*, frigate: Adm 1/5387
Adm 1/5338 Minutes of Court of Inquiry 20–23 January 1797 following complaint by US Government

Signals and Instructions for Ships Under Convoy, printed officially, 1797, author's collection
F.O. 22/40 Diplomatic Correspondence (includes letters and instructions from Secretary of State to ambassadors; dispatches, notes from Foreign governments) concerning events leading to Battle of Copenhagen.

Private Papers
Documents concerning Captain George Duff at Trafalgar, owned by the Misses Duff, Bolton Gardens, South Kensington
Documents concerning Rear-Admiral the Earl of Northesk and the *Britannia* at Trafalgar, owned by the Earl of Northesk
Memoirs of Midshipman W. S. Millard. A brief portion concerning the Battle of Copenhagen was published in *Macmillan's Magazine*, June 1895, unsigned. The full version was recently made available to the present author by Philip T. Millard, MB, FRCSE
Byng Papers (concerning Admiral the Hon. John Byng) at Wrotham Park, owned by Lady Elizabeth Byng
Osborn Papers, Bedford Record Office
Osborn MSS owned by Sir Danvers Osborn, Bt
'Abstract from Admiral Byng's Private Journal' in Martin Papers, British Library Add 41355

Admiralty Library
Progress Books and Lists of Ships: these give full details of construction and all repairs, dates and costs of RN ships
Papers Relating to Trial of Admiral Byng, cf 010

British Library
Morning Post 1801, *The Times* 1801, *The Gentleman's Magazine* 1801

Eg 3319, Journal of the Revd John Browne, in the *Majestic* at the Battle of the Nile

Add 41355, for Byng and Battle of Minorca period

Add 32860, intelligence relating to Minorca 1750–60

Add 35895, Papers relating to the trial of Admiral Byng

Spanish

Various, from Archivo General de Marina, Madrid, collection of Don Alvaro de Bazan, particularly concerning the West Indies

French

Bibliothèque Nationale, Paris, and various from archives at the Naval bases at Brest and Rochefort; Musée de la Marine, Palais de Chaillot, Paris

Danish

Rigsarkivet, Admiralty: Copybook of Admiralty and Defence Commission, 1801, Orders and Out-letters

Rigsarkivet, Crown Prince, Out-letters 1801

Rigsarkivet, Crown Prince, In-letters 1801

Rigsarkivet, Admiralty, 748/1801 series, ships' logs for Battle of Copenhagen

Rigsarkivet, Admiralty In-letters, Reports of the Commission for killed, wounded and pensions

PUBLISHED MATERIAL

Danish

Mindeskrift om Slaget paa Reden, P. C. Bundesen, Copenhagen, 1801

Collegial Tidende, by J. N. Muller, Christiania 1860

Berlingske Tidende, various issues of 1800 and 1801

British

The Naval Chronicle 1799–1819 (published throughout the war as a journal, and then in bound copies, these are one of the most valuable sources for details of actions, particularly the less important ones, biographical sketches of scores of officers over the years, lists of new constructions, articles by serving officers on tactics, new systems of gunnery, seamanship and conditions)

Naval Routine

Nautical Economy by Jack Nasty Face

The Naval Mutinies of 1797 by C. Gill, London, 1913

A Letter to the Rt. Hon. Lord Viscount Melville . . . connected with an improved system of management in H.M. ships . . . by a Post Captain, London, 1811

A Postscript to the 'Claims of the British Navy' . . . by the Same Old Post Captain, n.d.

Sea Life in Nelson's Time by John Masefield, London, 1926

A Social History of the Navy by M. Lewis, London, 1960

The Health of Seamen, by C. Lloyd, Navy Record Society, Vol CVII, London, 1965

England's Sea Officers, by Michael Lewis, London, 1939

Portsmouth Point, the Navy in Fiction, 1793–1815, C. Northcote Parkinson, London, 1948

Napoleon and his British Captives, by Michael Lewis, London, 1962

The British Tar in Fact and Fiction, by Cdr C. N. Robinson, London, 1909

Medicine and the Navy, by C. Lloyd and J. L. S. Coulter, vol III, 1714–1815, Edinburgh and London, 1961

Letters of the English Seamen, edited by E. Hallam Moorhouse, London, 1910

The Press Gang Afloat and Ashore, by J. R. Hutchinson, London, 1913

The Floating Republic by G. E. Manwaring and Bonamy Dobree, London, 1835

The Trade Winds, edited by C. Northcote Parkinson, London, 1948

War in the Eastern Seas, edited by C. Northcote Parkinson, London, 1954

The Black Ship, by Dudley Pope, London and Philadelphia, 1963

Britain's Sea Soldiers, by Col. C. Field, RMLI, 2 volumes, Liverpool, 1924

Instruction Manuals, Lists and Descriptions

Steel's . . . List of the Royal Navy, London, January 1799 (published quarterly)

Steel's . . . List of Privateers, taken from the hostile powers . . . London, 1799

Outline of Naval Routine, by Lt Alexander Fordyce, London, 1837

The Picture of Plymouth, being a perfect guide . . . etc., Plymouth, 1812, anon.

The Young Seaman's Manual and Rigger's Guide by Captain C. Burney, RN, sixth edition, London, 1869, and ninth edition, London, 1885

Minutes . . . of a court martial . . . of Captain John Moutray [for] the loss of a convoy under his charge . . . by Henry Parry, London, 1781

The Seaman's Manual . . . by R. H. Dana, London, 1841

The Seaman's Vade-Mecum and Defensive War at Sea, by William Mountaine, London, 1761

Steel's Naval Chronologist of the late war (1793–1801), fourth edition, London, 1806

The History of a Ship, from her cradle to her grave, anon. London, 1877

The Naval Gazetteer, Biographer and Chronologist of the late wars . . . compiled by J. W. Norie, London, 1842

The Royal Kalendar . . . for the year 1801 (including Rider's Merlin), London, 1801

Captain's Orders, HMS Euryalus, author's MS copy

Observations on Naval Affairs, by the Earl of Dundonald, London, 1847

A Treatise on Gunnery, by John Gray, London, 1731

British Naval Dress, by Dudley Jarrett, London, 1960

Portsmouth, Port Orders, by Sir Roger Curtis, with amendments by Admiral Sir Richard Bickerton, printed officially, author's collection

The Young Officer's Sheet Anchor, by Darcy Lever, London, 1819

The Anatomy of Nelson's Ships, by C. Nepean Longridge, London, 1955

Signals and Instructions, edited by J. S. Corbett, NRS volume XXIX, London, 1908

A History of Naval Architecture, by John Fincham, London, 1851

The Haven Finding Art, by E. G. R. Taylor, London, 1956

A Treatise on Naval Gunnery . . . by Maj.-Gen. Sir Howard Douglas, second edition, London, 1829

Instructions for the Exercise . . . of Great Guns (official publication), London, 1858

The Naval Surgeon, by William Turnbull, London, 1806

Steel's Ship-master's Assistant and Owner's Manual . . ., by I. Stikeman, 23rd edition, London, 1836

The Complete Epitome of Practical Navigation . . . by J. W. Norie, fourth edition, London, 1816

Professional Recollections on Points of Seamanship, Discipline and etc, by Captain F. Liardet, London, 1849

The Naval Service or Officer's Manual . . . by Captain W. N. Glascock, RN, two volumes, London, 1836

The Manning of the Royal Navy, Selected Public Pamphlets, 1693—1873, edited by J. S. Bromley, NRS volume 119, London, 1974

A Treatise on the office of A Purser on board His Majesty's Ships, by 'An old-established officer', London, 1788

Equipment and Displacement of Ships of War, J. Edye, London, 1832

Naval Tactics, anon., printed by David Steel, London, 1797

The Principles and Practice of Naval and Military Courts Martial . . ., by John McArthur, two volumes, London, 1813

The Sea Officer's Companion, by R. Waddington, London, 1778

Old Sea Wings, Ways and Words, by R. C. Leslie, London, 1890

Buckler's Hard and Its Ships, by 2nd Lord Montague of Beaulieu, London, 1909

Signal Book for Ships of War (Howe, 1790), official publication, author's collection

Signal Book for Ships of War (1799), official publication, author's collection

A Treatise on Masting Ships and Mastmaking, by John Fincham, London, 1843

Articles of War, London, 1825, author's collection

Regulations and Instructions Relating to H.M. Service at Sea . . . 1808, author's collection

An Universal Dictionary of the Marine . . ., by William Falconer, London, 1789, author's collection

Instructions for the Exercise of Great Guns on Board H.M. ships, handwritten volume, n.d., author's collection

The Surgeon's Mate . . ., by Dr John Wordall, London, 1617

The Mariner's Daily Assistance, by W. Turnbull, London, 1854

Seamanship and Naval Economy, by A. G. Griffiths, London, 1824

A Naval Officer's Guide for Preparing Ships, by C. Martelli, London, 1838

New Seaman's Guide, by John Diston, London, 1815

The Seaman's Sure Guide, by John Bettesworth, London, 1783

The Marine Officer, by Sir Richard Steel, London, 1840

The Log Book or Nautical Miscellany, anon., London, 1830

Action

The Campaign of Trafalgar, by Sir J. S. Corbett, London, 1910

The Year of Trafalgar, by Sir Henry Newbolt, London, 1905

Blue Book, Command 7120, published 1913, report of the commission appointed by the Admiralty to inquire into the tactics at Trafalgar; based on data in the *Logs of the Great Sea Fights*, edited by Admiral T. Sturges-Jackson, which was badly transcribed

The Trafalgar Roll, Col. R. H. Mackenzie, London, 1913

Bellerophon: the Bravest of the Brave, by Edward Fraser, London, 1909

A Narrative . . . *of the capturing of the* Hermione *frigate*, by Admiral Sir Edward Hamilton, Bt, printed privately, Sussex, 1899

The Enemy at Trafalgar, by Edward Fraser, London, 1906

Logs of the Great Sea Fights, 2 volumes, edited by Rear Admiral T. Sturges Jackson, NRS, Volumes XVI (1898) and XVIII (1900)

A Narrative of the Battle of St Vincent . . . by Col. Drinkwater-Bethune, 2nd edition, 1840

England Expects (US title *Decision at Trafalgar*), by Dudley Pope, London, 1959; Philadelphia, 1960

The Great Gamble: Nelson at Copenhagen, by Dudley Pope, London and New York, 1972

The Trafalgar Campaign, by Col. E. Desbrière, Paris, 1907; translated by C. Eastwick, Oxford, 1933

Biography

A Brief Memoir of the Life . . . *of William Marsden, DCL, FRS*, printed privately, London, 1838

The Life of Nelson, by 'The old sailor', London, 1836

The Life of George, Lord Anson, by Sir John Barrow, London, 1839

The Life and Services of Admiral Sir Thomas Foley, GCB, by J. B. Herbert, Cardiff, 1884

The Life of Admiral of the Fleet Sir William Parker 1781–1886 by Rear Admiral A. Phillimore, London, 1876

Narrative of a Captivity . . . in France and Flanders, by Edward Boys, London, 1831

The Life of a Sailor, by Captain F. Chamier, three volumes, London, 1833

Pages and Portraits from the Past, being the Private Papers of Sir William Hotham, GCB, Admiral of the Red, edited by A. M. W. Stirling, two volumes, 1909

The Narrative of a Chatham Pensioner (also called *The Seaman's Narrative*), by William Spavens, Louth, 1796

The Book of the Duffs by A. and H. Taylor, two volumes, Edinburgh, 1914

Naval Sketch Book; or the Service Afloat and Ashore, by An Officer of Rank [Captain W. N. Glascock], two volumes, London, 1826

Nelson and His Captains, by W. H. Fitchett, London, 1902

The Wynne Diaries, edited by Anne Fremantle, London, 1940

Memoirs of St Vincent, by J. S. Tucker

From the Gun Room to the Throne, by Philip d'Auvergne, Duc d'Bouillon, London, 1904

Three Dorset Captains at Trafalgar, by A. M. Broadley, London, 1908

Autobiographical Memoir of Sir John Barrow, London, 1847

Correspondence of Lord Collingwood, edited by G. L. Newnham Collingwood, London, 1838

Memoirs of the Naval Life and Services of Admiral Sir Philip Durham, by Captain A. Murray, London, 1846

Private Sea Journals, 1778–1782, by Captain Thomas Pasley, edited by R. M. S. Pasley, London, 1931

Anson's Voyage Round the World, edited by G. Williams, NRS vol. 109, 1967

Memoirs of Admiral Sir Sidney Smith, two volumes, London, 1839

Memoirs of Rear Admiral Sir William Symonds, edited by J. A. Sharp, London, 1858

The Life of a Sea Officer, by Baron Raigersfield, London, 1829

Landsman Hay, edited by M. D. Hay, London, 1953

Narrative of Captain O'Brien, RN, London, 1814 (reprinted from the *Naval Chronicle*)

Perilous Adventures and Vicissitudes of a Naval Officer 1801–1812, edited by Harold Burrows, Edinburgh and London, 1927

Memoir of James Trevenen, edited by C. Lloyd and R. C. Anderson, NRS volume 101, 1959

Above and Under Hatches, by J. A. Gardner, edited by C. Lloyd, London, 1955

Mariner of England, by William Richardson, edited by Col. Spencer Childers, London, 1908

The Private Papers of George, 2nd Earl Spencer, NRS, three volumes, XLVI, XLVII, XLVIII

A Naval Career During the Old War . . . Admiral John Markham, Anon. London, 1883

Royal Naval Biography, two volumes by John Marshall, 1823

At 12 Mr Byng Was Shot, by Dudley Pope, London and Philadelphia, 1962

A Sailor of King George: the Journals of Captain F. Hoffman, RN, edited by A. Beckford Bevan and H. B. Wolryche-Whitmore, London, 1901

Personal Narrative of Events, 1799–1815, by Vice-Admiral William S. Lovell, London, 1879

Thirty Years from Home, by Samuel Leech, London, 1843

Johnny Newcome in the Navy, by 'Jack Mitford', London, 1819

Nelsonian Reminiscences, by Lt G. S. Parsons, RN, edited by W. Long, London, 1905

A Naval History of the Patey Family, by Christopher Harvey, privately printed, n.d.

Autobiography of a Seaman by Earl of Dundonald, London, 1860–1

General

Sylva, by John Evelyn, London, 1664

History of the Post Office Packet Service, 1793–1815, by Arthur H. Norway, London, 1895

The Naval History of Great Britain, by William James (the six-volume edition to the Battle of Navarino; i.e. 1793–1827), London, 1902, is used; the first edition in five volumes was published in 1822

At War with the Smugglers, by Rear-Admiral D. Arnold Foster, London, 1936

The Impressment of American Seamen, by J. F. Zimmerman, New York, 1925

Builders of the Navy, by H. F. Burke and O. Barron, London, 1904

Wolves of the Channel, by W. Branch Johnson, London, 1931

The Tomlinson Papers, edited by J. G. Bullocke, NRS volume LXXIV, London, 1935

Fiction (a selection)

Tom Cringle's Log, by Michael Scott, 1829

The Cruise of the Midge, by Michael Scott, 1834

Frank Mildmay, by Captain F. Marryat, 1829

Mr Midshipman Easy, by Captain F. Marryat, 1836

Peter Simple, by Captain F. Marryat, 1834

The King's Own, by Captain F. Marryat, 1830

The Post Captain, anon. (John Davis), 1805

The Port Admiral, by W. J. Neale, 1833

Rattlin the Reefer, by the Hon. Edward G. Greville Howard, London, 1836

Land Sharks and Sea Gulls, by Captain W. N. Glascock, 1838

Tom Bowling, by Captain F. Chamier, 1839

Most of the more readily available standard biographies and naval histories have been omitted as they are kept in most libraries and tell little of the actual life of men at sea in the Royal Navy.

Index

NOTE: ships are listed under 'Ships'

Boatswain's call